HAMMERIN' HANK, GEORGE ALMIGHTY AND THE SAY HEY KID

The Year that Changed Baseball Forever

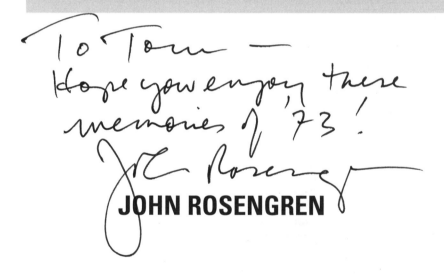

To Tom —
Hope you enjoy these
memories of '73!

John Rosengren

JOHN ROSENGREN

SOURCEBOOKS, INC.
NAPERVILLE, ILLINOIS

Published by Sourcebooks, Inc.
P.O. Box 4410, Naperville, Illinois 60567-4410
(630) 961-3900
Fax: (630) 961-2168
www.sourcebooks.com

Library of Congress Cataloging-in-Publication Data

Rosengren, John.
Hammerin' Hank, George Almighty and the Say Hey Kid : the year that baseball
changed forever / John Rosengren.
p. cm.
ISBN-13: 978-1-4022-0956-7 (pbk.)
ISBN-10: 1-4022-0956-8 (pbk.)
1. Baseball—United States—History. 2. Nineteen seventy-three, A.D. I. Title.

GV863.A1R627 2008
796.357'64097309047—dc22
                                        2007043486

Printed and bound in the United States of America.
VP 10 9 8 7 6 5 4 3 2 1

For my father,
who blessed me with his love of baseball

Man's mind cannot grasp the causes of events in their completeness, but the desire to find those causes is implanted in man's soul.

—LEO TOLSTOY, *WAR AND PEACE*

TABLE OF CONTENTS

LIST OF ILLUSTRATIONS

ACKNOWLEDGMENTS

The summer of '73, my father took me to watch the Twins play at Metropolitan Stadium in Bloomington, a twenty-minute drive from our house in suburban Minneapolis. As soon as the Twins announced their schedule, my father would buy tickets for the doubleheaders. Our favorites were the twilight doubleheaders, when we watched one game by daylight, the other under the night sky. Baseball was pure to me then: played outdoors on real grass. Seated beside my dad during those twin bills, I felt his love for the game seep into me and take root.

I turned nine years old that summer, just like Barry Bonds. As a matter of fact, we turned nine on the same day. I shared his birthday, but not his talent. As a Little League catcher with a weak arm, my destiny was to be a fan. I embraced my role happily the summer that Hank Aaron chased Babe Ruth and Reggie Jackson replaced Willie Mays as the game's dominant player. Baseball was magical to me—as it is for many boys in those years between the time we learn to read box scores and the day we discover girls.

When I first set out to write a book about the season when the confluence of several key events changed the course of the game forever, I dug out a box of baseball cards stowed in my basement. I pored over the Topps cards from 1973 and remembered the walks to the corner grocery store where my friends and I bought packs for ten cents apiece, then sat outside on the curb and tore them open, announcing with glee the prize cards "Catfish Hunter!" "Carl Yastrzemski!" "Rod Carew!" Looking at those cards again, over thirty years later, the magic I felt as a young boy rushed back.

That happened many times during my research for this book. Reading back issues of *Sports Illustrated*, *Sport* magazine and *The Sporting News*, talking to players from that era, listening to scratchy radio broadcasts of those games, and watching television footage from that season, I felt the innocent thrill that comes in middle age when one reconnects with a youthful passion. I hope that I have been able to capture that sensation and pass it along to readers in these pages.

There were many who helped along the way that I would like to thank. Kip Graff with the Major League Baseball Players Alumni Association put me in contact with some of the former players. Kristi Fick, Debbie Gallas, and Ken Pries of the Oakland A's; Michael Margolis of the Yankees; Tony Cook of the Kansas City Royals; and John Blake, Pam Ganley, and Dick Bresciani of the Boston Red Sox all provided information on their respective team's history or put me in contact with former players. Laura Hoke at the Shasta Country Library, Bill Nowlin, Stew Thornley, Jeff Horrigan, and Dawn Mitchell also helped in seemingly small ways that added up to a large contribution. Regalle Asuncion at AP Images, John Camarillo at Zuma Press, Andrew Newman at the National Baseball Hall of Fame, and Phoebe Sexton of the Boston Red Sox served up some fantastic photos. Ted Carmichael and Emily Williams at Sourcebooks helped keep things organized.

All of those who spoke with me provided insights not found in the printed word. Thank you Dick Bresciani, Fred Claire, Bob Costas, Ed Kranepool, Bill Lee, Paul Levy, Matt Merola, John Odom, Tony Oliva, Joe Rudi, Robert Sahr, Lon Simmons, Art Stewart, and Gene Tenace.

A special thank you to the entire staff of the Minneapolis Public Library, with its generous baseball collection. You tutored me in new technology, replaced the toner in the copier, and led me through the maze of stacks with unflagging patience and kindness. I appreciate that.

Every writer dreams of an editor who can provide wisdom, encouragement, and guidance. Mine came true in the person of Hillel Black, a venerable soul of publishing. Thank you, Hillel, for believing in this book and in me. I treasure your presence in my work and life.

My family supported me throughout long days and anxious nights. Heartfelt thank yous to my five-year-old son, Brendan, who checked out a children's baseball book to help me with my research; to my seven-year-old daughter, Alison, who cheered me on toward my deadline; and to my wife of nine years, Maria, for her understanding, patience, and confidence in me. Thank you for the love you each showed me in your own way.

Finally, this book would not have been possible without that first love from my father. Bill Rosengren not only bestowed in me my love of baseball, he gave me the love of his presence seated beside me at countless games during my youth and into adulthood. Cancer claimed him the summer I started writing this book. I regret that he could not read it, because I'm certain he would have enjoyed it, probably more than any of my previous books. I am grateful for one final expression of our mutual love, a pilgrimage to the National Baseball Hall of Fame we made the year before he died. We celebrated my—and Barry Bonds's—forty-first birthday in Cooperstown with my father again telling me stories of baseball as he remembered it from his youth. The magic flared once more.

Thanks, Dad.

Reggie Jackson smacks his second double of Game Six off Tom Seaver.

Chapter One

A MR. OCTOBER AFTERNOON

Listen. You can hear it in the crowd. The 49,333 at Oakland Coliseum that afternoon. Tense. Excited. Sold. They believe their A's can spoil this Mets miracle—the tremendous dash from last place at the end of August to within a game of the world championship. No matter, it's Game Six, the Mets up 3–2 in the Series. These fans have assigned their allegiance to these A's, the star-studded lineup of the defending champs: Bando, Tenace, Campaneris, Rudi, Hunter, Holtzman, Fingers, Blue, and Reggie. Reggie. Reg-gie! Reg-gie!! REG-GIE!

He steps to his place. First inning, man on, two out. Reggie digs in. The white Pumas anchor in the dirt, the Sonny Liston-sized biceps wiggle the 37-ounce bat in his powerful hands. Reg-gie! His swagger, his manner, his style—he's like no one else. He's Reggie.

He feels the eyes of the 49,333 on him, along with those of the millions in front of television sets from the Bay Area to Flushing Meadows. Feels good. His first World Series. The big stage. An October afternoon promise to supersize his status. Reggie stands poised to bust open his own image. Watch this.

The 1973 season had already proven itself a watershed year that changed baseball forever. Race, money, rules—raging factors in the country's social revolution—had marked the national pastime. A black man who had begun his career in the Negro Leagues threatened the supremacy of a white man's legend, a mythical landmark universally identifiable by a simple number, 714. In New York, a multi-millionaire shipbuilder with an ego the size of Yankee Stadium bought America's team at a bargain-basement price and began to flex his wealth in the league's largest market, sparking baseball's economic revolution. In a culture reluctant to change, American League owners had broken ranks with their National League counterparts and introduced the designated hitter, a marketing measure desperate to reclaim fan interest dissipated by the growing popularity of professional football. Already that season, baseball had undergone an extreme makeover that provided a demarcation in its history. There was baseball before 1973 and baseball after 1973—two distinctive eras.

Now Reggie at bat in the Fall Classic would animate the season's final act. While Willie Mays watched from the bench, Reggie would enact a changing of the superstar guard so complete that it would transform the media's coverage, the fans' perception, and the game's image. That afternoon, the age of the modern superstar was about to dawn.

———————

Willie Mays was the best player of his generation—some argue of all time. An All-Star 24 times, a two-time MVP, he was the kind of player for whom the Hall of Fame was built. *The Sporting News* had recently declared Mays the best player of the past decade. He held more Major League Baseball records in more categories than any other player in history. His day was nearly done. By October 1973, he was ready to retire, but he wanted to close out his career as a champion. In Game Six, the forty-two-year-old Mays watched Reggie bat from what had become Willie's customary spot at the back end of the Mets dugout.

Fail or triumph, Reggie did everything big. He was coming off an MVP season—batting .293 and smashing a league-leading 32 homers and 117 RBIs while scoring more runs (99) than any other American League player. Yet, that same season, he struck out 111 times, or once every fifth at bat. Shame claims the flip side of glory's skinny coin.

Reggie could be the victim of his own hype. After hitting 47 home runs in his sophomore season, he had started calling himself

Mr. B&B—as in bread and butter, the guy who delivered the big hits—then endured a three-year slump for a player of his potential, averaging fewer than 30 home runs and less than 75 RBIs a year. He batted .261 over those seasons.

Before the Series began, Reggie had announced to his teammates with characteristic swagger, "I'll take care of you."[1] But his bat had not been as large as his mouth. In the first five games, he had only five hits in 21 at bats, a .238 average. Worse, Mr. B&B had driven in only two runs and stranded 17 teammates on base. In Game Five, he had come to bat three times with men on and failed to bring any home, failed even to hit the ball out of the infield. Reggie faces Tom Seaver, the Mets ace, aware that he has failed to carry his teammates. If he doesn't show them his big stick today, he will be chastised as just a big mouth.

Minutes earlier, Reggie had stood at his locker, getting ready for the pre-game introductions. Teammate Gene Tenace walked over, placed his hand on Reggie's shoulder, and said, "I sure would like to play tomorrow."

Tenace walked away, but the message was clear: Back up your mouth. Win one for us.[2]

On the Mets bench, Willie watches to see what Reggie will do.

Reggie raises his 37-ounce bat. Seaver throws his fastball. Reggie slices a drive into left center. He hustles into second with a double, and Joe Rudi scores from first to give the A's an early lead.

It's what Willie would have done. Once upon a time.

———————

Reggie wanted to be Willie. Mays had been his boyhood hero. "I started thinking about playing ball when I found out who Willie Mays was," he said.[3]

In 1966, as a minor leaguer with the A's affiliate, the Modesto Reds, Reggie drove 100 miles to San Francisco with a teammate to watch Willie play. The twenty-year-old was mesmerized, following Mays's every move—admiring his basket catches, his big swings, even his casual trot toward the dugout. "I got to see Willie Mays play in person for the first time," he writes in *Reggie: The Autobiography.* "Willie Mays. In the flesh."

His teammates, having listened to Reggie's adulation of Willie, called him Buck, Willie's nickname.[4] Reggie didn't mind.

In a rare fit of humility, Reggie had once admitted that he would settle for being "one half the player Willie Mays is,"[5] but he was on his way to becoming close to Willie's peer. Jackson had a powerful arm, fast legs (he ran a 9.6 hundred-yard dash) and hit with power—in 1973, he hit a home run every 17 at bats, best in the majors. He was big and strong. At six feet and 205 pounds, he had an inch and 25 pounds on his idol. His biceps measured 17 inches around. He also possessed thunderous, 27-inch thighs that powered his big swing. Reggie didn't win batting titles—he would never hit better than .300 in a season—but when he made contact with the ball, he usually clobbered it. At forty-two, Willie knew how good he had been; Reggie, at twenty-seven, was just sensing his possibilities.

The two were marked by their different eras. Willie was born at the start of the Depression; Reggie was the first of the baby boomers. Willie was a rookie in 1951, shortly after Jackie Robinson had hurdled baseball's color barrier but when Jim Crow laws still ruled. A black man from the deep South, Mays came to the majors via the Negro League. Reggie, an African American with Puerto Rican roots, grew up in a Jewish suburb of Philadelphia and played college ball before breaking into the big leagues in 1967, amidst the turmoil of the Vietnam war and America's cultural revolution. Willie remained old school; Reggie epitomized the Seventies' Me Generation.

Willie performed; Reggie entertained. Reggie was such a hotdog, his teammate Darold Knowles said, "There isn't enough mustard in the world to cover Reggie Jackson."[6]

Both players could beat you. Willie would show you how. Reggie would tell you. He wanted you to see him beat you. He wanted you to revel in the glory of Reggie. Willie was legend; Reggie was hype—albeit hype that often delivered.

Reggie's ego drove the zeitgeist of the new superstar. Nobody else talked like Reggie; nobody else played with his style. Not in baseball. Not in any sport. Muhammad Ali came the closest. He brandished the same brash words, flaunted the same sparkling talent, and developed a media presence with daring charisma. But Ali was a lone wolf in the ring. Reggie did his thing among teammates, an even bolder stroke of ego. Among other team sports, Joe Namath, with his good looks, big-game talent, and famous Super Bowl III claim, approached Reggie as a peer, but Namath slurred his prediction under the influence. Reggie spouted his stuff stone cold sober. Nobody talked or played with his hubris.

You couldn't help but notice. If he could back up that talk on the field, his style would change the way reporters covered the game and the way other stars comported themselves. He would transform the very image of baseball. Jackie Robinson changed the color of the game; Reggie infused it with color. He broke the duller barrier.

Reggie comes to bat again in the third with two outs and Sal Bando on first. Once again, he raises his 37-ounce bat and waits for Seaver's delivery. Seaver, whose arm hasn't fully recovered from Game Three after only three days' rest, can't reach his usual high speeds on his fastball, his money pitch. He is pitching more with his head than his arm. He had wanted to rely on his outside fastball to strike out Reggie, but instead Seaver chucks sinkers over the plate, hoping to force a ground ball. Reggie lifts one of those sinkers to right center, slugging another two-out double. That scores Bando and puts the A's up 2–0.

In the top of the eighth, Catfish Hunter has set down the first Mets batter, and Seaver is due up. Mets manager Yogi Berra knows Seaver has spent what he had on the mound. He needs a pinch hitter. That is a role Willie could play.

By 1973, Willie's body—once powerful and seemingly chiseled from marble in the days before players lifted weights and gulped supplements—had started to break down. The speedy legs had slowed, the powerful arm had weakened, the sharp eyesight had dulled, the quick wrists had lost their snap. He still wanted to win as bad as ever, but these days his body denied him. That season, he had appeared in only 66 games, batted .211, punched six homers, stolen one base, and hit into 10 double plays. He had become a memory of himself.

But he was still Willie, one of the game's greatest clutch players. His 22 extra-inning home runs remain a record—far more than the next closest total of 16 hit by Babe Ruth. Willie is ready to bat for Seaver. Yogi looks down his bench, past Willie Mays, to Ken Boswell, a lifetime .248 hitter, who has managed only 25 hits in 1973. No doubt, Yogi figures the left-handed-batting Boswell will fare better than the right-handed Mays against the right-hander Hunter. Boswell makes good on Yogi's hunch, promptly smacking a single to right field.

A's manager Dick Williams replaces Hunter with Darold Knowles. Knowles gives up a pair of singles. Boswell scores, cutting the A's lead to 2–1. The Mets have the tying run on third and the go-ahead run on first—they are that close to clinching the World Series.

Knowles strikes out Rusty Staub on three consecutive fastballs. His work done, Knowles departs for Rollie Fingers, who records the final out of the inning. Willie can only watch.

Reggie leads off the A's half of the eighth.

He would finish his career with a .357 lifetime World Series batting average, nearly 100 points better than his career regular season average, and the best career World Series slugging average, .755. The higher the stakes, the better Reggie played. He loved the spotlight. The brighter the better. "When they turn on the light, they turn on Jackson," he said.[7] Yet in this, his first World Series ever, he still has something to prove.

He punches Tug McGraw's pitch into center field for a single. The ball skips past the Mets center fielder, Don Hahn, and Reggie races all the way to third. Two batters later, he scores standing up on Jesus Alou's sacrifice fly. A's lead, 3–1.

Reggie's first year in the big leagues had been Willie's last really good one. In 1966, Mays batted .288 and notched 159 hits, 29 of them doubles, 37 home runs; he knocked in 103 runs and scored 99. Then, he started his slow fade. In the last seven years of his career, he would never hit more than 28 home runs in a season (1970), drive in no more than 83 runs (1970), and never score as many runs. His production would trail off until his dismal final season.

But Willie could still win ball games. He had delivered the game-winning hit in the deciding game of the National League playoff that put the Mets into the World Series. Yogi had pinch hit Willie for Ed Kranepool in the fifth inning with the bases loaded and the score tied. Willie swung too big. He smashed the ball straight into the dirt. It leaped high into the air. By the time it came down into pitcher Clay Carroll's waiting glove thirty feet up the third baseline, Willie was safe at first and the go-ahead run had scored.

In the ninth, Fingers retires the first two Mets batters. Yogi wants to pinch hit for the right-handed Hahn. He looks down the bench. With his team down to its final out, Willie is ready. Yogi looks past Mays once again, to Kranepool. He opts for a left-handed batter against the right-hander Fingers. His hunch had worked last inning, perhaps it will work again.

Kranepool pops to second. Game over.

In the Mets clubhouse, the champagne stays corked. Willie quietly changes into his street clothes.

Across the way, reporters in the A's clubhouse gather around the game's hero, Reggie Jackson. He has accounted for all three of the A's runs, driving in two and scoring the third. Reporters crowd around him with their microphones and miniature writing tablets, ready to transmit his words to the world. Reggie joneses on the moment. Mr. October has arrived. Game Seven beckons.

Mike Burke and George Steinbrenner on January 3, 1973, announce their purchase of the New York Yankees.

Chapter Two

THE MONEY GAME

Flip the calendar to 1973. In January, President Richard Nixon was sworn in to a second term the week after members of his administration went on trial for the Watergate break-in. Shortly after the inauguration, the Administration signed a cease-fire agreement with Hanoi and began withdrawing troops from Vietnam, but it was too late—the war and Watergate had already erased the American public's innocence. The people had grown suspicious of their leaders.

A number of beginnings or firsts launched the country on an unknown course. The Supreme Court legalized abortion, NASA sent the space station Skylab into orbit, the World Trade Center opened, the federal government started the Drug Enforcement Agency, Federal Express began shipping packages overnight. KISS played its first concert, the United States Postal Service raised the cost of mailing a letter to ten cents, the pop top appeared on soda and beer cans, Schoolhouse Rock started teaching kids between Saturday morning cartoons, the bionic man—valued at six million dollars—debuted on the tube. And at the movies, something beyond comprehension was happening to a little girl, who could only be saved by the exorcist.

The shift from the familiar to the unknown provoked anxiety. In the year's top pop hit, "Tie a Yellow Ribbon Round the Ole Oak Tree," Tony Orlando sang about a man who fretted over how he would be received back home. Meanwhile, antiwar protesters taunted vets returning from Vietnam. Marlon Brando refused his Best Actor Oscar for his role in "The Godfather" to show his solidarity with the members of the American Indian Movement who had taken hostages at Wounded Knee. In a Gallup Poll, Americans voted New York Yankees fan and National Security Advisor Henry Kissinger, who won the Nobel Peace Prize for his role in brokering the Vietnam cease-fire, the most admired man in the world. Kissinger, who would later be accused of war crimes and human rights abuses, was even considered a sex symbol. Henry Kissinger, a sex symbol! Strange days, indeed.

The upheaval in society had extended to the national pastime, which underwent an extreme makeover in 1973. Labor clashes strained the owners' plantation mentality. Players explored new freedoms. The rules changed to allow one player on each team simply to bat but not to field. A black man in the South chased the hallowed record of a white man. The greatest player of a generation retired, replaced by a new breed of superstar. A powerful personality took the helm of America's team. The game's status quo crumbled in 1973, and it sought an altered equilibrium. The turbulent times induced the evolution of a new breed of baseball.

To assess the health of the game, one had only to look to its flagship team. The once proud Yankees, dynasty of past decades, had become losers. In 1972, they lost seventy-six games and a million dollars. The team's value plummeted. The Columbia Broadcasting System (CBS), which had purchased the Yankees in 1964 for $13.2 million, prepared to sell at a loss. *Forbes* magazine predicted that the national pastime would follow the fate of America's team and suggested that major league baseball "could well vanish from the scene in twenty years."[1] The magazine was correct in its perception of the Yankees as baseball's bellwether, but wrong about the direction the team and the game would head.

Forbes hadn't counted on the arrival of George M. Steinbrenner III. No sooner had the ball dropped in Times Square than the Yankees announced that a limited partnership headed by the Cleveland shipbuilder had purchased America's team. Mike Burke, who had been running the Yankees for CBS, told a gathering of the press at the Yankee Stadium club on January 3 that he and Steinbrenner, the two general partners in a limited partnership of fifteen owners, had purchased the Yankees for $10 million. (The final price would actually be less, $8.7 million, after CBS bought back a couple of parking garages.)[2] The purchase price—well below what the broadcast company had paid eight years earlier, though above the value CBS carried on its books[3]—seemed low to many, considering that owners had paid $10 million or more for expansion teams in Seattle and San Diego within the past five years. A considerable perk in the deal was New York Mayor John V. Lindsay's pledge of $24 million to renovate the crumbling forty-year-old Yankee Stadium over the next two years.[4] (The city's final bill would eventually run $106 million[5]—part of the $1.5 billion deficit Lindsay would leave his successor.)[6] Steinbrenner, the Yankees' fifth owner since the team began in 1903, bought the team at a bargain basement price.[7]

Ka-ching! The Boss had pulled off his first major deal in the game.

The following week at a lunchtime press conference, Steinbrenner and Burke introduced the other members of the partnership. The partners included John DeLorean, the General Motors vice president who would later introduce his own eponymous automobile; Thomas Evans, managing partner of the New York law firm where Nixon was previously a partner; James Nederlander, theater owner and Broadway producer who had teamed with Steinbrenner on the musical "Applause" starring Lauren Bacall; and Gabe Paul, past part-owner, president, vice president, and general manager of the Cleveland Indians who had initiated the Steinbrenner coup by introducing George to Burke. They staged the press conference at the "21" Club, the fashionable midtown Manhattan restaurant where athletes, sports bosses, and television movers and shakers populated the tables. The same place that previously had spurned Steinbrenner.[8] Prior to January 3, 1973, when his secretary tried to book a table for the Cleveland shipping magnate on his New York business trips, the best he could rank was an anonymous upstairs table at the obscure hour of four in the afternoon. Finally, his purchase of the Yankees provided the occasion for his coming out ball, making his entree into Gotham's social scene and stamping his mark on the game's landscape, one that he would completely reshape.

The Boss, driven by his thirst for power and fueled by love of profits, would make money the predominant factor in baseball, one that would eclipse the lively ball, lowered mound, and even juiced players in its influence. For this was a business, and nobody understood the race to the bottom line better than George M. Steinbrenner III.

George had learned at an early age how to make a buck. Born July 4, 1930, in an affluent area of greater Cleveland, he started in the egg business as a nine-year-old, gathering and selling the eggs of the 200 chickens, ducks, and geese his father had bought him. The young boy dutifully recorded the inventory and sales of the George Company in a notebook.[9] When George left for boarding school, he sold the chicken business to his sisters for fifty dollars.[10] Making money seemed the one way he was capable of pleasing his demanding father, whom his oldest child and only son, George, once described as "a superachiever that I would never match."[11]

Not to say he didn't try. The old man had graduated from the Massachusetts Institute of Technology. After completing his prep studies at Culver Military Academy in Indiana, George had his application to MIT denied. He attended Williams College instead. Henry was an NCAA hurdling champion. George practiced in his backyard on a set of hurdles he built in shop class, but he did not win the medals his father had garnered.[12] Instead, George excelled in the glee club with Stephen Sondheim. ("I had a better voice," Steinbrenner claims.)[13]

The closest George came to showing up his domineering dad was by rescuing the family business, Kinsman Marine Transit Company. George joined his father at the Great Lakes shipping company in 1957 after a two-year hitch in the air force and stints coaching high school baseball, semi-pro football, and college football at Northwestern University. The big steel companies were building fleets of their own to ship ore, endangering independent companies like Kinsman that worked the Great Lakes routes. In 1960, thirty-year-old George saved the family business by securing a commitment from Jones and Laughlin Steel of Pittsburgh for Kinsman's ore carriers to transport hefty annual amounts.[14] He eventually raised enough money to buy out his father.

In 1967, George led a group that took over the American Shipbuilding Company and merged it with Kinsman Marine. The company, with yards in Cleveland, Tampa, and six other cities, was struggling when George took over, but by the time he bought the Yankees, he had tripled its volume to more than $100 million.[15] His early practice in the egg business had paid off.

When George III bought the Yankees, he piqued the curiosity of New Yorkers and sports fans alike. They wanted to know more about this forty-two-year-old Midwesterner whom *The New York Times* reported was "involved in numerous activities, including business, politics, sports, show business and civic and charitable functions … considered one of the most effective fund-raisers in Cleveland, and, though a Protestant, was named man of the year for 1972 by Cleveland's Israel Bond Organization." Steinbrenner told them he grew up a closet Yankees fan. "Being in Cleveland, you couldn't root for them, but you would boo them in awe."[16]

Steinbrenner was not a stranger to the sports world. In addition to the coaching forays of his youth, he bred racehorses and was a part-owner and vice president of the NBA Chicago Bulls. From 1959 to 1961, he had operated the Cleveland Pipers of the National Industrial Basketball League and later the American Basketball League. The discerning observer could glean clues of

Steinbrenner's personality from his past involvement that revealed him to be an unusual owner: an intense competitor, an innovator, and a troublemaker.

The new Yankees owner expected to win. Kinsman Hope, his two-year-old thoroughbred, had won the Remsen Stakes two months earlier. His Pipers had won two championships. The new Yankees owner liked to work deals. He had signed Ohio State All-American Jerry Lucas, which prompted the NBA to include the Pipers as its tenth team, though the deal fell through when Steinbrenner could not raise the $250,000 entry fee. The new Yankees owner wasn't afraid to break conventions. He hired the first African-American coach of a professional team, John McLendon, to lead the Pipers. Like Branch Rickey, the Dodger general manager who signed Jackie Robinson as the first African-American ballplayer in Major League Baseball, Steinbrenner was driven more by a desire to win and attract fans than concern for civil rights. (McLendon, frustrated by George's meddling and domineering ways, quit less than two years later.)[17] The new Yankees owner also had trouble controlling his temper. He yelled at his players, the coach, and officials, sometimes leaving his seat to shout on the court.[18] He argued so disrespectfully with a referee during a Pipers game that the official threw him out, making him the first owner of a major sports franchise to be ejected from a game for arguing with an official.[19] *The Cleveland Press* deemed him "congenitally unsuited" to run the team.[20]

The writing on the wall was there for the astute observer to read between the lines when the new Yankees owner told reporters at the January 3 press conference he planned to be an absentee owner: "I'll stick to building ships. I won't be active in the day-to-day operations of the club at all. I can't spread myself so thin. I've got enough headaches with the shipping company."[21]

Steinbrenner almost didn't buy the Yankees. His first choice had been his hometown Indians. In 1971, Indians owner Vernon Stouffer had agreed in principle to Steinbrenner's $9 million offer to buy the team, but the deal fell through at the eleventh hour.

Stouffer sold the team the following spring to Nick Mileti, owner of the NBA Cleveland Cavaliers, for $9 million.

Gabe Paul, the Indians general manager, had been involved in Steinbrenner's unsuccessful effort to buy the Cleveland team. When Paul learned that CBS wanted to sell the Yankees, he hooked up Steinbrenner with Michael Burke, the Yankees president. CBS chairman William Paley had told Burke that he wanted to dump the Yankees, which had become an albatross to the media company, and he would sell the team to Burke for $10 million if he could come up with the financing. Burke, who didn't have that kind of capital himself, had not been able to find investors until he met Steinbrenner.[22]

George struck Burke as smart and savvy about numbers. He seemed stiff and square to Burke, who grooved more readily with the times, but also someone who could be a good fit. "At face value and taken at his word, George Steinbrenner appeared to have the ingredients of a good buyer and a good partner," Burke writes in his memoir, *Outrageous Good Fortune*. Burke's fault would be that he took Steinbrenner at his word.

But he was right that George was good for the money. Steinbrenner made two calls, enlisting the support of Bunker Hunt, one of the world's largest breeders of thoroughbred race horses, and Lester Crown, an insurance and real estate tycoon from Chicago who once owned the Empire State Building, for $2 million each, and banks tripped over themselves in their rush to loan the balance of $6 million.[23]

George walked into William Paley's office to make his formal offer on the afternoon of December 19, 1972, "scared stiff." Steinbrenner feared Paley would tell him he had decided not to sell or that the relatively young Midwesterner didn't have sufficient financing.

"What are you going to pay me with, Chinese money?" Paley said.

"No, sir," Steinbrenner replied. "I've got cash. Good old-fashioned cash."[24]

They had a deal.

When Steinbrenner told his father he had bought the Yankees, Henry said, "You're better off sticking to shipbuilding."[25] The ever hard-to-please father would relent, however, and later comment that George's purchase of the Yankees "was the first smart thing he's done."[26]

Steinbrenner had bought a team on the slide. Prior to CBS's ownership, the Yankees had won 15 American League pennants and ten world championships in eighteen years. During Burke's eight-year tenure (1965–1972), the Yankees had sunk to last place and finished higher than fourth only once. Those eight years had become the longest stretch without winning a pennant since the team's first in 1921. In 1972, the Yankees finished fourth and failed to attract a million fans for the first time since World War II. The Yankees' image sagged, and New Yorkers switched allegiance to the fashionable new team in Queens—the Mets drew 2,134,185 fans in 1972 to the Bronx Bombers' 966,328. Rumors swirled that the Yankees would relocate to New Jersey's Meadowlands.[27]

Steinbrenner, smiling widely at the press conference, was obviously happy with the deal. He knew what he had bought. "The Yankees are baseball," he said.[28] They would turn out to be a much better buy than the Indians. Thirty years later, Buster Olney, former Yankees beat writer for *The New York Times*, would observe, "Steinbrenner had recognized and exploited the financial potential of the Yankees, and by doing so he built the dominant superpower in a baseball universe increasingly inhabited by franchises with third-world finances."[29] Indeed, by 2006, *Forbes* valued the Yankees at $1.26 billion, the first baseball team to reach that amount.

So began 1973, with the Boss's arrival on baseball's scene.

Steinbrenner's purchase meant that Willie Mays would not manage the Yankees. The previous summer, several others had attempted to buy the club, including Herman Franks, the San Francisco Giants former manager. With an offer in the neighborhood of $13.5 million backed by the New York investment firm of Lehman Brothers, Franks thought his group would be the new owners—until Steinbrenner swooped in for the kill. Afterward, Franks revealed that one of his first moves as new Yankee owner would have been to ask his former center fielder, Mays, to manage the team.

Instead, Mays received from the Mets in early February a letter air-mail, special delivery. Don't report for spring training in St. Petersburg, it read. All of the Mets—indeed, all players of both leagues—received the same directive. Stay home. Spring training won't start as planned by March 1. The owners and the players' union had failed to work out terms of a new basic agreement. Another labor stoppage threatened the game.

A year earlier, the players had staged the first league-wide strike in the history of American sports. After a century of being held hostage by the owners, they had finally stood up to the bosses and walked off the job. Marvin Miller—who had represented the United Auto Workers and United Steelworkers as a labor economist before the players hired him as the players' union executive director in 1966—had convinced the players that the owners had exploited them by paying them less than their worth.

Miller decried their situation as worse than that of the grape pickers Cesar Chavez represented.[30] The media and fans failed to rally behind the players' cause. Dick Young of the *New York Daily News* spoke for many when he accused Miller of "brainwashing" the players, making them "zombies."[31] Others complained that he threatened to "destroy an American tradition."[32]

When the players seemed to waver in their collective resolve, Mays, the game's senior statesman, stepped up. The Giants player representative at the time, he told his younger counterparts at a meeting of the executive board of the Players Association (made up of one player rep from each team in the two leagues) that they must stand firm if they wanted to change the system: "I know it's hard being away from the game and our paychecks and our normal life. I love this game. It's been my whole life. But we made a decision

...to stick together, and until we're satisfied, we have to stay together. This could be my last year in baseball, and if the strike lasts the entire season and I've played my last game, well, it will be painful. But if we don't hang together, everything we've worked for will be lost."

The players followed Mays's counsel. The strike lasted thirteen days and cancelled 86 games before the two sides reached agreement. When they voted to strike on March 31, 1972, the players had sought $1 million from the pension fund's surplus earnings, derived from television revenue, to increase retirement benefits. The owners initially said, No, we're not giving you an extra cent. The two sides eventually met in the middle, agreeing on a $500,000 increase in retirement benefits, and the season began.

Mets chairman Donald Grant grumbled that "nobody won,"[33] yet it was evident that even though the players lost pay for the games not played, they scored a significant victory by sticking together to show they would no longer kowtow to management. *The New York Times* remarked on the strike's significance: "The compromise agreement between the club owners and the players is important not for who won and who lost in money terms, but for the implicit decision by management to accept players as grown-up men entitled to a collective voice in the determination of their own destinies."[34]

So, when the players stood firm the following spring in their demands and threatened legal action if the lockout continued past March 1, no matter how much the owners bristled at the players' impudence or resented Miller's style, they knew they had to reckon with their employees. This time, the two sides dickered over terms of a new basic agreement, the general contract that covered all collective working conditions. Miller had already negotiated two basic agreements, gradually improving conditions for players, half of whom were earning less than $17,000 when he started in 1967. This year, 1973, the players were seeking additional improvements to retirement benefits and an increase in minimum salaries, among other items. The previous three-year basic agreement had expired at the end of 1972. When the two sides failed to hammer out details of a new agreement by early

February, the owners voted to delay spring training. Commissioner Bowie Kuhn tried to downplay the delay as a "routine matter—mainly a case of logistics," but he sided with the owners and accused Miller of "a deliberate effort to create confusion in the minds of the clubs, players, and public regarding the status of the negotiations."[35]

The owners' worst fear was free agency. Even new Yankees owner George Steinbrenner, who would later sing another tune (surprise!), initially said, "I am dead set against free agency. It can ruin baseball."[36] In an effort to delay for three years any alterations to the reserve clause, which kept players bound to their teams, the owners offered players the bone of salary arbitration, whereby a player and club, failing to reach agreement on a contract, would each submit a number to an independent arbitrator who would choose one that both parties would be bound to honor. This was the first time the owners had put arbitration on the table for consideration.[37]

Reggie Jackson, the A's newly appointed player representative who was never shy about airing his opinions, worried that another prolonged shutdown could jeopardize the game's standing with fans. "We're hurting the game, both sides, and some people are going to turn their backs on baseball for good," he said after spring training had been delayed. "Look at it this way. I don't want to sit out. The owners don't want to lock out. They want to play and make money. That is only human. They are businessmen, and we're businessmen. This thing isn't all one way.… What I'm saying to both sides is please, please, let's get together and play ball."[38]

In less than three weeks, the two sides did just that. They worked out a deal in a flurry of meetings between Miller and owner representative John J. Gaherin, a former railroad negotiator, thereby escaping the players' threatened legal action. The owners approved a $610,000 increase in retirement benefits and agreed that any player with two or more years of major league service could submit his salary to arbitration. Owners also agreed to increase the minimum salary from $13,500 to $15,000, to raise the minimum World Series winners' share from $15,000 to $20,000, and to up daily meal money by fifty cents. The players also won the right for veterans of ten or more seasons—the last five with the same team—to veto his trade or sale to another team. Despite initial posturing to toughen their stance from the previous year, the owners had given considerably on each of these issues.

Arbitration was the players' biggest gain. It opened the door for contract negotiations. General managers, rather than risk having to accept a player's price, became more likely to negotiate. That gave players leverage they had not enjoyed in the past, when the clubs had simply named a price and said, "Take it or find another job." The players' only recourse had been to complain to the league president or commissioner, whose sympathies usually lay with the owners. *The New York Times* viewed arbitration as such a significant breakthrough that it anticipated Major League Baseball had established a precedent for other industries: "The pattern set on the diamond for use of arbitration to resolve pay conflicts should help induce other industries to adopt this same sensible method of ending contract stalemates without strikes."[39]

The two sides had argued about money, but the heart of the issue was independence. The concessions the players won from the owners in the basic agreement negotiated in 1973 marked a coming of age for the players. In 1972, they had cracked the owners' grip on their destinies; in 1973, they had proven themselves capable of determining their course. Three years later, they would do just that by writing their emancipation proclamation when they struck down the reserve clause that had bound them. That marked the beginning of free agency, when players truly became masters of their own destinies, able to purvey their services to the highest bidder on the open market.

———————

George Steinbrenner's new team began spring training on March 1 as the Las Vegas favorite to win the East Division title, the first time since 1965 the oddsmakers had picked the Yankees to win a title. The Yankees' status as favorites was more lucky coincidence for George—having bought a team that finished 1972 strong in the second half—than any indication of how bookies foresaw him impacting the team's standing. Few suspected at that early date how deeply involved he would become in the team's operations. The immediate concern at the Yankees camp in Fort Lauderdale was the absence of seven players.

The record number of holdouts—one or two was closer to the norm—was an indicator of the times and of the way those times were changing. Five of the seven holdouts had agents negotiating on their behalf, which increased their bargaining strength. Agents, recently unheard of, were fast becoming the norm in the game, which meant higher salaries also were becoming the norm. As *Forbes* magazine had observed: As the Yankees go, so goes baseball.

The players demanded more money and got it. Bobby Murcer, the Yankees' Gold Glove center fielder and top hitter, was the best player among the seven holdouts. He wanted a greater than 50 percent raise on his 1972 salary of $65,000. With Mike Burke's approval, Lee MacPhail, Yankees general manager, made Murcer the third Yankee in history to earn $100,000 annually. Murcer hit with comparable power as Joe DiMaggio and Mickey Mantle, the two previous Yankees to land $100,000 contracts, but his batting average lagged about thirty points behind theirs in the seasons that preceded their raises to $100K. By the time DiMaggio at thirty-five and Mantle at thirty-one earned that amount, they were both three-time MVPs; Murcer, twenty-six, would never be a contender for that award. (When adjusted for inflation, DiMaggio's 1949 salary was worth $183,000 in 1973; Mantle's 1963 pay worth $142,000.)[40] Murcer's landmark salary signaled the inflation in player compensation. By the end of spring training, MacPhail had signed all seven holdouts—at a cost. The Yankees carried the highest payroll in team history—nearly a million dollars.[41] On the eve of free agency, the trend would be irreversible.

But Steinbrenner was not happy giving away big money without being asked first. He called Burke from Cleveland and demanded to know if he had approved Murcer's contract. "Sure," Burke said. "What about it?"

"What do you think this is, a money tree?!"

The two shouted at each other over the phone, before Steinbrenner's attorney, also on the line, could calm them down.[42]

But George was not mollified. When the Yankees played their home opener against, fittingly, Cleveland, George would be there to watch Murcer come to bat in the bottom of the eighth with two outs and the tying run on base. He watched Murcer go down on a called third strike. "There's your goddamn hundred-thousand-a-year ball player," Steinbrenner fumed.[43]

Players quickly learned that George demanded their best, and even more.

———————

When George arrived in Fort Lauderdale for spring training, he didn't like what he saw. The forty-two-year-old military academy grad wore his brown hair feathered across his forehead, above the ears and off the collar. It was the Midwestern executive cut of the day: longer than their fathers' high and tight look but controlled and respectable, clearly setting them apart from the shaggy hippies that roamed college campuses. The new Boss was appalled that some of the players he purchased—yes, the Yankees now counted as one of his holdings—resembled long-haired ragamuffins.

He may have been a shipbuilder and not a baseball man, but he knew what he wanted. These shaggy kids didn't look like a team. They looked like, like dogs, he thought.[44] He grabbed a blank lineup card he found in the clubhouse and wrote down the numbers 17 (Gene Michael), 1 (Bobby Murcer), and 28 (Sparky Lyle). He handed the list to manager Ralph Houk and demanded he see that the players got haircuts.[45] Steinbrenner couldn't stick to building ships when he saw such sloppiness. It wasn't the Yankee Way he envisioned.

———————

Yankees players had something on their minds other than hair and money at spring training: sex. Not surprising for a group of virile young professional ballplayers. Sex was a staple of the game as common as peanuts and Cracker Jack. The whole country was in on it, actually. One out of four college guys bought *Playboy*, which began picturing pubic hair that year. Everyone enjoyed *The Joy of Sex*—on the page if not between the sheets. The *Kama Sutra*'s modern reincarnation had been a bestseller since its publication the year before.

Free love ruled, but this situation was unusual. The first week of spring training, two Yankees, pitchers Mike Kekich and Fritz Peterson, told their teammates they had exchanged wives, kids, houses, furniture, even dogs—a poodle for a terrier. "It wasn't a wife swap," Kekich explained. "It was a life swap."[46]

Kekich and Peterson, both left-handers, were good friends, always together it seemed. Peterson, the better of the two pitchers (he won 20 games in 1970; Kekich never won more than ten in a big league season), enjoyed practical jokes. Peterson ordered items out of catalogs—fishing rods, hunting gear—to be delivered to Thurman Munson at Yankee Stadium where the catcher opened them, baffled.[47] Peterson liked to stuff a hot dog in Gene Michael's glove so that when the shortstop, famous for his squeamishness over bugs and slime, stuck in his finger and squished the wiener, he screamed. Peterson called teammates in their hotels rooms, and, imitating a particular sportswriter's voice, requested exclusive interviews.[48] So, when Gene Michael's wife told her husband she'd heard Peterson and Kekich had traded mates, Michael thought it was another joke. "Don't believe that stuff," he told his wife. "Those guys are pulling some trick again."[49]

The Yankee brass only wished it were so easily dismissed. President Mike Burke, general manager Lee MacPhail, and manager Ralph Houk called beat reporters covering the team's spring training into a closed-door session in Houk's clubhouse office and tried to downplay the situation. "It's just a personal matter," they told the press in a preemptive effort. "No big deal, really."[50]

Sportswriter Maury Allen had passed on an exclusive story

two months earlier. He realized the two players and their wives had arranged details of their exchange at a barbecue in Allen's backyard on a Yankees' off day the previous July but kept their situation quiet for the remainder of the season. The players had posed, smiling, for family portraits with their wives and young children, at Family Day in Yankee Stadium that month. When Peterson called Allen in January to divulge the details, Allen said, No, thanks. He thought it was a private matter, not for public consumption.[51]

Allen, like the Yankees management, misread a public curious about scandal. In their reporting on Watergate, Bob Woodward and Carl Bernstein had changed the content of what the media reported and what readers wanted to know. Jim Bouton had exposed baseball's secrets only three years earlier in his tell-all, *Ball Four*. Despite the players' and their old/new wives' protestations that the situation wasn't "wrong," "cheap," nor "lecherous," the American people were eager to learn all about this high-profile sex thing.[52]

Houk, who called the situation the biggest surprise of his career, later admitted, "I should have just come out and said it all, because there's no way you can keep anything from the press. The less you keep from the press, the fewer problems you're going to have, because they're going to find it out anyway."[53] The press, recently accustomed to winking at celebrity indiscretions, was no longer willing to do so. The Kekich-Peterson wife swap became a national story.

Fans jeered the two pitchers in their respective spring training debuts. Peterson heard the boos even when he came to bat. Kekich said he blocked out the shouts when he struggled in the first inning and a fan shouted, "He's lost it, just like his wife!" George Steinbrenner heard the verbal assault on Kekich at the Yankees' Florida park, though he insisted most of the fans remained loyal to the team. After one man yelled, Steinbrenner said, "Right away some other fans turned around and shut him up."[54]

Eventually—exactly two weeks after the story broke—Bowie Kuhn, compelled to speak up as the "conscience of this game," responded to questions from a group at a private dinner. He said he had received about one hundred letters complaining about the situation, more than he had received over the designated hitter rule change. "I deplore what happened and am appalled at its effect on young people," Kuhn said.[55] It wasn't clear if he feared that high school students—prompted by the pitchers' example—would end up swapping prom dates, homework, and parents, but Peterson did promise the commissioner that he would try not to do it again.[56]

Peterson, thirty-one, actually seemed quite happy with his new wife, new kids, new home—or, rather, his friend's wife, friend's kids, friend's home. He and Susanne Kekich, twenty-seven, a tall, trim woman, planned to marry as soon as they could divorce their spouses of the past nine and eight years, respectively. For Mike Kekich, twenty-eight, the deal hadn't gone as well. He said he was doubtful things would work out between him and the petite, shy Marilyn Peterson, thirty-one, who had unsuccessfully begged Fritz to take her back.[57]

Sex. Money. The writers had plenty of material to keep their typewriters busy in the spring of 1973. Dick Allen had raised the bar for player salaries in late February. The 1972 American League MVP signed a three-year contract with the White Sox for $225,000 a season that made him the highest-paid player in baseball history—well above the salaries of Mets ace Tom Seaver, who signed for $120,000 in 1973, Willie Mays's $165,000, and even the $200,000 that Braves slugger Henry Aaron earned in pursuit of Babe Ruth's legendary 714 home-run record. Twenty-six players earned $100,000 or more in 1973, three more than had earned that amount the previous season.[58]

Baseball's rising salaries were in step with the other three major American sports, with MLB's average annual salary of $36,000 falling between the NFL's $27,500 and the NBA's $90,000 average salaries. But in 1973, baseball owners shared the smallest proportion of income with players, only 17 percent, lowest of the four major sports leagues. Given Marvin Miller's definition of exploitation, "measured by the difference between what your labor is worth and what you are paid,"[59] baseball players did deserve a larger cut of the pie, but the average American worker, who earned $9,000 in 1973, harbored little sympathy for the plight of the exploited professional athlete.

Dick Allen's signing prompted the media's widespread criticism of inflated salaries. *Los Angeles Times* columnist Jim Murray complained, "Richard Anthony Allen is a moderately skilled outfielder-first baseman with the Chicago White Sox. He's not precisely a 'superstar' because 'superstars' never get shopped around and traded in the prime of their careers. Franchise owners would find a way to accommodate Dracula if he could bat .400. Richard has a lifetime batting average of .299, which is no threat to Ty Cobb's .367 or Rogers Hornsby's .358. Richard could catch them only if he batted .480 a year from here on out…. No one ever compared him to Joe DiMaggio in the field, and he's a cool 426 home runs behind Babe Ruth. He's 2,071 lifetime hits behind Cobb."[60]

Much as they disliked it, there was nothing they could do to slow the rapidly-rising pay. While Allen's 1973 salary of $225,000 seems a pittance compared to Alex Rodriguez's $27.7 million salary for 2007, it was the biggest money of the day, and the game's watchdogs (prophetically) feared where it would head. "Sports is a Big Rock Candy Mountain," Murray wrote. "It is possible to see the new economic elite makes its fortunes in cleats."[61]

That day—when the players in cleats summited the Big Rock Candy Mountain—wasn't far off. Though stars like Willie Mays would not play long enough to reach that peak, he and those who stood with him in 1972 and 1973 staked out the approach for those who followed. Mays and company belayed the power shift from owners to players.

That spring, not only was the mountain they climbed green, the players who stood atop it wore the same. Garish as their uniforms may be, the defending champion Oakland A's were the team to topple in 1973.

The Mustache Gang, 1973

Chapter Three

THE TEAM OF THE TIMES

On Friday evening, April 6, 1973, the Oakland A's ran up the center field pole at Oakland-Alameda County Coliseum a large green and gold flag that declared them world champions. The 15-by-37-foot flag dwarfed the American flag next to it. Proud and confident, the A's opened the season before a hometown crowd of 38,207, the second largest crowd in Oakland A's history. Reggie Jackson, the team's emotional mascot, trotted to his position in right field with the smooth stride of a winner. His white shoes flashed against the freshly mowed grass. His golden yellow double-knit uniform trimmed with green sparkled under the light standards. His afro bushed from under his green cap. He sported a beard, which he liked because he thought it made him look mean, as if the A's cleanup hitter wasn't imposing enough to opposing pitchers.[1] Reggie's teammates—best friend Joe Rudi; the competitive captain, Sal Bando; '72 Series MVP Gene Tenace; the practical-joking and dominant Catfish Hunter—took their positions. Catfish fired the first pitch—a fastball called for a strike—and the rowdy and wrasslin', shaggy and unshaven, green and gold began the defense of their title.

Reggie and his teammates opened the 1973 season not only as the team to beat; the A's were the team of the times. The way they quarreled and grappled with one another, their clubhouse resembled Altamont more than Alameda. They disregarded authority with exuberant contempt. Their uniforms and personalities splashed the game with color at a time when black and white thinking was giving way to a broadening palette of ideas. With mangy mops and fuzzy faces, they could have passed for the cast of the musical Hair, which had ended its Broadway run the previous summer but still played on the West Coast. The Yankees may have been America's team in deference to tradition, but the A's of 1973 more closely embodied the nation's identity.

The A's fought one another with verbal jabs and closed fists. When third baseman Sal Bando booted a ball, relief pitcher Rollie Fingers taunted him on the bus after the game, "Hey, steel-glove, when you gonna get a new mitt?" Pitcher Blue Moon Odom called Bando a "fat wop," and Bando retorted with "dumb nigger."[2] The taunts led to shoves, which occasionally escalated into wrestling matches and fistfights. Blue Moon once threatened reserve outfielder Tommie Reynolds with a Coke bottle.[3] As a rookie in 1968, Reggie had squared off against Bando on the bench. In 1972, Jackson crossed out Mike Epstein's ticket request on the team pass list, and the A's 220-pound first baseman attacked Reggie. Their teammates in the clubhouse gathered around—not to break up the scuffle—but to watch, like junior high kids magnetized on a playground—fight! Epstein landed nearly a half dozen punches[4] before manager Dick Williams burst into the room and busted up the fight.[5] They couldn't even win in peace. Moments after the final game of the '72 Series, Moon and Blue tussled.

The A's didn't just fight among themselves; they brawled against other teams as well. Shortstop Bert Campaneris missed Opening Day because he was serving a seven-game suspension for throwing his bat at the Detroit pitcher in last year's A.L. playoffs. Reggie injured a rib in a fight against the Royals in early August 1972. He missed 18 games, and the persistent soreness in his side robbed him of his home-run stroke down the stretch.[6]

The A's distrusted authority. While the nation's youths thumbed their noses at parents, cops, college administrators, and politicians, the ballplayers not only criticized one another, they questioned and disrespected the umpire, their manager, and their owner. Late in the 1972 season, after a game with Boston, Williams chastised Jackson for not throwing the ball into the infield while the tying run scored. "What were you doing out there?" the manager charged.

"None of your goddamn business," Reggie said.

"I'm running this ball club," said Williams, who prized the discipline and order authority brought.

"Like hell you are," Reggie retorted. "We all know who's running this ball club."

He meant Charlie Finley, of course, the A's megalomaniac owner. The remark snapped Williams like a wet towel.[7]

After purchasing the Athletics while they were still based in Kansas City and phasing out the Athletics in favor of the A's, Finley had designed new uniforms for the A's. His "Kelly green and Fort Knox gold" creations injected color into baseball's drab world of gray and white. The boom in color television coverage accentuated the contrast. By 1973, 60 percent of the televisions in American households were color sets—a revolutionary increase from three percent ten years earlier.[8] Americans no longer saw the world in black and white; they viewed it in full spectrum. The A's brilliant green and gold vibrated off their living room screens.

Players griped and critics sniped at the cartoonish costumes. An airplane circled Cincinnati's Riverfront Stadium during the first game of the 1972 World Series towing a banner that read: "Oakland has Weird Uniforms."[9] When Mickey Mantle first saw them, he mocked the players wearing them, "They should have come out of the dugout on tippy-toes, holding hands and singing."[10] But there was no denying the colors' transformative impact. Just as rock n' roll, the sexual revolution, the Vietnam war, and the Watergate scandal had shattered the black and white paradigm of society's values and mores into a variety of shades, the A's colorful uniforms reflected the new spectrum. By the end of the decade, other teams would be sporting uniforms in every color of the rainbow.

They also followed suit with Finley's shoes. He had introduced the bright white—"albino kangaroo"—shoes that contrasted sharply with the traditional black spikes worn for decades. By 1973, many other teams were in step with the A's, making the switch to colorful footwear that matched their uniforms.

The A's made their boldest statement with their hair. The youth of America had expressed their freedom and rejected traditional values with their follicles. So, too, the Oakland nine spawned a generation of new growth with their hair, both cranial and facial. Their locks tumbled out of their caps and over their shoulders. For black players like Reggie and Blue Moon, their tight curls bulged under the edges of their caps. While long hair had symbolized a break with traditional values for white youth, afros symbolized black power. Hair became an expression of values, politics, and style. The A's flaunted theirs, especially in their beards and mustaches, where they truly reflected the face of society.

Sal Bando had looked the prototypical ballplayer in his early days with the A's: close-cropped hair, conservative clothes—the athletic professional. By 1973, his mustache covered his upper lip, his hair flopped over his collar, bell bottoms swamped his shoes, and the lapels of his shirts sprawled over trendy sport coats. "My hair is growing over my collar," he confided in A's beat writer Ron Bergman before spring training. "It's going to cover my ears."[11] Bando represented the trend that had taken over the team and would soon sweep baseball—a trend Reggie had started. His mustache proved the tipping point in baseball fashion.

Others before him had tried to break baseball's unwritten ban on facial hair, but not even Dick Allen nor Pete Rose had proven brash enough to defy decades of decorum. Washington Senators pitcher Allen Benson had worn a beard briefly, for two games in 1934. One had to go back another twenty years to 1914 to find a mustachioed player during the regular season: Wally Schang, a catcher for the Philadelphia Athletics.[12] Perhaps it was fitting that another Athletic would revive the suspended fashion almost sixty years later.

Major League Baseball had no official policy outlawing facial hair. There was simply strong peer pressure—and sometimes team policy or mandate, as in the case of the new Yankees owner—to conform to the clean-shaven standard. Pressure so strong that after Dick Allen appeared on the cover of *Sports Illustrated's* 1970 season preview issue with a mustache and mutton chops, none of his St. Louis Cardinal teammates dared to follow his lead. Allen shaved before opening day. Pete Rose trespassed the Cincinnati Reds' strict dress code when he arrived at spring training in 1972 with a Vandyke. Team president Bob Howsam and manager Sparky Anderson coerced him to shave before the season started.[13]

That same spring, Reggie arrived at the A's training camp in Arizona with a mustache he had started growing during the 1971 American League Championship series. A's owner Charlie Finley didn't like it at first. He told manager Dick Williams to make Reggie shave it off. Reggie characteristically told Williams where to go.[14] Unlike with Allen and Rose, Reggie's mustache survived Opening Day. And beyond.

Once the 1972 season was underway, the A's players seated together on a chartered flight grumbled that Reggie's mustache—and the beard he had started to grow—violated team rules. The others might have to abide by them, but he seemed to think himself above them. That rubbed his teammates wrong. "Catfish decided to address the issue in proper Oakland A's fashion," Williams recalled in his memoir, *No More Mr. Nice Guy.* "He decided to rat on him."

Catfish walked to the front of the plane where Finley sat and conveyed the players' grievance to the owner. Finley dismissed his star pitcher's complaint, seemingly uninterested, but by the time the plane landed in Chicago, Finley had figured out a way to capitalize on the situation.[15] Always keen on a new promotion, Finley announced at a May press conference Major League Baseball's first "Mustache Day." For the A's home game on Father's Day in June, he offered a $300 bonus to any player who grew a mustache by that day and free admission to any fan with a mustache.[16] Wacky promotions spelled profits in Finley's book. He figured "Mustache Day" would attract younger, long-haired fans to the Oakland Coliseum and that seeing players who looked like them would make the fans want to come back.[17]

Finley likely had an ulterior motive. Knowing how Reggie set himself apart as an individual, Finley figured that Reggie would shave his mustache once his teammates grew theirs. "I think Finley wanted to get him to shave it off," Gene Tenace told *The Sporting News*.[18] That was classic Finley: playing one end against the other.

Several of the players balked at Finley's promotion. *What? Try to be like Reggie?* Finley approached the resisters and repeated his desire that all players have mustaches. They relented.[19] Others, like relief pitcher Rollie Fingers, whose two-week paycheck was only $1,200, found a $300 bonus hard to refuse. They happily sprouted mustaches and pocketed the extra cash.[20] Even Dick Williams, known for his tough stance against facial hair, grew a mustache, figuring it might lessen the gap between him and his players. "The world had changed, and baseball had changed with it," Williams said. "If I could identify with my players with a mustache, why not?"[21]

Only Vida Blue, still bearing a grudge against Finley stemming from their acrimonious contract dispute that had Blue hold out until May 2, refused to satisfy the owner's wishes. He alone among the twenty-five players on the A's roster remained clean-shaven for Mustache Day on June 18, which also happened to be the day the team photo was taken. The portrait recorded MLB's first fully—well, almost; Blue excepted—mustachioed team since before World War I.

Finley had figured his players would shave after they collected their bonus checks.[22] Some did, but most kept their mustaches. Even Williams, the son of a rigid military man, stayed mustachioed. Then, they went on a winning spree, and superstition took over—the mustaches became a sort of rabbit's foot worn on the upper lip. "We didn't dare take them off," Tenace said.[23]

The promotion gave Rollie Fingers his trademark, a handlebar mustache as inextricably linked with his identity as Marilyn Monroe and her mole. The following season, Fingers negotiated the $300 mustache bonus into his contract. Finley, seizing upon the opportunity to create a return on his investment, issued a tongue-in-cheek press release: "Rollie not only got a substantial increase in salary, but his 1973 contract also includes a year's supply of the very best mustache wax available. In fact, this is what held up the final signing. I wanted to give Rollie $75 for the mustache wax and he wanted $125 for it." They agreed on $100, enough for the A's relief ace to wax the famous tips of his mustache twice daily.[24] The genie was out of the bottle, thanks to Reggie's defiance, Catfish's resentment, Finley's greed, and Fingers's tips. The A's had given baseball a new look.

Sportswriters dubbed the A's the Mustache Gang. One manager quipped that they were "a baseball team that came to look like a protest march."[25] Pundits billed the 1972 World Series matchup of the hirsute A's against the clean-cut Reds the "Hair versus Square" series.[26]

Nothing sparks a fashion like winning. The '72 champs' facial fashion quickly caught on. Around the baseball circuit, players' faces bloomed with all varieties of facial hair—mustaches, mutton chops, Fu Manchus, Vandykes, mountain man beards, you name it. The trend resulted in a decade of baseball cards that cataloged the sport's whiskered creativity.

Some of the old-timers decried baseball's new look. "They worry more about their hair dryers than their equipment," charged Bob Feller, the Cleveland Indians Hall of Fame pitcher.[27] But the times were a changin', nowhere more visibly than on the players' faces, and the youth weren't asking for the old guard's blessing to grow their hair the way they wanted.

Of course, some teams tried to enforce the old ways. The San Francisco Giants, California Angels, and Cincinnati Reds imposed rigid dress codes. The press ballyhooed the way those teams met the long-haired, bearded, and mustachioed players when they reported to training camps. Barbers on hand sheared them like sheep. The old guard aside, public sentiment on this issue favored the players. *Sporting News* columnist Art Spander argued that players wanted to look like part of society, not "like a man just released from a concentration camp. If management desires fans to identify with a big first baseman, it best allow that first baseman to wear his hair the way he wants."[28]

Even the Yankees joined in, within their new owner's limits. The man who had issued haircut orders through his manager had nothing against mustaches. Steinbrenner fixated on hair length and smooth chins. The Culver Military Academy graduate viewed the longhairs as more Manson than Samson. His efforts to impose his standards, like those of an overbearing father with his rebellious teenage sons, eventually caused public disputes with Don Mattingly, Thurman Munson, and Dave Winfield, among others. Once Reggie Jackson became a Yankee under the Boss's employ, he used his beard to get under Steinbrenner's skin.

Finley, meanwhile, tried to win the players' hearts through their beards and mustaches. He had a newspaper photo of the San Francisco team shaving off mustaches, beards, and sideburns tacked to the A's clubhouse bulletin board along with a note: "To the World Champion A's: How would you like to be a 'Giant' and be told how to dress?" He signed the note Charles O. Finley.[29]

It would take more than a mustache, however, for Finley to win his players' hearts. They hated him. Therein lay the secret of their success.

The A's may have battled one another, but a common enmity toward their owner united them. "All people are the same color to Charlie Finley—green," Reggie Jackson told *Sport* magazine. "We win in spite of him. He's a financial empire, and I respect him for that. But we know the kind of man we play for. We just bind together and win for each other."[30]

What kind of man was Charlie O.? He was a competitive, self-made man driven to win and desperate to make a buck.

He devised so many wacky promotions that Minnesota Twins owner Calvin Griffith called him, not endearingly, "the P.T. Barnum of baseball."[31] Charlie O. not only dressed his players in gaudy green and gold, he outfitted ballgirls in hot pants (Reggie Jackson dated them), concocted the artificial nickname "Catfish" for the Southerner Hunter, offered Blue $2,000 to take the first name "True,"[32] and devised a mechanical rabbit (christened "Harvey") to deliver baseballs to the umpire. Charlie O. schemed innovations endlessly, some that stuck—nighttime All-Star games, World Series night games on weekdays, the designated hitter—and some that didn't—designated runners, different colored bases, three-ball and two-strike counts. Some proved too early for his time—in 1973, he stumped for interleague play, which wouldn't happen until 1997.

Charlie O.'s pet cause at the outset of the '73 season was orange baseballs. He passed out boxes of the Charles O. Finley Baseball, manufactured by Spalding, to his players. He lobbied that batters would be able to see better a ball painted deer hunter orange, particularly at night, which he reasoned would result in more hits, more action for the fans, more revenue for the owners. More than thirty years earlier, Larry MacPhail had experimented with orange baseballs for night games in Brooklyn, but Finley claimed the idea as his own.[33]

In late March, Finley had convinced the American League to let him use the orange balls in an exhibition game with the Cleveland Indians that commissioner Bowie Kuhn was on hand to watch. George Hendrick hit three of Finley's orange balls over the fence in the A's 11–5 loss. Only five days earlier, Finley had traded Hendrick, one of the A's underachieving center fielders in 1972, and catcher Dave Duncan to the Indians. Finley might have expected that Hendrick would credit better visibility of the ball for his three dingers. Instead, Hendrick told Kuhn afterward that he couldn't pick up the spin on the orange ball the way he could pick up the red seams spinning on a white ball. "I think he did that just to get back at Charlie," Dick Williams mused. "Call it 'invention killed by a grudge.'"[34]

Charlie's cheapness fueled his employees' contempt. He wouldn't spend a penny he could pinch. He had pared down his operation to the bare necessities. He employed a skeletal front office staff of eight or nine people in Oakland. He employed himself as chairman, president, general manager, scout, and ticket manager. The clubhouse had a bare floor, no carpet. Players wore last year's uniforms. He doled out two caps and 24 bats at the start of the season—don't break them all before October. No free stock of baseballs for players to autograph. No stamps for players to answer fan mail. No phone in the clubhouse. He offered fewer frills than Motel 6. When the lockout delayed the start of spring training, Finley, who didn't make any money on the exhibition games, praised the delay—it meant he saved the money he would otherwise have to pay his players for meals, motels, and $57 each in weekly Murphy money to cover expenses.[35] "Lord, the man was cheap," Reggie said.[36] "He could squeeze a nickel out of you, and when he did that, he'd go for a dime."[37]

Another player groused anonymously to a *Time* reporter, "Charlie Finley is the cheapest son of a bitch in baseball." To which Charlie retorted, "The guys are a bunch of spoiled brats."[38] So raged his rapport with players.

Finley's penny-pinching may have pissed off his players, but it also yielded earnings. Finley turned a $1.3 million profit on his 1972 team even though the World Champions failed to draw a million customers to the Oakland Coliseum. He did have a knack for making a buck, as he'd proven with his multimillion-dollar insurance business. His net worth in the mid-Seventies was estimated to be at least $30 million.[39]

Yet Cheap Charlie was prone to occasional fits of generosity, paying out impulsive bonuses or buying expensive gifts. In the clubhouse after the first game of the '72 Series, when Gene Tenace had popped off two homers in his first two at bats—the first player ever to accomplish the feat—Finley whispered in his ear, "That was good for five grand," and sure enough, he delivered a check for $5,000.[40] When a line drive in the 1967 minor league opener struck Rollie Fingers in the face and laid him up with a broken jaw just nine days after the young pitcher had wed his high school sweetheart, Finley called and told the newlyweds to take a honeymoon anywhere they wanted in Florida—he would pay for it all.[41] He spent $80,000 on the '72 World Series rings—the most extravagant ever designed to that point, with a full carat diamond in each—and the half-carat diamond pendant bracelets for the players' wives, girlfriends, or mothers. Charlie flew to Arizona to personally pass out the rings and pendants during spring training.[42]

But none of that generosity infused his contract negotiations with players, which had a way of ending ugly. After Reggie slugged 47 home runs, drove in 118 runs, scored 123 more–best in the league–and batted .275 in 1969 for $22,000, he asked for a raise to $60,000 for the 1970 season. Charlie offered $35,000. Reggie seethed. He had grown up poor in Philadelphia, sniffed big money when Finley lured him away from Arizona State University with a $95,000 signing bonus, and was ready to cash in on what he felt he was due. Charlie offered another $5,000 but then held firm.

They remained at an impasse when spring training started. Reggie threatened to quit. Charlie offered another $5,000. Reggie blinked first and signed. Charlie had shown him who was boss. When Reggie slumped early, Finley had him benched. Reggie snubbed the owner's annual barbecue at the La Porte, Indiana, family ranch; Finley announced his plans to demote his star to the minors.[43] Reggie refused to go, and the commissioner backed him. Finley ordered the manager to pinch hit for Reggie against left-handed pitchers. In an early September game in Oakland, Reggie pinch hit with the bases loaded, bottom of the ninth. He clobbered a grand slam to win the game. Crossing home plate, he stopped, glared at the owner, and flipped him off. The owner threatened to have Reggie suspended if he didn't sign the apology Finley had drafted. Reduced to tears, Reggie signed.[44] But he felt humiliated, not remorseful. "I want to be traded," he told reporters. "I don't want to play for Charles Finley."[45]

Absent other options, Reggie stayed, and by 1973, he had tried to suppress the grudge which renewed annually with contract talks.

"I've got too much going for me now to let that SOB spoil it for me," Reggie told sportswriter Glenn Dickey over lunch before the '73 season began. "I know there are certain things we have to put up with in Oakland that we wouldn't have with other clubs. I know I'd probably be a $100,000 ballplayer with another club and I'm earning about $20,000 less here, but those are the circumstances that prevail, and I have to put up with them."[46] He sounded more bitter, and perhaps more honest, in his 1974 memoir, *A Season with a Superstar*: "An owner like Finley puts it to you whenever he wants to. It's legalized rape."

Charlie repeated himself with Vida Blue in 1972. Having won the Cy Young Award in 1971 with a 24–8 record, a 1.82 ERA, and a $14,750 salary, Blue wanted a raise. Charlie didn't think Blue deserved a $100,000 bump in pay.[47] Blue held out. Charlie barely budged. Blue finally signed in early May. Charlie blasted Blue in the press. Blue fumed. He spurned Charlie's mustache promotion and had a lousy season. Charlie had signed his star pitcher for a discounted price—and secured another resentment. The two haggled again over money before the 1973 season, and Blue missed most of spring training. Charlie threatened to trade him. Blue finally signed. Charlie bullied Blue, Reggie, and the others with his checkbook. Arbitration would give them another recourse, but they could not invoke that privilege until after the season, when seven A's— more than from any other team—would seek arbitration. For '73, Reggie and his mates still had to endure Finley.

One by one, or sometimes collectively, Finley antagonized his players, whether by money or manipulation. The animosity didn't end there. His manager resented his meddling and second-guessing with daily phone calls to the clubhouse, dugout, hotel room, or home. His staff mutinied against his autocratic style. In his first fifteen years of owning the A's, Finley burned through five scouting directors, seven farm directors, ten publicity managers, and sixteen broadcasters.[48] He had kissed his wife, Shirley, on the roof of the A's dugout last season when his team won the World Series, but he sat with Miss California when his wife wasn't at games. Shirley, mother of their seven children, would later file for divorce and testify that her husband of nearly thirty years had beaten her regularly.[49]

Even the fans hated him. When Finley announced plans to move the Athletics from Kansas City to Oakland for the 1968 season, fifty Kansas City residents sent letters of condolences to the Oakland mayor.[50] Senator Stuart Symington of Missouri, who had called Finley "one of the most disreputable characters ever to enter the American sports scene,"[51] declared Oakland "the luckiest city since Hiroshima."[52] In Oakland, fans complained about the ballpark's dismal conditions and stayed away. In 1972, the A's averaged 11,888 fans for home games—fewer fans than any other world champion since the 1944 St. Louis Cardinals, when World War II stunted attendance,[53] and fewer than the league average. Finley responded by raising tickets by fifty cents in 1973, putting the cheapest seats in Oakland Coliseum at $2.00, matching the Texas Rangers for the highest-priced tickets in the American League.[54] He prized profits before popularity.

Charlie O. did things his own way, goddamnit. He made a mule the team mascot. Wearing a green cowboy hat, he rode the mule into cocktail parties, through hotel lobbies, and onto the baseball field, where the mule made a habit of crapping in the foul territory west of the left field line. Dick Williams had to tell opposing managers before games that when horsehide met horseshit, the ball was still in play.[55] Finley called the mule Charlie O. "His detractors think it's a terribly cruel thing to do to an animal," *Sport* magazine cracked.[56]

For all of his odd and ostracizing ways, Charlie was the owner who hoisted the World Champions flag at the outset of the 1973 campaign. He was *The Sporting News*'s pick as 1972's Man of the Year. A month after the '72 Series win, the La Porte Chamber of Commerce sponsored a 1,000-person party in his honor and presented him with a bronze bust of himself. Two months later, 670 guests in Oakland toasted him at another gala. President Nixon sent a laudatory telegram. An Oakland city council member proposed that the team's stadium be renamed "Charlie O. Finley Coliseum." He served as Grand Marshal of San Francisco's St. Patrick's Day parade. Whether they saw him as visionary or asshole, nobody denied Charlie's ultimate asset: finding and signing talent. Witness Reggie Jackson, Sal Bando, Bert Campaneris, Catfish Hunter, Gene Tenace, Joe Rudi, Paul Lindblad, Rick Monday, and Rollie Fingers—all Finley discoveries. That singular strength proved the foundation of the dynasty he assembled. It served his insatiable desire to win.

Despised, controlling, competitive to a fault—sounds a lot like Steinbrenner, huh? Indeed, George and Charlie had a lot in common. They fixed one eye on the bottom line, the other on winning. Both demanded that things be done their way. Steinbrenner would become notorious for burning through managers; Charlie already was—he averaged an annual manager firing his first ten years with the A's. Both owners feuded publicly with players, who usually ended up hating them. George also shared Charlie's talent for making staff tense, firing them compulsively.

Both dreamed of owning their own baseball team, and both failed in their first attempt to purchase a club. George missed with the Indians; Charlie missed with the Philadelphia Athletics, Detroit Tigers, Chicago White Sox, and California Angels before snaring the Kansas City Athletics for $2 million in 1960. Both men were forty-two years old when they bought their ball clubs. Both men also owned or operated professional teams in different sports: Steinbrenner dabbled in basketball with the Bulls and Pipers in addition to his racehorse hobby; Finley owned the Memphis Tams in the American Basketball Association and the National Hockey League's California Golden Seals—he changed both teams' uniforms to green and gold that matched his A's fashion statement. The press had enjoyed lampooning Charlie since he arrived on the sports scene. Once the media discerned George's flamboyant foibles, they pounced on him with equal alacrity.

But the two men were certainly not cut from the same cloth. Charlie pushed green and gold; George defended navy pinstripes.

Charlie wore loud, checkered sport coats; George favored blue blazers. Charlie rode a mule; George raised thoroughbreds. Though a dozen years younger, George was old school, Charlie a circus act.

They shared Great Lakes beginnings, but George was born into privilege; Charlie was raised in Birmingham, Alabama, and Gary, Indiana, with steel mill grit in his teeth. Both in the egg-selling business as boys, George's father provided his inventory; Charlie searched out rejected, discolored eggs he bought for a nickel per dozen and resold for fifteen cents a dozen.[57] George jumped hurdles at Williams; Charlie played semipro baseball for the La Porte Cubs and attended classes at Gary College. George found his niche in the family business; Charlie hustled his way into the millionaire ranks by selling group disability insurance to doctors. Living on a 12,000-acre farm in La Porte, sixty miles west of Chicago, Charlie was an absentee owner; George frequently stayed at the Plaza Hotel to increase his presence at Yankee Stadium. Charlie bought out the remaining owners of the Athletics within a year of purchasing the team; Steinbrenner simply silenced his limited partners.

Reggie, who would eventually leave Finley to spar with Steinbrenner in New York, delineated the difference between the two owners with a gunfighter analogy: "Charlie would plug you right between the eyes. He didn't have to tell you he was tough; it was just there, all over him.... George wanted to intimidate you because he didn't really want to fight. He didn't want to look you in the eye and fire."[58]

Charlie Finley, Major League Baseball's reigning maverick, and George Steinbrenner, the new king on the block, were inevitably headed on a crash course before the year was over. But, first, the season had to get underway.

———————

Finley the finagler had arranged for a former POW to throw out the first pitch on Opening Day, a popular move by clubs that spring, but Finley managed to one-up other teams and the press with his ceremonial hurler. Finley enlisted Lieutenant Commander Everett Alvarez, Jr., a Navy pilot who was the prisoner held for the longest time by the North Vietnamese. Charlie had reached Alvarez at a naval hospital in Oakland when no reporters were allowed access.[59] Finley had the infamous POW throw out an orange ball.

Pleased with his coup, Finley watched Reggie trot out to his position. He wondered how Reggie's legs would fare. Reggie had shredded his left hamstring in the final game of the 1972 American League Championship Series on a slide that scored the tying run, then he developed tendonitis in his right knee working out in the off-season. He had left spring training briefly to have his legs examined by the team physician in Oakland. By his own admission, Reggie still couldn't go 100 percent an entire game[60] on what *Sports Illustrated* called his "gimpy legs."[61] Finley knew the team's success that season could hinge on those legs.

Finley had boasted that his team would repeat as World Series champions, but he harbored his own private doubts. Reggie trotted to right field, not center, where he had filled in last year. That was supposed to be Angel Mangual's position, but in 1972, Angel so frequently misjudged fly balls that Williams shifted Jackson, never a Gold Glove candidate, to center. George Hendrick had played center during the first five games of the World Series, but he hit so infrequently that Finley had traded him to the Indians. Reggie had requested the switch back to right to avoid the strain center field put on his legs,[62] so Finley had secretly secured the rights to Billy Conigliaro, who had quit the Milwaukee Brewers the previous June when he had not seen his name in the posted starting lineup.[63] Finley had publicly expressed his confidence in Conigliaro, but he couldn't be sure.

There was another hole at second base. Williams had auditioned 11 players at second in '72—including six in one September game—but none had outright won the job. Dick Green started the '73 season there. No one knew how long he would last. The previous season, he had played only two dozen games there. Even if Reggie's legs remained sound, second base could prove the Athletics' Achilles' heel for '73.

First base raised more questions. In November, Finley had traded the A's regular first baseman, Mike Epstein, who was too outspoken for Charlie's tastes, to Texas for Horacio Piña, the only pitcher in the majors with an underhand delivery. Without a first baseman, Finley decided to move regular catcher Gene Tenace to that spot for '73. Finley's explanation for the move foreshadowed the controversy he would ignite later that season in the '73 Series. Tenace couldn't catch any more, see, because he had confided to the owner at the La Porte gala that his arm had gone bad, couldn't make the throw to second any more. And, what do you know, the team doctors confirmed the sorry state of Tenace's throwing arm for the owner with a diagnosis of tendonitis, so he had to move Tenace to first.[64]

True, Tenace had strained his shoulder late in the '72 season, and he had taken cortisone shots during the playoffs and Series. Williams had moved him to first for Game Seven and replaced him behind the plate with Dave Duncan, explaining Tenace couldn't throw. Tenace had played quietly in pain rather than tell his owner of his injury. "I wouldn't say something like that," Tenace said. "I never had any leverage to play any position other than catcher." He figured a winter of rest would heal his arm, and by spring it felt strong again.[65] Finley's relocation of Tenace—who would go on to catch another 748 games in his career—to first base and the owner's explanation raised eyebrows and questions about Charlie O's believability.

The one place where no one doubted the A's dominance was in its pitching corps. The starting rotation consisted of Catfish Hunter, Blue Moon Odom, Vida Blue, and Ken Holtzman. The best bullpen in baseball had been strengthened by the additions of Paul Lindblad and Horacio Piña, who joined Darold Knowles and Rollie Fingers. On the strength of his pitching alone, Williams had predicted another World Series win. "We're going to win it again," he promised in spring training. "We have the best pitching in baseball."[66]

On the other half of the battery, Dave Duncan angled for more money as the top catcher. Finley refused. Duncan had embarrassed him the year before on a team flight. Duncan held out. Tenace traded his new first baseman's mitt for his catcher's mitt, and his shoulder seemed healed. Late in spring training, Finley swapped backstops, sending the uppity Duncan to the Indians for veteran Ray Fosse, whom Dick Williams called "the best catcher in baseball."[67] Tenace went back to first base. For his part, Duncan declared, "I feel like I've been released from prison."[68]

Finley and Williams claimed the '73 edition of the A's was superior to last year's version, but not everyone believed it. The naysayers pointed to the holes in center and at first and second base. They suggested Finley had given up too much when he traded first baseman Epstein, the A's home run leader in '72, for Piña, who was 2–7 the same year. There was also no clearly designated designated hitter. No, they said, not the A's again. They fingered the White Sox as the front-runners to represent the American League in the Fall Classic.

The gimpy legs hadn't subdued the swagger in Reggie's tongue. On the eve of Opening Day, he declared his intention to have a $100,000 season. He explained to reporters that if he stayed healthy, he could hit 30 home runs "without trying," bat .300, and drive in 100 RBIs. That would be good for a contract worth a hundred grand in '74. "This isn't pie in the sky talk or the pot of gold at the end of the rainbow," Reggie said. "I don't think I'm expecting too much for myself."[69]

No, maybe not, especially coming off his best spring ever, when he led the team in homers and batted close to .400, but he may have been expecting too much generosity from Finley. Reggie's biggest feat would be prying a $30,000 raise from the tightfisted owner.

The A's did not play like World Champions on Opening Day against the Minnesota Twins. They beat themselves with mistakes, and their stars failed to shine. Second baseman Dick Green botched a double play in the first inning, an ominous E-4. Newly acquired Ray Fosse, the "best catcher in the league," threw the ball into left field trying to catch a runner stealing third. Three more players chipped in with errors. Catfish lasted three innings plus two singles in the fourth, yielding six runs. Fingers hit a batter. The night ended darkly, with the A's on the wrong end of the 8–3 score.

Reggie Jackson's legs appeared healthy, but his bat looked anemic. In his first at bat, Reggie struck out with two men on base. He came to bat again in the ninth with two out and a runner on first—and struck out again. His performance was hardly an effort worthy of a hundred grand. If Reggie wanted to earn the big money and the A's wanted to repeat as champions, the superstar needed to perform in the clutch. The season would prove Reggie's worth.

Orlando Cepeda joins the Red Sox in January and becomes the first player to sign as a designated hitter.

Chapter Four

THE DESIGNATED HITTER HAS HIS DAY

Elsewhere around the major leagues, the 1973 season officially started on Thursday, April 5, with a showcase game in Cincinnati, where the San Francisco nine beat the defending National League champs 4–1. Full play in both leagues began Friday. After the Senators fled Washington, President Nixon adopted the California Angels as his team. He made the forty-five-mile drive from the Western White House in San Clemente to Anaheim, where he handed the ball to Major David Luna, a North Vietnamese prisoner for eight years. Luna, also the first pitcher to throw a no-hitter for nearby Orange County High, tossed out the ceremonial first pitch. Meanwhile, in Pittsburgh, the Pirates retired No. 21 before a crowd of 51,695 in homage to Roberto Clemente, the Pirates right fielder who had died in a plane crash on New Year's Eve on his way to deliver aid to earthquake victims in Nicaragua. In Atlanta, a mere 23,385 fans, the smallest crowd in the National League, showed up. A few rednecks in the outfield section slung racial slurs at the Braves right fielder, Hank Aaron, criticizing his $200,000 salary. At Shea Stadium, George Steinbrenner watched the Mets' Tom Seaver beat Steve Carlton, the National League's 1972 Cy Young Award winner, and the Phillies 3–0. Willie Mays started in center field, batted third, and went oh-for-three.

Boston, where the Red Sox hosted the Yankees, was the focal point of the Opening Day offerings. There, where the American

Revolution took shape, the rules of the national pastime changed forever. During the first inning of a windy afternoon game, Yankees starter Mel Stottlemyre watched from the dugout bench while Ron Blomberg batted in his place—as he would do for the Yankee pitchers all afternoon. Blomberg took a base on balls and secured his place in history as the first designated hitter to bat in a regular season game. The other American League teams playing that day would all use designated hitters for their pitchers, but in a game that started at 1:30 p.m. on the East Coast, Blomberg became the first.

Quick with his wit, Blomberg joked that he was cut out for the DH role. "I taught myself to hit by pulling blackberries off a bush in our front yard and hitting them with a stick," he said. "I got to be a pretty good hitter, but no one ever hit the berries to me so I could learn to field."[1]

In truth, Blomberg's at bat was an unintended, almost embarrassing way into the record books for the twenty-four-year-old with real aspirations to play first base for George Steinbrenner's team. Yankees manager Ralph Houk had said at the outset of the season he would select his designated hitters on a daily basis, determined by the ballpark and opposing pitcher. That historic day in Boston, Houk had picked Felipe Alou, not Blomberg, to play first base because he hit well in Fenway. Houk inserted Blomberg into the number six spot in the lineup as the designated hitter because he wanted another left-handed hitter up against Boston's starting pitcher, right-hander Luis Tiant. It was a new assignment for Blomberg; he hadn't batted as the DH in any of the Yankees' spring training exhibitions.[2] Blomberg, the accidental answer to a trivia question, would not prove to be the measure of the new designated hitter rule.

That distinction belonged to the DH in the Red Sox lineup, Orlando Cepeda. Cepeda, a seven-time All-Star beyond his prime, was the quintessential designated hitter. He had believed he was finished, his career sabotaged by bad knees. But then, days after the American League owners had voted to implement the controversial DH rule for the 1973 season, Boston had called. Even if Cepeda couldn't run or field, he could still hit. A fifteen-year veteran at that point, he had the poise to handle the pressure of the role. The Red Sox signed Cepeda, the first player hired specifically as a designated hitter. He would be the means by which the critics and supporters would judge the success of the designated hitter experiment. He carried the fate of the new rule on his bat like a weighted doughnut.

Rule 6.10 stated "a hitter may be designated to bat for the starting pitcher and all subsequent pitchers in any game without otherwise affecting the status of the pitcher(s) in the game."[3] It was a desperate measure. By the time the owners gathered for their winter meeting after the 1972 season, baseball was in a bad way. The national pastime had lost its grip on the country's imagination. Television, by now a standard fixture in American living rooms, had diverted fan attention to fringe sports like golf, drag racing, and alpine skiing. *Sports Illustrated* duplicated the coverage, forsaking features on baseball during the season for coverage of yachting and horse races. Opening Day 1973 competed with the fifth annual Masters golf tournament for headline space in the dailies, along with hockey and basketball playoffs, which had spilled into April.

Football represented the biggest threat. The NFL had surpassed MLB as the land's number-one attraction. Blame television. Football played well to the little screen. Baseball didn't. Baseball, as its defenders argued, was not meant to be viewed but to be absorbed. "Baseball is a day in the sun, with a couple of beers and camaraderie," Art Spander wrote in his *Sporting News* column.[4] Baseball was a ballpark sport, Dick Young argued in *Sports Illustrated*. As such, "There is the sublime moment baseball turns from a spectator sport to a participant sport" when the fan rides the manager for a critical decision.[5] You couldn't do that to a TV. Well, not with any satisfaction. Despite the pundits' apologies, football was winning the ratings war. In 1972, twelve million homes tuned into

"Monday Night Football" while national broadcasts of baseball games on Monday nights averaged barely more than seven million homes. Saturday afternoon's "Game of the Week" reached little more than four million homes weekly.[6]

Commentators from Harry Caray to Howard Cosell complained that the game dragged on television. For all of the arguments that baseball's beauty transcended the tube's confines, owners heard the siren call of Madison Avenue. Bigger television audiences translated into bigger advertising revenues. Major League Baseball's brass tried various means to hurry the pace—players ran hard to and from their positions, golf carts chauffeured relief pitchers from the bullpen to the mound. But the game remained too slow, too dull for the average viewer at home, and owners failed to cash in.

Baseball also suffered from a public relations crisis. The labor wars had eroded fan interest. While the owners and players had haggled over pensions and arbitration instead of starting spring training, Furman Bisher had written for *The Sporting News*, "Baseball is developing all the fan appeal of coal mining."[7] Baseball commissioner Bowie Kuhn warned that "the American fans are fed up with this disruptive annual exercise of the players and clubs rending at each other…. Neither baseball nor any other sport is an indispensable part of the American scene. All of us had better recognize it." Indeed, an independent research firm that surveyed public opinion on baseball's labor dispute found that "fans could live without baseball."[8]

So they were, tuning into football games, reading about golf, and planning Sunday picnics in places other than the ballpark. The pain was felt most acutely in the American League, where attendance had dropped 14 percent in 1972 from the previous season.[9] The junior circuit trailed the National League in attendance by 26 percent.[10] The disparity may have been explained by the larger fan bases for NL teams in more heavily populated metropolises than their AL counterparts, as Joseph G. Preston posits in *Major League Baseball in the 1970s*. But the prevailing wisdom of the day was that offense generated interest. There were more home runs, doubles, and triples hit and more runs scored in the National League. It followed that those games would attract more fans. Meanwhile, American League owners were losing out at the gate, where they faced a crisis of attrition, antipathy, and apathy.

The cavalry that rode to the rescue straddled a mule. Charlie O. Finley proposed the solution: the permanent pinch hitter. "The average fan comes to the park to see action, home runs," Finley reasoned. "He doesn't come to see a one-, two-, three- or four-hit game. I can't think of anything more boring than to see a pitcher come up to bat, when the average pitcher can't hit my grandmother. Let's have a permanent pinch hitter for the pitcher."[11]

Granted, there were pitchers who could hit, but not many. In '72, American League pitchers struck out nearly 30 percent of the time, and their collective batting average was almost one hundred points below the league average for all hitters. The permanent pinch hitter Charlie proposed would erase the tedium of the pitcher at the plate and boost entertainment with more hitting. That meant action, which played better on television and lured fans to the park. The idea was perfect: more offense, more fans, more profits. Bingo!

Not so fast, Finley. You're attacking the game's foundation. Baseball had been played with nine men per side for over a century. Pitchers batted—that's how the game was played. It was a time-honored tradition. Replacing a pitcher at the plate with a designated hitter would fundamentally change the game. Why, that would be like celebrating Christmas in July. It just wasn't done. The idea rubbed against the sensibilities of baseball's protectors.

They feared this erosion of tradition might lead to other wacky proposals. What would Charlie want next, designated runners? Actually, yes. An MLB committee studied that Finley suggestion in 1973, but the idea did not come to fruition other than on the 1974 A's roster in the person of Herb Washington. Some saw baseball going the way of football, which at that point hadn't specialized much beyond the place-kicker but by the twenty-first century would be insanely specialized down to pass-rushing linemen and third-down ball carriers. Although the designated runner idea didn't pan out, the permanent pinch hitter would eventually open the door for a substrata of relief pitchers.

There was also concern for the record books. Inserting a designated hitter into the batting order would alter the way the game was played and tinker with its statistics, baseball's holy code. The rule change would impact the number of runs scored, batting averages, runs batted in, complete games pitched, and strikeouts. Consider that California Angels pitcher Nolan Ryan led the majors with 329 strikeouts in 1972, but many of those he fanned were pitchers. Had the DH rule been in place and had Ryan faced more effective hitters, *Sports Illustrated* posited at the outset of the '73 season that Ryan may not have struck out as many as the 310 that Phillies ace Steve Carlton whiffed in the National League.[12] The rule would introduce a new asterisk era in the minds of baseball purists, much the same way the 162-game schedule had. "After all, what keeps baseball going?" Yankees great Mickey Mantle asked rhetorically. "It's the records. People are always talking about records, and if you eliminate the records, the game loses a lot of its romance. Yet that's what they're doing. They are making records easier to erase."[13]

The debate raged vigorously, the arguments stacked one against the other. A designated hitter would relieve the boredom that resulted from the parade of pinch hitters and relief pitchers late in a game, but it would also eliminate the strategy of when to pinch hit and for whom. The rule change would mercifully relieve the fans from having to watch a pitcher try to bat, but it would also prevent pitchers from having the chance to help themselves win a game at the plate. The change would make bunting more of a surprise than a routine, but it would reduce bunting overall—designated hitters would be signed not for their finesse but for their power. The DH spot would extend the careers of aging sluggers but slow the development of younger players.

Some owners, like the Dodgers' Walter O'Malley, opposed the idea simply because Charlie wanted it. They disliked him so much that they automatically rejected whatever he proposed.[14]

In the end, as with most any business decision, the proposed rule change came down to the bottom line. The National League, with its potent offense, was doing record business.[15] Owners were not motivated to change. They supported the status quo and voted against the idea. The American League owners, on the other hand, were hungrier to recoup dwindling earnings. In January, they voted 8–4 to implement the designated hitter as a three-season experiment.

The permanent pinch hitter was not, in fact, a novel idea. The AAA International League had used a designated hitter for the entire 1969 season with mixed results. The change had sped up the game and increased the number of runs scored per game by 12.6 percent. A fan survey showed that over two-thirds of fans approved the designated hitter and only 7 percent opposed it (the rest were neutral),[16] but attendance for the season had dropped by almost 20 percent, which killed the experiment.[17] That had happened in a relatively obscure minor league. The change at the big league level fired the American imagination in a much greater way. This was the first major change in the game's rules in eighty years.

Bowie Kuhn quickly voiced his approval. "The effect will be to improve hitting and give us a classic balance between pitching and hitting," the commissioner said.[18] "I would have preferred that both leagues did it, but if it's successful in one, then I hope the National follows suit."[19]

Players, on the other hand, feared that the change could mean job cuts. With starting pitchers able to last longer, avoiding late-inning, pinch-hitting substitutions, the thinking was that the designated hitter might reduce the need for at least two relief pitchers, tempting owners to trim rosters down to twenty-three players.[20]

Others feared for their personal safety. If pitchers never had to bat, they could throw at batters without being subject to retaliation. "It's legalized manslaughter," Red Sox star Carl Yastrzemski said. "The only thing preventing pitchers from throwing at hitters now is that they must come to bat themselves."[21]

Still others opposed the designated hitter on higher grounds, saying it dumbed down the game. Baltimore Orioles manager Earl Weaver, a wily tactician, complained that there was no basis for the rule. "I might be from the old school, but I don't think baseball needs saving," Weaver said.[22] He would find a loophole in the rule, listing a pitcher as the DH in his starting lineup. That way, if the opposing pitcher changed before the DH's turn at bat and he wanted to use, say a left-handed batter instead of a right-handed batter, he hadn't wasted a hitter without using him.

Rhetoric boiled over on both sides. One accused the traditionalists of being too square to evolve with the times, Neanderthal types who would be content squatting around campfires gnawing on bones. The other side countered that the radicals had no respect for tradition, the very problem with society and the reason for its unraveling moral fabric. "Probably not since the Roman Catholic Church switched from Latin to English Masses has any break with tradition caused more vigorous argument in this country," William Leggett observed in *Sports Illustrated*'s season preview.[23]

The integrity of the game was at stake. The experiment would determine whether or not baseball could survive the change. Ultimately, the question would be answered at the turnstiles. If the designated hitter caused them to spin more frequently, the game would be saved in the American League. But, the future did not show promise. A *Sporting News* survey at the outset of the 1973 season revealed that fans were skeptical about the new rule. Sixty-one percent polled said they opposed the designated hitter.[24] The experiment seemed doomed before it began.

––––––––––

Orlando Cepeda was an unlikely candidate for the American League's savior. Once upon a time, maybe. In 1958, Cepeda had torn up the National League his first year with the Giants, their first away from Brooklyn. The twenty-year-old outfielder had batted .312, slugged 25 home runs, knocked in 96 runs, and was the unanimous choice for Rookie of the Year. The son of a Caribbean baseball legend nicknamed Bull and often called the "Babe Ruth of Puerto Rico," Baby Bull was a natural talent who got better each year. By 1961, he led the league in home runs (46) and RBIs, capturing the Triple Crown with fellow Puerto Rican Roberto Clemente, who won the batting title. Cepeda's 142 RBIs that year still stand as the most hit by a Giant—not even Barry Bonds has bettered the mark. Charismatic and enthusiastic, able to bust up a clubhouse with a Spanish cheer, Baby Bull became more popular in San Francisco than Willie Mays. With St. Louis in 1967, Cepeda powered the Cardinals to the World Series title with a unanimous MVP season. He became the only player ever to be chosen unanimously both as the Rookie of the Year and the Most Valuable Player.

Had you picked him then as the Great Puerto Rican Hope of the American League, it might have been unanimous. But in 1973? No way. Sure, he still had the great bat and the quick smile, but by then he also had the bum knees. Four surgeries had left scars on both sides of both knees—those joints had been carved up more than a November turkey.

Cepeda had enjoyed a good season in 1970 with the Atlanta Braves, batting .305, hitting 34 home runs, and punching in 111 runs. He started 1971 strong. By the end of May, he had hit 14 homers and knocked in 44 runs, but then he wrenched his other knee, the "good" knee. Cepeda tried to play with the pain, but he surrendered to surgery before the season ended. He rehabbed the knee with some winter ball in Puerto Rico. It still hurt that spring. He wanted to play but got only sporadic starts and pinch-hitting calls. In June, the day after he hit two home runs, he didn't see his name in the starting lineup. *¿Qué pasa?* Cepeda was batting .298, but they wouldn't play him. *¡Bastante!* He quit. "They treat me like garbage," he said and went home.[25]

The Braves talked him into returning. Ten days later, they shipped him to Oakland in exchange for Denny McLain, a former MVP himself—the first time that two MVPs had been exchanged for one another. But McLain, a 31-game winner in 1968, was washed up by age twenty-eight—on the down side of a gambling habit and without any resemblance to his earlier, talented self. Cepeda was deemed his equal, baseball's equivalent of milk past its expiration date.

Technically, McLain and Cepeda were not traded for one another, since the trading deadline had passed. Instead, Finley worked a deal where he agreed to sell McLain to the Braves in exchange for the purchase of Cepeda, contingent upon both players first clearing waivers. Any of the other twenty-two teams could have picked up Cepeda, but none considered him worth the $25,000 waiver price. Baby Bull became one of Charlie O's A's on June 29, 1972.

Cepeda's career had come full circuit—almost. He was back where he began, in the Bay Area, only Oakland seemed a long way from San Francisco. He realized he was "no longer a star, but an injured veteran on the decline."[26]

Finley soon made the same discovery. His original plan was to platoon Cepeda at first base with Mike Epstein, which fueled Epstein's resentment toward the owner.[27] Cepeda's rickety legs botched the plan. He could barely stand without his left knee hurting. The 90-foot run to first base was a gauntlet of pain. He played a week for the A's, with three hitless appearances as a pinch hitter. Cepeda needed another surgery, his fourth. Discouraged, he missed the rest of the season. Finley did not include Cepeda's name on the list of players to receive World Series rings.

In December, Finley sent a telegram to Cepeda in Puerto Rico. *Call me within three days* (at your expense, of course), *or you'll be released*. Seventy-two had been a frustration. Benched by the Braves. Released. No one wanted him on waivers. Three plate appearances with Oakland. As a pinch hitter, not a player. Knees hurting the whole time. Another surgery. Then, there was the owner. He was *loco*. Difficult in every way.[28] Charlie had told Cepeda he didn't want to pay him because he couldn't play every day.[29] By releasing him in the winter, he wouldn't have to pay any more of his $90,000 salary. Typical Finley. Cepeda didn't call.

Finley claimed it wasn't about the money. "Cepeda's salary didn't bother me," Finley told the press. "What bothered me was that our team physician (Dr. Henry Walker) who performed the operation said that all of the cartilage in his knee was gone—that it was almost bone on top of bone. Dr. Walker advised me that it was very, very questionable whether he could hold up."[30] Finley said he feared that Cepeda would never play again because of his knees.[31]

Of course, money was always a factor with Finley, regardless of what he said, but his concern about Cepeda's knees was legitimate. Cepeda didn't fit Finley's definition of the ideal designated hitter: able to make frequent contact with the ball, hit to all fields, knock out homers, and have a certain amount of speed.[32] Ixnay on that last one. *Adios*, Orlando.

Finley placed Cepeda on waivers. Once again, there were no takers. Cepeda was cut loose. A free man. Adrift. At thirty-five, he figured he was finished. Not that he wanted to be, but the way his knees ached when he got out of bed and nagged him throughout the day, he was ready to quit.[33] December 18, 1972, the day Finley let him go, would be the date etched on the tombstone of his career. "I was completely discouraged," he wrote in his memoir, *Baby Bull*. "I wanted out of baseball."[34]

Then, in January, the Red Sox called. *¡Sorpresa!* Down in Puerto Rico, Cepeda hadn't heard that the AL had implemented the DH rule only days earlier. That gave him another chance to play ball. Over the holidays, he had realized baseball was all he'd ever known, all he'd ever wanted to do. *Sí*, he would fly to Boston for a doctor to examine his knees.[35]

Thomas Tierney, MD, the Red Sox team physician, poked and tugged Cepeda's legs. They appeared fit enough. "His knees will stand up all season," the doctor pronounced.[36]

No one could be certain, of course. Both sides knew it was a gamble. Cepeda told Red Sox general manager Dick O'Connell that he wouldn't regret signing him.[37] He asked for $100,000. O'Connell offered $85,000 and a Mercedes as a signing bonus.[38] Cepeda signed—and became the first hired-gun designated hitter. Baby Bull, also known as Cha Cha, met the press in loud plaid pants and a matching vest over a white turtleneck—looking every bit 1973. His bushy sideburns and moustache completed the mod look. Only the Boston cap squashed over his afro looked out of place.[39]

Skeptics thought he was out of place on the Boston payroll. They knew how good Cepeda was—or had been. They had seen what he could do as the MVP of the Cardinals team that beat their miraculous Red Sox team in the 1967 Series. But what about those knees? They weren't worth eighty-five grand today. *You kiddin' me?* Didn't matter what the Sox doc said, those battle-scarred knees were ticking time bombs. The barstool wisdom in Beantown was that the former National League star wasn't fit for the junior circuit, even if he would play only half of the time. He hit over .300 nine times? Drove in over 100 runs five times? Scored more than 90 runs five times? So what? That was then. A then so long ago. *Nope, guy ain't got a chance. Gimme another pint.*

On the circuit, Cepeda's signing drew criticism for other reasons. Some players scoffed at the idea of being simply a hitter. Frank Robinson, the only player to be named MVP in both leagues, told *The New York Times* that anybody who did not play in the field was not a complete player.[40] The irony of Frank Robinson's statement would play out in the 1973 season, when he batted in 127 games as the Angels' designated hitter.

Others did not want to be stigmatized as a designated hitter, because it usually meant one of two things: they fit the stereotype as an ailing veteran in his final days or their glove was so bad they weren't worth the risk in the field. When the Rangers' rookie manager Whitey Herzog later said he had landed the perfect DH in Rico Carty, the thirty-three-year-old outfielder with the weak arm and the highest batting average among active players (.315) retorted, "I'm no invalid. I want to play both ways."[41]

Even players for whom the DH role seemed to be invented said they wanted to do more than simply bat in a game. "I'd rather hit and play in the field, too," said the Minnesota Twins' Tony Oliva, a thirty-four-year-old, three-time batting champion with battered legs and the agility of a Ming vase. "When you play in the field, you're more in the game. Your body stays loose, you're more with it. Everything is better."[42]

Cepeda said initially, at his signing press conference, that he wanted to play regularly, but almost as quickly, he defended his integrity as a designated hitter. "To me, hitting is baseball," Cepeda told *The New York Times*. "If you hit, you're a good player. If you can't hit, you're nothing. I am a complete baseball player."[43]

Cepeda knew that was the only way he could still play. He just had to prove it. Spring training would be his first test. He played a little first base in Florida, but quickly abandoned his hope of being a two-way player.[44] Some reporters doubted that Cha Cha would even make the team.[45]

Red Sox manager Eddie Kasko had tried to put him at ease when training camp opened. Kasko didn't like the new DH rule. He hoped it would be rescinded after the season. But he believed Cepeda could help his club.[46] The first day of spring training, Kasko told his new but not young hitter that he wanted him to be his own man. "Get in shape the way you know how," Kasko said. "You know what's best for you." Cepeda appreciated that sort of respect.[47]

He lifted weights to strengthen and support his knees. He batted .346.

Good, yes. But it was still spring. Those were exhibition games. Meaningless. Pitchers had gotten a late start because of the lockout. Wait to see what he does in the regular season. That would be the true test.

————

Along came Opening Day. That historic afternoon game at Fenway. Blomberg beat Cepeda into the record books, but both of their bats were shipped to Cooperstown. Not that Cepeda had done much with his. There, too, Blomberg showed him up. The Yankees DH added a single to his walk, reaching base twice in four trips to the plate. The Red Sox had won big, 15–5, but Cepeda's bat had been silent. Listed fifth in the Boston order, the Red Sox' expensive designated hitter had come to the plate six times and walked back to the dugout six times without reaching base. He tried to beat out one ground ball—laboring, straining, barely moving—but was easily thrown out. It was painful just to watch. The 32,000-plus Fenway faithful shook their heads. Cepeda finished the first day of the experiment oh-for-six.

His second day did not go much better. In a replay of Opening Day, the sun shone impotently, the cold winds whipped, the Sox routed the Yankees, and Cepeda went hitless. He did manage two sacrifice flies and a base on balls, but Boston wasn't paying him the big money to hit long outs. After two games, the Red Sox had scored 25 runs on 33 hits, but the team's designated hitter hadn't contributed one hit. Cepeda was oh-for-eight, and doubts about the DH experiment loomed as large as the triple zeros in his batting average. Boston fans taunted him from the bleachers. Sportswriters tagged him the designated out.

The mockery continued on day three. Once, twice, thrice, Cepeda failed to hit. Kasko had stuck with Cepeda in the number five spot, but he decided he would sit Cha Cha tomorrow and use Ben Oglivie. Cepeda came to bat again in the ninth oh-for-eleven on the season. His knees ached in the cold. He didn't think he could run. He would be lucky to beat the throw to first if he banged a ball off the Green Monster.[48]

Cepeda faced Sparky Lyle, on the mound in his first appearance at Fenway since the Red Sox traded him to the Yankees a year earlier. Lyle had come into the game three innings earlier, trailing 3–2, but the Yankees had evened the score in the top of the ninth.

He wanted to give his team a chance to bat in the tenth and avoid being swept by their hated foes. Even more, Lyle wanted to show the Red Sox what a mistake they had made in letting him go.

Cepeda watched Lyle's first pitch. Ball one. He watched the second. Strike one. The pressure mounted. Lyle threw a slider, his money pitch. Cepeda swung—and connected. The ball lifted into the wind and muscled its way over the tall left-field wall. Home run! Boston 4, New York 3.

The Fenway crowd "erupted into a frenzy." Cepeda's teammates rushed out of the dugout to congratulate him at home. Cha Cha stopped short of the plate, then toed it with his right foot in a celebratory dance step. His teammates mugged him happily.[49]

Cepeda made his first hit as the league's representative DH count, but one hit—even a dramatic game-winning home run—does not a season make. He had boosted his batting average to a meager .083. Around the league, his fellow designated hitters had gone 23-for-104 collectively over the first three days of the season, a .220 average. Not an impressive debut. It was still too early to judge the outcome of the experiment, but Cepeda would have to improve his hitting significantly to instill faith in the doubters who believed the new rule impugned the game's purity. The season was still young—it would prove a mighty test for the old player.

The hate mail, verbal taunts, and death threats **Aaron** endured throughout the 1973 season had him frequently looking over his shoulder.

Chapter Five

CHASING THE GHOST

On a late April evening in Atlanta, Hank Aaron chased Babe Ruth's ghost, haunted by the specter of racism. The floodlights glistened on the nape of his dark chocolate skin. A black man at bat in the capital of the South, he stood within reach of Ruth's home run record of 714 home runs, the most hallowed mark in American sports, but centuries of hatred stood between him and that milestone. The challenge to the right-handed batter with the quick wrists was not only to knock the ball over the left-field fence thirty-seven more times but to press through the force of American history. The legacy of slavery, Jim Crow, and the Ku Klux Klan formed the greatest challenge to his pursuit of baseball's most prized record.

In 1973, the nation remained conflicted over race. The American public wanted to see itself as the Waltons, that benevolent, warm, and welcoming family on the hottest new TV show of the year. The white ruling class had let the Negroes sit in the front of the bus, drink from the same fountains, and eat at their restaurants. But "All in the Family," animated by Archie Bunker's bigoted riffs, remained the country's most popular show. The new laws may have white-washed discrimination, but they had not erased America's prejudice.

In his first at bat against the Mets on April 27, 1973, Aaron made a routine out. He took his spot in the outfield for the start of the next inning. A few hometown rednecks in the right-field bleachers started in on him. There weren't many fans in the stands that night, fewer than 8,000, and Aaron could hear the individual voices.

"You're not as good as Babe Ruth!"

"You're making too much money, you SOB!"

"Did you forget how to hit, nigger?"

Aaron had heard those taunts since Opening Day. He stared straight ahead.[1]

Aaron batted again in the fourth. The Mets had threatened to score in their half of the inning. Willie Mays had singled, breaking out of an oh-for-eighteen slump, and so had the batter after him, but the next batter stranded the runners on base. The score remained tied at zero. Tom Seaver, the Mets' dominating pitcher, had not given up a hit. Aaron faced him with two out. Seaver threw a curveball that broke a fraction of a second too late. Aaron plunked it over the left-field fence for the game-winning hit, his fifth home run of the season and 678th of his career. He needed only thirty-six more to tie Ruth.

Aaron had started the season with 673 career home runs, forty-one short of Babe Ruth's record. He had averaged 35 home runs a year over nineteen seasons but hit almost forty-one a year over the last four seasons. Only two years earlier, in 1971, he slugged forty-seven, the most he'd ever hit in a season. Most people figured Hammerin' Hank would reach 714 sometime in 1974, but after he hit his fifth tater against Seaver, Aaron was on pace to hit forty-five for the season. The mark was certainly within reach in 1973.

Some astute followers pointed out that Aaron should have started the season at 674, with one more home run to his credit. They referenced a game against the Cardinals in 1965. Aaron had nailed a changeup onto the right-field roof of Busch Stadium, but when Aaron crossed home plate, the ump shouted, "You're out." While Aaron circled the bases, Cardinals catcher Bob Uecker had shown the ump the spike marks where Aaron had stepped outside of the batter's box when he swung. The ump, Chris Pelekoudas, took away what could prove the difference between Hank and the Babe, should Aaron fall one homer short.[2]

Aaron began the season powerfully motivated. For starters, he felt the "sheer ambition of breaking such a monumental mark."[3] That alone was enough to make him work hard in spring training, eager for Opening Day. He had said in February at his thirty-ninth birthday party, where they served him a cake at the Braves offices, that he planned to play only two more years.[4] He wanted to make those count, playing the best he could and staking his claim on the home run title. If he stayed healthy, it would certainly be his, and he could exit the game gracefully, the way he had played it for so long.

Aaron also realized the opportunity to find the spotlight that had eluded him. His accomplishments to date certainly merited lavish attention. He was a smooth fielder with a strong, accurate arm. He ran well, stealing more bases than most power hitters. He hit for average as well as power—the first player to collect 3,000 hits and 500 home runs. Yet he remained overlooked and underrated. A star in small markets—first Milwaukee, then Atlanta after the Braves moved there for the 1966 season—he had never received the attention he would have if he'd played for a team in a larger city on one of the coasts. He also played with seeming ease and without flair, much like the great DiMaggio, but, as a black man, without the adulation. "It was odd that Joe DiMaggio was also quiet and deliberate, and yet in DiMaggio's case these traits were perceived as dignity and grace, which translated into American heroism," Lonnie Wheeler wrote in Aaron's autobiography, *I Had a Hammer*. "In Aaron's case, the same qualities translated into comparative invisibility." Aaron knew the closer he moved to 714, the more he would garner the attention he deserved and desired.

He had reason to be happy already. He had a new love in his life, Billye Williams. They had met the previous season, when she interviewed him on her morning television show, "Today in Georgia." He had impressed her with his "quietness, with his unassuming attitude, the fact that he seemed not too taken with himself or his accomplishments." He struck her as "genuinely nice" and a "family kind of man."[5] By the time the Mets came to town in late April, Aaron and Williams were engaged, planning to marry after the season.

Something deeper than love and ambition motivated Aaron that spring: his sense of duty to his race.[6] Aaron had cracked the Braves lineup in 1954, seven years after Jackie Robinson had broken Major League Baseball's color barrier. That year, the U.S. Supreme Court ruled in *Brown v. Board of Education* that a black girl could attend the white school in Topeka, but in the South, white men still lynched black boys who whistled at white women. America may have set aside the "separate but equal" standard, but it was not color blind.

Aaron would play five years in Milwaukee before the last MLB team finally integrated its roster. He slept in separate hotels from his white teammates, ate in separate restaurants. He heard the hatred that lynched his brothers in the jeers of the Atlanta crowd. He read it in his mail. What Jackie had begun twenty-six Aprils earlier had not been finished.

As a boy, Aaron had idolized Robinson, who opened baseball's door for him. "He gave every black kid in America something to look forward to," Aaron said.[7] As an adult, Aaron's admiration deepened for "the man whose judgments I valued more than anybody's."[8] When Aaron was a rookie and the black players stayed in hotels determined by skin color, not team colors, Robinson had welcomed the young man into his circle. They started a conversation that lasted until shortly before Robinson's death about how an African-American ballplayer should carry himself and represent his race. Robinson urged Aaron never to allow himself to be "satisfied with the way things are," but to strive to improve conditions for himself and all African Americans.[9]

Robinson's funeral the previous fall, in late October 1972, further engrained Aaron's motivation. Aaron attended the service at Riverside Church near Harlem, as did Willie Mays and a handful of active players. Aaron was shocked that more current players did not pay their respects to the man in the casket who had made it possible for them to play the game. "It made me more determined than ever to keep Jackie's dream alive, and the best way I could do that was to become the all-time home run champion in the history of the game that had kept out black people for more than sixty years," he wrote in *I Had a Hammer*. "I owed it to Jackie."

Each time he stepped to the plate in 1973, Aaron saw himself as Robinson's successor in the struggle for equality, carrying on where Robinson had left off. Rachel Robinson, Jackie's widow, deemed Aaron worthy of the role. "Despite the odds against them, (Jackie and Hank) became not just outstanding ballplayers, but men of determination and courage," she said. "These qualities and their resilience enabled them to endure and transcend obstacles with dignity and pride."[10]

Every bigoted slur hurled from the bleachers, every racial indignity cast toward his people, deepened Aaron's resolve. He would break Ruth's record and use his role as the Home Run King to improve conditions for his people.[11]

The Braves beat Seaver and the Mets Friday night, 2–0, on the strength of Aaron's homer and another by Darrell Evans on the next pitch. Aside from those two pitches, Seaver had pitched well that night, giving up just one other hit. He had given up five home runs already in April, but those were all solo shots, the only five runs he had yielded in the five games he had started. His teammates had given him little support, scoring only six runs in those games. Though he had pitched well during the month, he had won only two games and lost two. After the game, he was pissed. "Get away from me," he barked at a reporter. "Get away from me before I start yelling."[12]

The next night, Saturday, the Braves led 2–1 going into the eighth inning. Willie Mays came to bat with a runner on first, no outs. Mays had broken out of his slump the night before and already had a hit in the game. This time, he lined the ball to center field for a double, his first extra-base hit of the three-week-old season. Two batters later, Mays scored the go-ahead run, and his season brightened, slightly. The two hits that night raised his average to .118.

For two decades, Aaron had starred in Mays's shadow. Mays, with his flash on the field and say-hey personality, had played on the larger stages in New York and San Francisco. His style—the basket catches and hat flying when he ran the bases—gave kids an image to imitate and sportswriters entertaining copy. Mays was a star on the rise when Aaron arrived. As Tom Stanton observes in *Hank Aaron and the Home Run that Changed America*, "Aaron broke into the majors three years after Mays and continually found himself one step behind." Aaron was named NL MVP in 1957; Mays had won the award three years earlier, in 1954. Mays repeated as MVP in 1965; Aaron never did. Aaron won his first batting title in 1956; Mays had won his first two years earlier. Aaron led the NL in home runs in 1957; Mays had led the league in home runs in 1955. Aaron won a World Series in 1957; Mays had won the World Series in 1954. Aaron won the first of three Gold Gloves in 1958; Mays won his first of twelve in 1957. Seemed everything Aaron did, Mays had already done. Aaron wrote in his autobiography, "I had to wonder if I would ever get out of that man's shadow."[13]

Until June 10, 1972. That Saturday, Aaron parked a Wayne Twitchell pitch into the stands for his 649th career home run, one better than Mays. That made Aaron the National League's leading home run hitter of all-time and positioned him closest to the major league record of 714. In '72, Mays hit only eight home runs. He had already dropped out as a contender to Ruth's mark. Others who had once been mentioned as a threat to reach the pinnacle of baseball's achievement—Mickey Mantle or even Eddie Mathews, now the Braves' manager—had also bowed out. That left Aaron alone to challenge the Babe. "I think the press and the fans were reluctant to concede the point, because they had always imagined that a challenger to Ruth would be a charismatic player like Willie or Mickey Mantle—somebody they knew was coming," Aaron wrote. "I had sort of tiptoed along all those years. All of a sudden they looked up and saw me treading on sacred ground, only a hundred homers away, and they wondered how it was possible. What's Aaron doing here?"[14]

Aaron knew he belonged there. At six feet and 190 pounds, he was a solid but not imposing figure. He did not hit towering home runs. He swung off his front foot with a lunge that pushed balls over the fence. But Aaron had played well for nineteen seasons, avoided serious injury after breaking his ankle late in his rookie year, and racked up hits, home runs, RBIs, and runs scored in record amounts. He studied opposing pitchers and remembered their tendencies with encyclopedic accuracy. He had Ted Williams's savvy of the strike zone and the discipline not to chase bad pitches. He was patient enough to wait for his pitch. When it came, he usually didn't miss. His supple wrists whipped his bat quickly— not swinging out of his shoes like Reggie Jackson—but with the speed and strength to pull more balls over the left-field fence than any batter in history.

Pitchers had trouble fooling him. "Trying to throw a fastball by Henry Aaron is like trying to sneak a sunrise past a rooster," said Cardinals pitcher Curt Simmons.[15] Or maybe it was Dodgers pitcher Don Drysdale, who gave up 17 home runs to Aaron. Or Joe Adcock. The quote has been attributed to all three. No matter who said it, the truth of the statement remains unaltered: Aaron was a constant force at the plate.

Once Aaron passed Mays in home runs, others began to notice and speak up. "As far as I'm concerned, Aaron is the best ballplayer of my era," Mickey Mantle said. "He is to baseball of the last fifteen years what Joe DiMaggio was before him. He's never received the credit he's due."[16]

By the time the 1973 season had started with Aaron only forty-one homers this side of Babe Ruth's mark, *The Sporting News* declared, "Aaron is the number-one story in sports."[17]

Along with that long overdue attention came heightened scrutiny of his play. Those watching closely noticed that Aaron, a .305 career hitter, had started the season slugging more long balls than base hits. They observed that in the first month, seven of his nine hits were home runs and his average slumped around .200. They accused him of swinging for the record. They said he was playing for his place in history, not for his team's place in the standings. That stung. Aaron had never been a selfish player. He wanted to break the record, but he did not want to be seen as one who played for personal glory rather than the good of the team. His goal had been to bat .300 that year. He didn't want to break the record batting .240, reduced to a one-dimensional player in the game's memory. But the hits just weren't coming.[18]

Saturday night, April 28, the second game of the three-game series with the Mets, Aaron went oh-for-four at the plate, and his average sagged lower. The rednecks in the right-field stands needled him. The same crap they'd been slinging at him since the season started: he didn't deserve his salary, he couldn't carry the Babe's bat, he was washed up. The longer the game went on, the more he failed at the plate, the more beer they consumed, the uglier the comments became: nigger this, nigger that. Things you couldn't repeat to your children. Again that night, the crowd was small—fewer than 10,000—and the plaintive shouts shrilled in his ears.

Aaron burst that night, April 28. The white man had pushed him too far. *Enough with these loudmouth rednecks. I don't have to take this crap.* In the ninth inning, his team losing 4–2 with him hitless for the night, Aaron walked over to the outfield fence with his fists clenched. He found the voice in the stands, a white man about his age. "If you don't shut your damn mouth, I'm going to come up there and kick your ass," Aaron said. Security officers escorted the man out of the stadium before Aaron had to use his fists.[19]

Maybe that wasn't what Jackie would have done, but Aaron wasn't going to back down. Dick Young from the *Daily News* had flown to Atlanta to watch Aaron in the series with the Mets. Aaron told him afterward that he would not put up with the "loudmouth redneck" slurs. Young saw the pressure tainting the star's pursuit. He wrote, "Just as it was with Roger Maris (when he chased Ruth's single season home run mark of sixty-one), the beauty of baseball is turning into something ugly for Hank Aaron, something inexplicably hostile, something he feels the urge to flee from."[20] Young failed to note the difference: Maris was a white man. He did not have to endure the wrath of the country's pent-up racial hatred the way Aaron did. That is what turned baseball ugly in 1973.

Sunday, April 29, was "Hank Aaron Poster Day" at Atlanta Stadium. The Braves printed 20,000 posters of the future Home Run King to give to the first 20,000 kids entering the park that afternoon.[21] They had plenty left over. Total attendance for the game, adults and kids, was only 12,152.

Atlanta did not seem interested in the Braves that season. More specifically, the city's baseball fans ignored Hank Aaron. Through the first two months of the season, the Braves averaged fewer than 8,000 fans per game, though they drew double that on the road—many of those fans drawn to see Aaron in particular.[22] Aaron took the small crowds personally. "Atlanta overwhelmed me with its indifference," he said. He concluded that fans that weren't willing to pay one dollar, the price of a general admission ticket, spurned him because of his race. "If I were a white man going for the record, the place would have 15-20,000 every night," Aaron said.[23]

The taunts, the indifference—which persisted—angered Aaron so much that he made a public statement in May that charged America with being a racist country and said all that Atlanta had to offer was hatred and resentment.[24] "Some people can't stand the infringement of a black man on this kind of a record," he said. "I know it happens all over the world, but I'm only concerned about Atlanta since that's where I play most of my games."[25]

He knew age and the constant threat of injury conspired against him reaching Ruth. He felt more than ever his body breaking down. But the bigotry should not have been another force he had to battle. He decided to speak out against it—and use it to motivate himself to pass Ruth. "I had to do it for Jackie and my people and myself and for everybody who ever called me 'nigger,'" he wrote in *I Had a Hammer*.

Aaron had not made a name for himself as an outspoken or angry man. Quite the contrary, he was a quiet introvert who preferred a small circle of friends to large crowds. He was friendly to other players, always saying "hello" to the opposing catcher when he came to bat, and ready to give younger players advice.[26] He was a gentleman that *Sports Illustrated* called "the most dignified of athletes."[27] He had an easy, gentle smile, but his eyes glared daggers at someone who crossed him. Aaron could no longer remain quiet about the hatred directed at him.

Aaron came to bat in the bottom of the ninth on "Hank Aaron Poster Day." The Braves trailed 1–0. If they lost, their record would drop to 7–13 for April, not a promising beginning. Aaron, batting in his customary number three spot, was hitless in his first three attempts that day, stymied by the Mets' Jerry Koosman.

Aaron approached the plate slowly, deliberately, batting helmet in one hand, bat in the other. He paused before the batter's box, rested his Louisville Slugger against his thigh and, with both hands, pressed his blue helmet in place over his cap, eyes fixed on Koosman. Aaron twisted the spikes of his right shoe in the dirt at the back of the box and set his left foot. He waved his bat over the plate, loosening his famous, quick wrists. He was ready.[28]

Koosman threw four pitches. Aaron waited patiently, working the count to three and one, before he saw a fastball he liked. Aaron swung and connected. The ball sailed over the left-field wall—foul. He positioned himself back in the batter's box. Koosman shook off two signals and threw a changeup. Aaron swung again but popped the ball up to the second baseman.[29]

That ended the game and the Braves' April. Aaron, down about his hitting, his team's play, and Atlanta's poor reception, turned to the fan mail that poured into the Braves' stadium. That often lifted his spirits. But not always. "Dear Nigger," he read.

George M. Steinbrenner III
The new owner of the Yankees said he would stick to building ships,
but during the 1973 season the Boss became intimately involved with
running the club and trying to cover up his illegal contributions to
President Nixon's reelection campaign.

Chapter Six

THE COVER-UP GAME

W hile Hank Aaron chased Babe Ruth's ghost in Atlanta, George Steinbrenner cleaned the house that Ruth built in the Bronx. On Sunday, April 29, George III completed the Cleveland coup at Yankee Stadium and claimed outright his title as the team's sole and undisputed boss.

During the first game of a doubleheader that day, a Yankee employee handed out a five-paragraph statement to reporters in the press box. The release announced the resignation of Michael Burke, the one-time CBS executive who had overseen the Steinbrenner purchase of the Yankees and stayed on as president. The day Burke had introduced the sale of the Yankees, he stood alongside Steinbrenner smiling like a frat boy who'd just lost his virginity to Raquel Welch. At Sunday's game, the fifty-three-year-old Burke sat alone in a box, set off from other team officials and fans, his face serious and eyebrows puckered. He left after the fourth inning without talking to reporters.

The statement set the press box abuzz with speculation. The reporters weren't talking about the Yankees' sweep of the double-header. They speculated about what had happened behind the scenes that had caused Burke to quit. The statement had not stated any reasons for his departure. It only stated he would retain his five percent ownership share, estimated to be worth approximately $1 million, and would become a "special consultant."[1]

At the "21" Club press conference in January, Steinbrenner had said he would not be active in the daily operations of the club. No, that would be Burke's job. George would stick to what he knew, building ships. But Steinbrenner also knew how to run a business, and the Yankee business proved too great of a temptation for him to keep his word—if he had ever intended to do so.

In the week between Steinbrenner and Burke's announcement of the Yankee purchase and the introduction of the other partners, Steinbrenner had surprised Burke with the news that he had added three partners, including Gabe Paul. Paul, the Cleveland Indian executive who had brought Steinbrenner and Burke together, had bought a five percent interest in the Yankees, the same as Burke's share. George assured Burke over the phone that Paul was sixty-three and intended to retire in Florida with his wife in a couple of years, as Burke remembers it. Only the morning before the "21" Club press conference did Burke learn at a partners breakfast meeting that Paul expected to become president of the Yankees, something George had promised him. No way, Burke said. He prevailed, for the moment.[2]

The press immediately speculated that Paul, a long-time baseball man, would soon be running the team. "Oh, no," Burke said at the "21," trying to save face. "This is a nice way for Gabe to close out his baseball career." Burke recited the lines George had provided. "He's sixty-three and intends to retire to Florida in a couple of years. We'll simply use his baseball knowledge as constructively as we can." Burke tried to shift the thrust of Paul's threat to another guy's job, that of his deputy. "We have one general manager, and he's Lee MacPhail."[3]

Steinbrenner said that he and Burke would rank as general partners.[4] The Yankees media guide pictured them as such. The implication was that they would work together as equals. But that was not the case. Burke shouldered none of the financial responsibility that a general partner typically carries. The partnership agreement clearly stated that there was only one general partner in the new

Yankees ownership, only one man who would assume financial responsibility and run the business, one man who "in his full and exclusive discretion shall manage, control and make all decisions affecting the business and assets of the Yankees."[5] That man, of course, was not Michael Burke; it was George Steinbrenner. He alone would write the checks and dictate the decisions.

In January, George had insisted when he introduced the other investors, "We are all equal partners,"[6] but Burke would soon find out what it meant to be in a partnership with Steinbrenner. He would soon understand why one of the other original partners, John McMullen, who later owned the Astros, would declare, "Nothing is more limited than being a limited partner of George's."[7]

George blamed the flowers. When he first walked into the team's offices at Yankee Stadium, he saw freshly cut flowers on every desk. "What the hell is this?" Steinbrenner demanded. "Is it Flowers Day? Is it Secretary's Day?" One of the employees explained that Mr. Burke did that for his employees every day. Wasn't it wonderful? Hell, no, George thought. "When I saw the flowers, that was the trigger," he explained years later. "I got involved."[8]

George had to have things his way. Burke felt the strain from the beginning, well before Steinbrenner started sending letters and memos with instructions during spring training.[9] He and Steinbrenner were two strong-willed men cut from different cloth. *The New York Times* liked to describe Burke as "long-haired, mod-attired and dashing." Steinbrenner played his blow-dried, blue-blazered foil.

Inevitably, they clashed. Steinbrenner wanted the players to wear their hair shorter; Burke didn't think hairstyles on a ballplayer mattered. Steinbrenner hired a clown to entertain fans before games; Burke didn't find the clown's act funny. They disagreed on how to set up television deals. But the biggest friction between the two occurred over Gabe Paul's role. Steinbrenner wanted Paul involved in the daily operations; Burke, who oversaw those operations, did not.

George knew he needed a baseball man at the helm. As much as he wished he were a baseball man and would pretend otherwise,

Steinbrenner had no experience with the game outside of being a youth starstruck by the Yankees coming to Cleveland. George knew Michael Burke was not a baseball man. Burke had been a college halfback, a wartime spy, a circus operator, a film writer, and a television executive, but he was not a baseball savant.

He had proven that during his eight-year tenure overseeing the Yankees on CBS's dime. Burke had taken over a winner—a team that had won the pennant fourteen of the last sixteen years—and overseen finishes between fourth and tenth place, with one seemingly respectable second place, except that the team finished 15 games out of first. During those eight years, the team lost more money than it was worth, a whopping $11 million in operating expenses. Steinbrenner even charged that Burke had managed to louse up the team's television and radio rights despite the fact that a broadcast company owned the team.[10] The Yankees were *paying* the station that carried their radio broadcasts and collecting only $200,000 for television rights—far below market value, as evidenced by the crosstown Mets' $2 million television contract.[11]

No, Burke wouldn't do. But Paul would. Here was George's baseball man. Paul had started out as a batboy for the Rochester Red Wings in the International League in 1919. He had moved up the administrative ranks in the minor leagues, got his shot in the Bigs with the Cincinnati Reds as the team's first public relations manager, and worked his way to the general manager slot by 1951. He spent a brief stint in Houston as the startup's general manager in 1961, then he landed in Cleveland, where he had served as general manager, vice president, and president. He had also acquired a share of the team.[12] Now Paul, there was a guy who knew baseball. When George offered him the chance to work in the Big City with large sums of money, Paul couldn't resist.

Soon as the Yankees announced that Paul would be jumping from Cleveland to New York, the American League insisted that he sell his Indian stock, a 7 percent interest valued at roughly half a million dollars, before the start of the 1973 season.[13] Paul did so, but that didn't clear up questions about when he had switched his allegiances from the Indians to the Yankees. See, back in late December, after Paul had introduced Steinbrenner to Burke and shortly before Steinbrenner made his offer to CBS, Paul, then the Indians general manager, had traded Graig Nettles and Jerry Moses to the Yankees in exchange for Charlie Spikes, John Ellis, Jerry Kenney, and Rusty Torres. Cleveland fans immediately complained that they had gotten "nothing" in exchange for Nettles, a future Gold Glove third baseman.[14] Eighty-two percent of callers to the *Cleveland Plain Dealer* after it reported the trade opposed the deal.[15] Spikes was considered a legitimate though unproven prospect, but Ellis, Kenny, and Torres had not updated their résumés with any significant achievements lately. George himself went so far as to say that as a Cleveland fan—who had not yet finalized his purchase of the Yankees—he was sorry to hear Nettles would no longer play for the Tribe.[16] Call that Steinbrenner sincerity.

The deal smelled sufficiently rotten for Bowie Kuhn to summon Paul to his office for an explanation. Paul defended his actions before the commissioner and the press. "I'm not concerned in the least about any suspicion that people may have," Paul said at the "21" Club press conference. "When you are right, there is nothing to be afraid of. And I was right. That deal was of benefit to both clubs."[17] Still, it did make for an auspicious beginning of Paul's days with his new club.

Burke had tried to resist Paul. In January, he rebuffed Steinbrenner's plan to name Paul team president. George couldn't oust Burke immediately. He needed Burke around to close the deal with CBS. Yet Burke had unwittingly signed his own resignation by crossing the Boss.[18] Once the purchase was completed, Steinbrenner squeezed off Burke's responsibilities. "When Burke didn't relinquish the business and baseball ends, we thought it would be best for him to concentrate on public relations," George explained later.[19] Burke's pride couldn't take that. He buckled and quit.[20]

Steinbrenner could not be found for comment at the Yankees' Sunday doubleheader. Burke, the ex-COO, had left the stadium. But reporters did find Gabe Paul seated next to Lee MacPhail in the enclosed mezzanine box reserved for Yankees officials and guests, empty except for themselves. Paul feigned surprise at Burke's announcement. He did offer a parting shot at the man who had suggested he would retire soon in Florida. "I think he [Burke] will be around quite a lot from what I understand," the new team president said. "We value his judgment and assistance."[21] Message to Burke: Who's going to pasture now, Mike?

The New York Times concluded accurately, "Burke's departure leaves Steinbrenner clearly as the number one man in the Yankee hierarchy." Paul confirmed that's the way it had been from the outset. "There's been one general partner," he told the *Times*. "George has been the only general partner."[22] So, George had formalized full control and appointed Gabe Paul as his right-hand man.

How good was Gabe? Within four years, he would have the Yankees back on top of the American League. For his part, Steinbrenner would usher in the age of free agency by signing Catfish Hunter to an eye-popping (at the time) $3.75 million contract for five seasons and sign other stars for whopping sums, entitled to spend so lavishly by his shipping profits and his team's marketplace, the richest in the country. Yankees critics complained that Steinbrenner had bought the pennant, but few recognized that Gabe Paul was responsible for over half of the players on the Yankees' 1976 roster. Paul had an eye for talent and an ear for the inside scoop. He acquired 13 of the 25 ballplayers in trades, including Lou Piniella, Oscar Gamble, Mickey Rivers, Carlos May, Chris Chambliss, Fred Stanley, and Willie Randolph.[23]

Two weeks after Burke's abrupt exit, the Yankees staged a press conference to explain the situation. While George smiled and Burke frowned, Steinbrenner left no doubt who ran the show. "Mike didn't agree with everything I wanted to do," he said, "so I fired him."[24] That basically laid out Steinbrenner's management style and foreshadowed his future relationship with Yankees employees from the top down.

Burke did clarify that while the team had lost $11 million on his watch, the net loss had been only $5 million. He had recouped some of the difference with income from advertising and stadium rental to the NFL's Giants.[25] But, obviously, regaining half of your losses was not the kind of bottom line that would satisfy his former boss.

Amazingly, George convinced Burke to say it was his idea to resign. Steinbrenner softened the blow with a $25,000 annual consulting fee, good for ten years, for which Burke wouldn't have to put out, despite George's claim that he would continue to seek Burke's valuable insights. "A lot of times making someone a consultant is putting him out to pasture or a settlement," Steinbrenner said into the microphone. "This isn't the case here. Mike Burke is going to be of great value to the club on a consulting basis."[26] A familiar barnyard smell wafted into the room.

But George couldn't quit the bullshit there. He proceeded to shovel a bogus sentiment that he and Mike remained good buddies. "It may be difficult to believe, but we are closer personally than ever before," George said.[27] That was the kind of close, personal friendship George would go on to cultivate with future employees like Billy Martin and Reggie Jackson.

Burke would later characterize Steinbrenner's affection as the sort Brutus showed his friend Julius. Not long after the press conference, Burke ran into Gabe Paul and his wife, Mary, at a New York restaurant. Mary Paul asked Burke how he was doing. "I'll feel a lot better as soon as I get this knife removed from my back," he reportedly said.[28]

For all of his shortcomings, Burke's Yankee legacy would last four decades. Credit him with the renovation of Yankee Stadium. The venerable park, glorious when it opened in 1923, had faded into disrepair. The concrete showed cracks. Pillars obstructed views from many seats. The fifty-year-old stadium needed a makeover, and Burke arranged it. He had convinced his friend, Mayor John Lindsay, to put up city funds for the renovation of the city-owned stadium, initially committing $24 million but eventually paying $106 million, thanks to inflation, mob-run unions, and other cost overruns.[29] When the new and improved Yankee Stadium opened on April 15, 1976, Steinbrenner had Burke to thank.

Burke credits himself with one more chapter in Yankees lore. In late April 1973, he stood with George on the field watching the crowd depart from an afternoon game and discussing the final details of Burke's exit. Perhaps George expected Ralph Houk would not be able to endure Steinbrenner's meddling because Burke remembers him asking whom he should hire as his next manager. Billy Martin, Burke said.[30] George would, of course, do that, hiring and firing Martin five times over the next two decades.

The Sporting News, among others, expressed sadness at Burke's departure. In a farewell editorial, the publication praised Burke for being "closer to the thinking of young America than perhaps anyone else in the upper echelons of baseball." Four years earlier, Burke had presented a plan for reorganizing baseball's executive structure. He had lobbied baseball to establish an "image of freshness, vigor and excitement to survive," but the old guard had resisted his modern ideas, just as Steinbrenner did.[31]

Despite plans for the stadium's makeover, the reconstruction had not begun and rumors persisted that the team would relocate to the Meadowlands in New Jersey. Steinbrenner assured the press at the Burke press conference on May 13 that the Yankees were not leaving New York. Why would they? The stadium renovation was too sweet of a deal to pass up. Besides, George said, his purchasing group had inherited the thirty-year lease that Burke had signed with the City of New York, so they were bound to stay. Sort of. George wanted you to know that he would not be pushed to do something he didn't want to do. "We could've gotten out of it and they [the city] could've, but we chose not to," he said.[32] He would not be bound by anything not in his best interest.

So, with Burke gone and Paul in place, George could return his attention to Cleveland, where his shipping business beckoned. He repeated his claim, first made four months earlier, that he would leave the baseball business to those in charge. "Some people may find it hard to believe, but I don't intend to project myself into it," he told the assembled media. "They'll see no interference from me. I think we have it working now in a way that will be the best for the Yankees."[33]

Does anybody see a pattern developing here?

———————

In resignations elsewhere on April 30, 1973, President Nixon demanded those of his two closest aides, H.R. Haldeman, White House chief of staff, and John Ehrlichman, chief domestic advisor, both of whom had been implicated in the Watergate scandal by testimony from White House counsel John W. Dean III. The President fired Dean the same day. On national television, Nixon accepted responsibility, but not blame, for the Watergate scandal.

A month earlier, Watergate judge John Sirica had publicized a letter he received from John McCord, Jr., one of the burglars who had broken into the Democratic National Committee's headquarters. McCord wrote that members of the Nixon Administration had pressured him and other defendants to plead guilty and keep silent about the break-in. McCord named Attorney General John Mitchell as the "overall boss" of the bungled operation. McCord's letter suggested a massive cover-up that eventually would be exposed as the country's largest political scandal.

———————

Watergate provided rich material for standup comedians that year and inspired several board games, as toymakers cashed in on the scandal. The Watergate Game (last person to stay out of jail is declared the winner) sold out its first issue of 10,000 games in four days. The Watergate Scandal Game was advertised as "a game of cover-up and deception for the whole family." In the Watergate

Caper Game, players earned investigative points by indicting and convicting various officials.[34]

That April, when Steinbrenner wasn't ushering Michael Burke out of Yankee Stadium, he was busy playing his own cover-up game in Cleveland. At the American Shipbuilding Company, the business Steinbrenner claimed he knew best how to run, local corporate corruption kept pace with national political impropriety.

Three years earlier, AmShip had started awarding bonuses to employees, chosen for their loyalty, who in turn wrote personal checks to support a slate of political candidates identified by the Boss. Steinbrenner had assured his employees that the illegal practice did not violate any federal laws.[35] The first round of bogus bonuses was awarded on September 27, 1970. Steinbrenner received his bonus two weeks later, divided into two payments of $37,500, one dated October 9 and the other October 12. The two dates straddled the close of the company's fiscal year on October 10, so that they could be recorded in separate years. During that three-year period, AmShip did not award any bonuses other than those used as political contributions.[36] Steinbrenner's bonuses totaled $75,000. Remember that amount for later.

George was not a Republican. He counted prominent Democrats Senator Ted Kennedy and Congressman Tip O'Neill among his close acquaintances. Steinbrenner had chaired the 1969 and 1970 Democratic Congressional Dinner, a major Washington fund-raising event. In a huge success, the event raised over $800,000 the first year and $1 million the next. In 1970, Steinbrenner testified before Congress on behalf of the Maritime Acts, and the Democrat-dominated legislative branch updated and passed legislation that benefited Great Lakes shippers, namely AmShip.[37] That gave George more money to spend on political favors.

Steinbrenner had done right by the Democrats, but he figured he needed to work the other side of the political fence as well. He was prepared to make a contribution to Nixon's re-election effort in 1972. Steinbrenner said the donation was an attempt to shake Nixon's cronies off his back. He claimed they pressured him to dish up dirt on their political opponents. "Not only stories about the politicians but about their wives. Drinking. Sex. Very damn distasteful if you ask me," Steinbrenner told Roger Kahn. George refused. Nixon's men threatened him with anti-trust investigations of American Shipbuilding and with personal and corporate tax audits. Steinbrenner tried to buy them off with a generous contribution to CREEP, the Committee to Re-elect the President, in his version of events.[38]

Maybe. More likely, Steinbrenner thought his contribution might lubricate the cogs in Nixon's administration to start working in his favor. The Justice Department's anti-trust division was curious about AmShip's interests in purchasing the Great Lakes Towing Company and an Erie shipyard, both of which would give AmShip a considerable—perhaps monopolizing—market share. The Labor Department was investigating a fire in one of AmShip's shipyards that killed four workmen. And the secretary of commerce had denied AmShip's request for the government to pay a $5.4 million cost overrun on the construction of the oceanographic survey ship *Researcher*.[39] Steinbrenner could use some help from Nixon's guys.

As luck would have it, George had a friend in the right place. His Williams College classmate, Thomas W. Evans, who also happened to be a member of the American Shipbuilding board of directors, was CREEP's deputy finance director. Evans, who would become one of Steinbrenner's partners in purchasing the Yankees, set up a meeting for George with Herbert Kalmbach, Nixon's personal attorney and fundraiser, in mid-March of 1972. Kalmbach told Steinbrenner he wanted $100,000, donated in thirty-three $3,000 checks and one $1,000 check. The checks could be made out to any of sixty committees he listed that had been set up to funnel contributions to Nixon's campaign.[40]

The law required names of all people who made political contributions over $3,000 to be publicized. That would change on April 7, 1972, so that candidates would have to name all donors. Kalmbach told George he wanted his $100,000 before April 7. On April 6, 1972, Steinbrenner had bogus bonus checks made out to eight loyal employees, for a total of $42,325.17. After taxes and other mandatory deductions, the employee bonuses totaled exactly $25,000. The dutiful employees wrote out personal checks to the Nixon campaign worth $25,000. Steinbrenner wrote twenty-five personal checks for $3,000 apiece, each to a different pro-Nixon committee. His contribution came out to $75,000, the exact amount of his bogus bonuses in 1970.[41] Nifty, huh? George had his $100,000 contribution package delivered on April 6 and phoned Kalmbach the next day to make sure it had arrived on time.[42]

It had, but perhaps the $100,000 hadn't been enough. Less than a week after Steinbrenner delivered his contribution, the Justice Department requested details of AmShip's $7 million purchase of the Great Lakes Towing Company. Within a month, the Labor Department fined AmShip $10,000 for violating federal safety laws in the fatal shipyard fire. The new secretary of commerce billed AmShip $208,000 for late delivery of the OSS *Researcher* to the U.S. Coast Guard and slapped the company with an additional $22,000 in other penalties.[43]

Despite the $5.4 million overrun that the company had to eat and the $230,000 in penalties it incurred on the OSS *Researcher*, American Shipbuilding's board approved the bonuses to George and others who would use them to make Nixon campaign contributions "for effective settlement of the U.S. Coast Guard claim." That is until April 1973, when Steinbrenner decided that looked perhaps too blatantly bogus and he directed the company secretary, Robert Bartlome, to change the meeting minutes to read "for effective operation of the company during the year just ended." Just to be safe, Steinbrenner had Bartlome backdate the change to the date of the original board meeting.[44]

Also in April 1973, Steinbrenner had the company treasurer gather records of the bogus bonuses and deliver them to him. George personally destroyed those company records.[45]

Steinbrenner had the corporate counsel draft a statement for recipients of the bogus bonuses to sign, assuring anyone who might later be interested in them, say the FBI or a grand jury, that the bonuses were "in no manner, either directly or indirectly, conditioned upon or subject to the making by me of any contribution, whether charitable, political or otherwise." Furthermore, the statement continued, at no time had "any director, officer or supervisory employee of the company, directly or indirectly, directed, requested or suggested that I make contributions to any charitable or religious group or organization or to any political organization or candidate and that any contributions so made by me during the year 1972 were entirely voluntary and of my own choosing."[46]

The eight loyal employees who had recycled their bonuses into political contributions at George's instruction couldn't believe the audacity of the statement. But they signed it, backdated to December 30, 1972.[47]

Steinbrenner had embarked on his own Watergate game—see if you can cover up your company's illegal campaign contributions so that federal investigators won't be able to discover it. Within a year's time, he would see if his efforts would be as successful as those of the man whose re-election he had helped finance.

While on the disabled list, **Willie Mays** reads his mail at Shea Stadium in the team's clubhouse.

Chapter Seven

ONE UP, ONE DOWN

The fates of two future Hall of Famers diverged on opposite paths the first three months of the 1973 season. Both men felt the curse of age in their knees. Both had wondered if the previous season had been their last. Both closed out their remarkable careers with teams other than those of their glory days. Yet, while one appeared a pathetic image of his former self, the other enjoyed a renaissance, recast in a new role.

Orlando Cepeda followed his dramatic game-winning homer against the Yankees with a strong April. He hit five home runs in 10 games. His .333 batting average was best on the Red Sox. The team's hottest and most productive hitter, his at bats led the Red Sox in biggest ovations. Boston's designated hitter opened May even stronger.

On May 1, the Red Sox hosted the Texas Rangers at Fenway. Cepeda batted in the bottom of the fourth with Boston trailing 3–0, one out, and two runners on base. Boston's designated hitter doubled to drive in a run and make the score 3–1. He moved to third on a single that scored another run. Boston trailed 3–2. Red Sox catcher and 1972 AL Rookie of the Year Carlton Fisk tried to hit a sacrifice fly to left field, but it seemed too shallow. Cepeda tagged up. Boston's third base coach Eddie Popowski feared the aging star with the bum knees might be thinking he could score. He screamed at Cepeda to stay put.[1]

But Cepeda knew left fielder Rico Carty from their days together with the Braves. Cepeda knew Carty did not have a strong arm. He also knew his team hadn't been playing well. The Red Sox needed a run to tie the game and a win to boost their morale. Cepeda gambled that his worn knees could beat Carty's weak arm. Soon as the ball landed in Carty's glove, Cepeda left third for home.[2]

Carty threw wide. Cha Cha scored standing up. His calculated daring tied the game. The Fenway crowd loved it. They gave him a standing ovation. The barstool skeptics raised their mugs to him. *Guy's lookin' better every day.*

He was. On May 2, Cepeda came to bat in the bottom of the third with the Red Sox leading 1–0. He had singled in the first inning. Now, he batted with the bases loaded and two out. Crack! Boston's DH blasted a home run, the ninth grand slam of his career. The hometown crowd cheered mightily. Circling the bases, Cepeda soaked it up. They loved him in Boston. After thinking he had been done with baseball, this was looking to be a wonderful year for Cha Cha.[3]

Sportswriters who had begun the season calling Cepeda Boston's "designated out" now wondered if he could hit 40 home runs. He had done that only once in his career, a dozen years earlier when he led the league with forty-six, but they noted he had started 1973 on pace to hit nearly 50 homers. Seemed no matter how Cepeda played, whether he struggled or triumphed, they heaped more pressure on him.

He felt it. First, in his knees. He lived that season in a two-story house in Boston. Some days his knees hurt so bad he could barely make it down the flight of stairs from his bedroom to the front door. He didn't know how he would make it to first base. He also felt the pressure in his mind.[4]

The designated hitter faces a pressure peculiar to his position. If any other player strikes out with runners in scoring position or messes up a bunt, he has the chance to redeem himself in the field. Not so the DH. His only chance comes with the bat. He's paid to hit. He knows that's what is expected of him every at bat, even though he also knows odds are he will fail more often than succeed.

There is not a great margin for error at the plate. For a man who comes to bat 550 times in a season, the difference between batting a solid .300 and a weak .245 is only 30 hits. Fail to hit thirty times over the course of a 162-game schedule—have Brooks Robinson stab a line drive down the line or Bobby Murcer chase down a long fly or Catfish Hunter fool you on a two-strike curve—and you're out of a job. They don't reserve a spot in the batting order for .245 hitters. You've got to produce or make way for those who can. And if you fail that first time at the plate, there's just more pressure to come through in the next at bat.

Cepeda knew the situation, and he felt the pressure.[5] Those first 11 at bats of the season aside, he had gotten off to a terrific start. But he knew it was a long season. They may love him now, but he was only a slump away from turning their cheers into jeers. "People remember today for my home run which won the game," he had said after his dramatic first hit of the season. "Another day they will remember I failed."[6]

He kept lifting weights to strengthen his legs. He smoked a soothing joint after games to ease his mind.[7] Cepeda had started smoking pot as a teenager in Puerto Rico.[8] After first hurting his knee in 1965, he found the wacky weed helped take the edge off the pain. He regularly smoked it after games since.[9]

No big deal, at the time. By 1973, cannabis was commonplace in society and baseball circles. One of the biggest celebrities of the day, Paul McCartney, admitted he grew pot on his farm in Scotland. Babe Ruth and other legends of the game a generation or two earlier may have preferred liquor—and some ballplayers still did— but for many a player who came of age during the psychedelic days, marijuana was the drug of choice. Cepeda and other players enjoyed its medicinal and recreational benefits. Pot was illegal? So was alcohol during Prohibition, but ballplayers still imbibed. Players who smoked dope scoffed at the moral argument that marijuana was bad stuff. But in the wake of McCartney's bust—in March, the former Beatle pled guilty to raising marijuana—they knew they had to be careful not to get caught. Cepeda's luck would run out shortly after his knees gave out.

Cepeda continued to stare down the pressure during May. He had fallen off the forty-homer pace but was looking good for 30 dingers and 100 RBIs. So far as Boston was concerned, this designated hitter rule was definitely looking like a good idea.

The designated hitter experiment was showing signs of success all around the league. The composite DH batting average through May 26, roughly the first quarter of the season, was .236, close to being the projected 100 points better than the composite pitchers' batting average of .146 in 1972. The biggest increase was seen in power—already, the AL's designated hitters had swatted more home runs than all pitchers and pinch hitters for them had hit in 1972.[10] The Angels' Frank Robinson and Twins' Tony Oliva had hit consistently and delivered dramatic home runs. Cleveland's Ron Lolich and Minnesota's Danny Walton had joined Cepeda in hitting grand slams from the DH slot. But Cepeda, with his .289 average and 22 RBIs, had become the league's showcase designated hitter and one of the season's top stories.

His success was winning over the critics, not just in Boston, but around the league. Detroit sportswriter Joe Falls, who also penned a column for *The Sporting News*, initially had spoken out against the new DH rule as a baseball purist, but the "lovely sight" of Orlando at bat had helped reverse his position. "He hobbles around the bases like a wounded buffalo," Falls wrote. "But, oh my, can he still swing that bat! Point him toward the left-field wall in Fenway Park and watch the fun."[11]

The fun continued through June. Cepeda closed the month with a .293 average, tops on the team among regular players, 12 homers, 12 doubles, and 40 runs batted in. The Red Sox had played only .500 ball to that point, miring them in fourth place, but Cepeda gave the Boston faithful reason to feel good.

––––––––––––––

There was a time, not so long ago, when Willie had been a giant among Giants, considered worth the entire Mets team—and more, as George Carlin joked on his 1966 album, "Take-Offs & Put Ons." "In the sportlight spotlight tonight," sportscaster Biff Burns reports, "first, a baseball trade: The San Francisco Giants today traded outfielder Willie Mays to the New York Mets in exchange for the entire Mets team. The Giants will also receive $500,000 in cash, two Eskimos, and a kangaroo." Mays had listened to the routine and laughed.[12] Coming off his 1965 MVP season, it didn't seem such a stretch that he was better than the entire Mets team, which had won only 50 games in its fourth season. To think the Giants would trade their franchise player was unthinkable, not even for an entire franchise.

Yet the preposterous turned Carlin prophetic when Mays received a phone call from a reporter in May 1972 telling him he had been traded for Charlie Williams—a minor league pitcher!— and $50,000 in cash. That was hardly the value Carlin had appraised Mays at in 1966, but by '72, Mays's skills had lost their luster and a young crop of promising players had squeezed him out of the San Francisco outfield.

Initially, Willie felt betrayed. Horace Stoneham, the Giants owner who spoke of the team as a family, had traded his prize player without talking to Willie. Mays's feelings softened with Stoneham's explanation that he was losing money but wanted to ensure Willie's financial future before he sold the team.[13] Stoneham couldn't afford to pay Mays his $165,000 annual salary as a part-time player, but he knew the Mets could. The Mets gave Mays a contract good for $165,000 a year as a player and $50,000 as a coach for the balance of ten years, the most ever offered a baseball coach. Mays liked that, and he liked the idea of his career coming full circle.[14] As *The New*

York Times pointed out, the trade "returned Mays to the New York baseball scene where he had started his career twenty-one years and 646 home runs ago."[15]

The press spun the story as a happy homecoming. Newspapers quoted cabbies and grandmothers rejoicing over Willie's return. They thought maybe the great Willie Mays could secure a pennant for their Mets. But not everybody thought Mays belonged back in New York. Lon Simmons, the long-time Giants radio announcer for KSFO, traveled to New York to cover San Francisco's series against Mays's new team. When Willie stepped onto the field to warm up with "Mets" stitched across his chest and glanced up at Simmons in the broadcast booth, tears filled the broadcaster's eyes. "It just didn't look right," Simmons said. "You look at a player in a different uniform when you've seen him in that uniform for years and star in that, and it's just not right."[16] He spoke for Giants and Mays fans across the country.

But patrons at Shea Stadium delighted in the sight of Mays wearing the blue and orange. With Mays on the bench for his first game, they chanted, "We want Willie," when the New York pitcher was due to bat in the eighth inning. Yogi Berra went with a left-handed pinch hitter on that occasion, but the Mets manager did insert Willie into the lineup two days later against his former team. Willie homered in his second at bat of the day to win the game. He had three game-winning hits in his first 12 at bats as a Met. The baseball gods seemed to have written a fairy tale ending to Mays's storied career, but fate discarded the script.

Mays finished 1972 with a .250 batting average, and he wondered if he should call it quits. The legend had too much pride to be a hanger-on.[17] He showed up for spring training in 1973 with leather and steel braces on both knees—one to protect his damaged left knee and the other to keep him from favoring his "good" right knee.[18] He asked his former manager and trusted friend, Herman Franks, to come down to St. Petersburg and offer his opinion. Franks watched Mays for a few days and told him he thought Willie had another season in him.[19] Mays seemed to confirm Franks's assessment, batting .323 during the preseason tune-up and proclaiming his knees sound. Others weren't so optimistic. In March, Mays had left camp without permission on a Thursday afternoon to visit his wife at their home in the San Francisco Bay area. With a Friday off, Mays figured he could return in time for the team's Saturday morning workout, but his flight was cancelled and weather delayed the next one. He didn't return until Saturday afternoon, after the workout was over. Yogi fined Mays an estimated $1,000. Cynics joked that the fine broke down to $100 for leaving and $900 for coming back.[20]

Willie's first eight at bats of the regular season forecast the story for the year. He made seven outs—eight, if you counted the double play he grounded into—in his first seven at bats. Then, he came to bat in the bottom of the ninth with the score tied, two outs, and a runner on second. Willie punched a slider into center field for a game-winning single.[21] He failed these days more than he succeeded, but he still had the knack to win ball games.

The swing was there, but it was more often poetry in motion than beauty in action. He was no longer the hitter, fielder, and runner that Leo Durocher had admired twenty years earlier. His legs tired quickly. He taped them before games, but he could not turn them over any faster. He needed to have fluid drained regularly from both knees. After games, he returned to his high-rise apartment overlooking the Hudson River and soaked in a hot tub. His wife, who had joined him in New York, rubbed ointment into his legs and throwing arm.[22]

Willie's right shoulder, sore since spring training, hampered his throwing. He took cortisone shots but still could not throw like he used to. In early May, he leaped to catch a fly ball but misjudged his position. He crashed into the wall and aggravated his already aching shoulder.[23] On his forty-second birthday, May 6, his shoulder hurt so bad that after he caught a fly ball, he had to toss the ball underhanded to the infield. The runner advanced easily from first to second. Such a play contrasted starkly with his whirl and hurl after the famous '54

Wertz catch. The rifle had been reduced to a pea shooter. The next inning, Willie asked Yogi to take him out of the game.[24]

Mays couldn't throw or swing a bat. The Mets placed him on the fifteen-day disabled list. He had reached another milestone in his career: that was the first time he had landed on the disabled list.[25]

Was Willie done? Looked like it. What was a center fielder who couldn't throw? Were he playing in the American League, he could have assumed the role of a designated hitter, though his paltry batting average would have discouraged any manager from inserting him even there for regular duty. But that was hypothetical. Mays was in the National League, where the DH was scorned and not an option. Willie brushed off rumors that he was done. His shoulder just needed some rest, that was all.

Yet he couldn't help but think of hanging it up.[26] Maybe Franks had been wrong. Maybe Willie should not have tried to play another season. That's what the critics were saying—that he was washed up, an embarrassment. His pride had endured about all he could bear. But he didn't want to go out like this, with a whimper. He would be back, he told reporters.[27]

Willie wasn't the only Met hurting. Injuries struck first baseman John Milner, backup first baseman Ed Kranepool, catcher Jerry Grote, backup catcher Jerry May, right fielder Rusty Staub, left fielder Cleon Jones, backup left fielder George Theodore, shortstop Buddy Harrelson, pitcher Jon Matlack, and Willie Mays. At one point, the team had only a dozen healthy players. Manager Yogi Berra was so desperate for bodies to fill out his lineup that one night in early June, he asked Willie, who had rejoined the team a couple of days earlier, if he would try to play in Cincinnati. Willie agreed, though he was concerned about hurting himself worse. "If I get hurt, I get hurt," he said. "But this team needs me, and I'm going to try."[28]

Tension crackled between the legendary Mays and the manager only six years his senior. They had a *tête-à-tête* the second day of spring training, when Berra cut Willie some slack on his workout load compared to the younger players, but Mays, accustomed to calling the shots for himself, seemed to bristle at Berra's authority.[29] The fine Yogi slapped on Mays when he went AWOL on his conjugal visit seemed a warning not to test the manager's authority. But Mays continued to question it.

Against Cincinnati, Willie walked and scored in the first inning. In the third, he grounded into a fielder's choice, which eliminated the lead runner at second. He stole second, his first stolen base of the season, but was stranded there. In the sixth, he hit a fly to right field that was caught for the Mets' first out but advanced the runner to third. He came to bat again in the top of the eighth with the score tied 2–2 and a runner on first. Yogi wanted him to bunt.

Bunt? Willie wasn't a bunter. He wasn't a player whose role had been to advance runners. The man with 1,879 career RBIs and a record 22 extra-inning home runs was a reliable power hitter who drove in runs. At least, he had been. Willie tried to bunt, but he popped up to the catcher, Johnny Bench.

Willie batted again in the top of the tenth, the score still tied 2–2 and a runner again on first. Yogi again wanted him to bunt. This was not the sort of thing Willie worked on in batting practice. He popped out to the first baseman. Bench won the game in the bottom of the tenth with a three-run homer.

After the game, Willie, who was becoming increasingly grouchy as the season wore on, questioned Berra's strategy. "I think I sacrificed only ten times in my career," Mays said. "And never twice in one game."[30] The rift between Mays and Berra widened.

Later that week, Willie shined with flashes of his old self. On Saturday, June 9, the Mets staged an old-timers game before they hosted the Dodgers at Shea Stadium. A crowd of 47,800 turned out to watch past Mets greats play legends from the Yankees and Brooklyn Dodgers, but it was Willie Mays, older than a dozen of the old-timers, who put on a show in the game that mattered. He started in center field for the first time at home in over a month. In the top of the third inning, with the scored tied 2–2, he made a tumbling circus catch.[31] In the Mets half of the inning, Willie homered to put his team ahead to stay. As he had done so many times before, he won the game with his glove and bat.

Yet these days, his feats served more to measure how far the hero had fallen. His spectacular catch would have been routine in the old days, but he initially misjudged the straightaway fly to center. Finally picking up the ball's flight, he backpedaled in time to make the catch over his head, then fell backward and rolled twice across the dirt track at the wall.[32] His home run was the 655th of his career but only his first since the previous August, a four-month drought. Willie had become more memory than performing legend.

The game two days later, when San Francisco came to town on Monday evening, June 11, showed how low he had slipped. Mays started in center field for the third game in a row, "an endurance test he hadn't tried in six weeks," the *Times* noted.[33] The fourth inning "exposed one of the Achilles' heels that have [sic] bedeviled them (the Mets) this season: Willie Mays can't throw," Joseph Durso, who covered the Mets for the *Times*, observed.[34] Mays chased a ball to the wall in left-center, nearly 400 feet from the plate, but, rather than heave it back to the infield, he lobbed the ball ten feet to rookie left fielder, George Theodore, to relay in. Theodore was so startled by Mays's unusual move that he bobbled the ball, and the runner advanced to third. Mays drew an error on the play. In the bottom of the ninth inning, Mays came to the plate with the Mets trailing 2–1 and the tying run on first. He grounded out to second base to end the game and drop his batting average to .094. The man who had batted over .300 ten times wasn't hitting half his weight.

The June 11 game prompted Roger Angell to remark in *The New Yorker*, "The horrible truth of the matter was that Mays was simply incapable of making the play (in the field) . . . his failings are now so cruel to watch that I am relieved he is not in the lineup every day."[35]

The Mets struggled along with Willie. They had finished April in first place of the National League's East Division but then had fallen apart. The injuries had reduced their consistency. The batters couldn't score runs to support pitching ace Tom Seaver, and Tug McGraw, their screwball All-Star reliever, had plummeted into a baffling slump. On Friday, May 4, McGraw had relieved Jerry Koosman in the eighth inning with the Mets leading 5–2. McGraw had saved 27 games in 1972 and posted a 1.70 ERA. He was Yogi's go-to guy in this sort of situation. McGraw came in with the bases loaded and walked three batters to tie the game. Yogi yanked him before he could do further damage. McGraw's performance went south for the next several months, along with the team's.

Mets fans were frustrated with their team's floundering. They found places other than Shea Stadium to amuse themselves. An irate Giants fan in Redding, California, about a two-hour drive north of Sacramento, employed another, more extreme method of venting his frustrations. Gerald Bishop watched his Giants lose their third game in a row, a 2–1 loss to the Houston Astros that threatened to drop the Giants out of first place. Upset with the Giants' failure, the forty-two-year-old Bishop fired seventeen rounds from his rifle into his television set.[36] After police arrested Bishop, he said, "Didn't you ever want to shoot your TV?"[37]

Mets fans felt Bishop's pain. On June 29, the Mets lost to the Cubs and dropped into last place, 12 games out of first. Willie and the Mets had hit bottom. That's where they would stay for the next two months.

The two men, Cepeda and Mays, played out the contrast of sport's fickle fortune, with yesterday's prize no guarantee for tomorrow's take. They would both fight to navigate their courses through the end of the season, Cepeda trying to stay abreast of his wave of success and Mays trying to resuscitate his mighty talents. But Mays was six years Cepeda's senior, the oldest player in Major League Baseball, and in the age before an emphasis on stretching and nutrition extended careers, time was not on Willie's side.

Jackson in his element, posing for the press.

Chapter Eight

YOU'RE SO VAIN

Losing all three games of their opening series against the Twins, the world champs looked more like chumps. The A's flew to Chicago for their next series, but on the hour-long bus ride from the airport to their hotel, the players did not seem worried. Reggie Jackson and the others horsed around in the back of the bus, joking and gibing. That worried Dick Williams, who hated losing. The manager turned from his seat in the front and lit into his team. "You better bust your rears," he chided them.[1]

The A's walloped the White Sox the next day, 12–2. Jackson respected Williams's smarts and drive to win, but he wasn't ready to give the manager credit for the team's first victory. "I know what you're going to write," Reggie said sarcastically to Ron Bergman of the *Oakland Tribune*. "You're going to write that because Dick Williams yelled at us on the bus, we won. Can't you give us a little credit?"[2]

Reggie, who had gone two-for-four at the plate and recorded four putouts in right field, didn't want to share the glory; he reserved that for himself. He played amidst a strong cast, Sal Bando and Catfish Hunter preeminent among them as team leaders, but Reggie ranked as the dominant personality and the talent to carry the A's. In pursuit of his personal goals for a $100,000 season, Reggie played for ego and money. He put the "me" into team—the consummate new superstar.

The origins of Reggie's ego can be traced to Cheltenham High in greater Philadelphia, where he was a football and baseball stud. He averaged eight yards per carry as a halfback and scored 30 touchdowns in his three seasons on the Cheltenham varsity. Forty-eight colleges, including powerhouses like Notre Dame and Penn State, offered him football scholarships. On the diamond, he threw three no-hitters and batted .550 his senior year. Four pro baseball teams wanted to sign him.[3] Reggie liked the way those achievements turned pretty heads and bowed macho ones.

The ego grew at Arizona State University, where he accepted a football scholarship but switched to baseball. Reggie hit gargantuan home runs that continued to turn heads. He broke the school record for most home runs in a season and became the first college player to drive a ball out of Phoenix Municipal Stadium when he smashed a ball 480 feet.[4] In 1966, Charlie Finley signed him to a pro contract after his only varsity season sophomore year.

Reggie scored his first hit of the national spotlight when he challenged Roger Maris's single-season home run mark in 1969. Reggie hit 37 homers by the All-Star break. By September 1, he had hit forty-five. The media swarmed him, and everyone from the President to the team owner fawned over him. In the two weeks before the All-Star Game, reporters demanded a hundred interviews. *Sports Illustrated* featured him on its cover in July. President Nixon sent him a personal note after Jackson hit two homers in a game Nixon attended in Washington. Reggie's teammates stood to cheer him when he walked into the clubhouse after a Friday night game in Boston where he hit three home runs, two singles, and a double, driving in 10 runs. On July 2, in Seattle, after Reggie hit three homers in a game, Finley wrapped him in a hug.[5] The attention and adulation intoxicated Reggie.

But he overdosed on it. The pressure attendant to such attention stalled his home run drive and landed him in the hospital with a case of shingles in September.[6] He hit only two more homers that month and finished the season with forty-seven, third in the league.

No matter. In only his second season, his early hot streak had catapulted his status from potential star to proven superstar. He wanted more of the fame trip.

In the days when players played for the same team often for their entire career and became identified with that team—Hank Aaron was a Brave, Al Kaline was a Tiger, Roberto Clemente was a Pirate, Willie Mays was a Giant (even after he pulled on a Mets uniform)—Reggie set himself apart from his teammates. His talent alone would have been enough for that. They stood in awe of it. One day, Joe Rudi, the A's left fielder, and Dave Duncan, the backup catcher before Finley traded him during the spring of 1973, stood at the batting cage and watched Jackson crush one pitch after another during practice. Rudi turned to Duncan, "How could God give one person that much talent?"[7]

Reggie went further to distinguish himself. He grew the mustache, then the beard. He wore Pumas when Finley signed a deal for his players to wear Adidas. He spoke the loudest in the clubhouse. He strove to establish himself as the alpha dog, which he did better with his lungs than his fists. "Reggie would lose every fight on the team," A's pitcher Blue Moon Odom recalled. "He had muscles, but all of us on that team had muscles and knew how to use them."[8] Nevertheless, Reggie's vocal presence and mighty talent transcended his team. He was not Reggie Jackson of the A's; he was Reggie. As in Reggie the candy bar he would one day have named after him.

Reggie also set himself apart from other stars of the day. Long before athletes praising themselves in the third person came into vogue, Reggie sang his own praises readily. "Guys like Frank Robinson let their bats do the talking," Odom said. "Reggie would pat himself on the back perhaps before someone else would. That was Reggie. He wanted to let people know he was better than another person."[9]

His style reflected his ego. Fans today have become accustomed to players thumping their chests or watching their home run blasts like little boys enamored of their own turds, but in 1973, fans expected players to trot around the bases modestly with their heads down, the way Frank Robinson, Harmon Killebrew, Hank Aaron, et al. did. But Reggie couldn't contain himself that way. He shouted, pumped his arms, or otherwise hot-dogged it around the bases when his turn came. Look at me!

There were other flamboyant personalities in his day, perhaps most notably the highly paid Dick Allen of the White Sox. But Allen failed to put up as many numbers as headlines for his troubles. Reggie had the skills and the durability to back his mouth. He talked more than any other future Hall of Famer of his day, and he played better than any personality of his time. Reggie's combination of talent and talk distinguished him from his contemporaries and forged a prototype for players to come.

Dick Williams saw through him, or thought he did, anyway. "His constant talking gave his teammates something to both laugh at and rally behind, and the best thing about it was that it was an act," Williams wrote about Jackson in *No More Mr. Nice Guy*. "Reggie was really just a talented but very sensitive and insecure person. In other words, get through his bullshit and you found a guy who would play his ass off for you."

Williams also recognized that Reggie needed some extra tending. Not only was the young superstar sensitive, he was going through some personal difficulties in early 1973. The previous year, Reggie had split up with his wife of four years, whom he'd met in college and married when he was twenty-two. Reggie had wanted to reconcile, but they finalized their divorce in February 1973.[10] The break-up and battles with Finley had led Jackson to a psychiatrist, who perhaps trimmed his messianic complex but hardly tempered Reggie's grandiosity. "He made me realize that R-E-G-G-I-E doesn't spell J-E-S-U-S," Jackson wrote in one of his memoirs. "He made me see that I had strengths, too, that I could use. I had to become the best ballplayer I could be. I felt if I could be the best I could control my destiny."[11]

That desperation to be the best prompted his $100K pronouncement and a decision to have his finest season ever, convinced he could control his own destiny. Williams saw that Reggie's moods were often as inconsistent as his play. One day, Reggie would be sullen and unresponsive around teammates, the next he'd be joking and snapping towels outside the shower. He would be jubilant and joking after a big hit, grouchy and grumbling if his name wasn't in the lineup. Williams recognized his role was to help Jackson exorcise his demons. "Having Reggie in an up mood was essential to the success of the Oakland A's," Williams said. "My job was to bring out that talent, remove those doubts, allow Reggie to fulfill his destiny."[12]

Reggie worked the press to keep his name in the paper. "One of the things Reggie figured out early on was that he was an entertainer," his teammate Joe Rudi said. "Playing in Oakland, he was playing in relative obscurity. He was doing everything he could to build up a national image."[13]

Rudi, who roomed with Reggie on the road, came to see Jackson as one of the guys when they were alone. Soon as Reggie got in a group or around the press, that changed. "The personality came out, and he was performing," Rudi said. "If people were watching or the press was writing, he was going to be Reggie the superstar."[14]

Not all of Jackson's teammates passed off his grandstanding as an act. They resented the extra attention he drew, perhaps even resented his additional talent. "We all knew we contributed, but we were also aware of who contributed the most, who was the one player we couldn't afford to lose, the one player who really was most vital to our success," catcher Dave Duncan said. "That was Reggie."[15] The jealousy caused tension that also set Reggie apart from his teammates.

The media lapped up Reggie's lip and lavished him with their attention. In the cliché-addled world of professional sports, where some athletes were dumber than a bag of laundry, here was a guy with an IQ of 160 willing to speak his mind. They could count on

Reggie for good copy. Reggie had learned to work them and seemed to approach every interview as a chance to add another plank to the national platform he was building. These days, "SportsCenter," YouTube, and fan blogs can catapult a player to national celebrity instantaneously, but in 1973, the opportunities were more limited. A player could make a name for himself with a tremendous performance on a nationally broadcast "Game of the Week," in the All-Star Game, or in the World Series. Reggie did all that and served up a generous portion of quotes. Bergman, the A's beat reporter, tagged Reggie his MVQ, or Most Valuable Quote.[16] Reporters in other cities soon discovered Reggie's loquacious quotient and sought him out.

Even when he didn't play, the reporters flocked to him, which provided more fodder for his teammates' jealousy and resentment. In the 1972 World Series, the television cameras trained on the injured Jackson sitting with his crutches on the bench, and sportswriters asked his views of the games. When the A's captured the Series crown, Reggie spoke for the team in the clubhouse. He proclaimed the start of a new dynasty.[17]

On the second weekend of the season, the designated hitter made its debut on national television when the A's played the Twins on NBC's "Game of the Week." It was the first chance for fans in places without an American League team to watch a regular season game featuring the new rule. On a cool, Minnesota Saturday that also happened to be "Snowmobile Day" at Metropolitan Stadium, millions of television viewers watched both teams' designated hitters go one-for-four. Reggie upstaged them. He rapped two hits, including a two-run homer that won the game. On the flip side, he struck out twice. "I'm not thinking home runs this year," he told reporters after the game. "I'm thinking base hits, a .300 average, and a $100,000 salary next season. I know I'm strong enough to hit the ball out if I make contact. I'm trying to cut down on my strikeouts even though I had two today."[18] That was Reggie: two whiffs, a game-winning homer, and a proclamation that he was aiming for base hits to score more money.

The win was only the A's second in seven games. The designated hitter slot revealed a hole the team needed to fill. The first month of the season, Williams tried six different players in the role, but none claimed the spot as his own. The frontrunner was Angel Mangual, who had proven last year with his poor fielding in center field that he had the glove for the DH role, but he was hitting a meager .235. Finley had dumped his two best prospects for the role: Mike Epstein out of spite and Cepeda out of stinginess. Charlie needed a designated hitter and, as he was so often able to do with players, he found one, Deron Johnson. Finley traded a minor league pitcher to the Phillies for the thirty-three-year-old Johnson, who had played for Finley twelve years earlier in Kansas City.[19]

Johnson immediately made Finley look good. On May 4 in Cleveland, Johnson's first game back with the A's, he hit three singles and drove in four runs. That first week, he hit .406, slugged three homers, and drove in nine runs. The A's won seven of their next nine games.

But as soon as Finley filled one hole, another opened, this time in center field. Billy Conigliaro, whom Finley had signed for the role before the season, had started strong, batting .295, but then hurt his knee sliding into second base on April 21. He wound up on the disabled list May 8 and had surgery the next week to repair damaged cartilage in his knee. Billy C. was lost for two months.[20] Mangual replaced him but then pulled a chest muscle and couldn't play in the field. When the muscle healed, Williams put Mangual back in the field as the manager had promised him he would, but Mangual dropped the first ball hit to him and went hitless in eight at bats. Williams replaced him with Bill North, another Finley off-season acquisition. The switch-hitting North had speed but had hit only .181 with the Chicago Cubs in 1972 between trips to the minors. Williams was desperate enough to declare: "Bill North is my center fielder. He stays in there unless he falls flat on his face."[21]

North stayed. He started hitting, stole bases, and—with his speed—caught balls Mangual wouldn't have reached. During May, North made two spectacular diving catches. His play won Reggie's admiration. "He covers more ground in center than anyone we've ever had," Jackson told reporters.[22] Reggie mentored North, and the two became friends.[23]

The following season, the two men would come to blows in the clubhouse before a game. North was declared the winner: he played in the game; Reggie didn't.[24] As of 1973, though, they were friends.

With center field settled, that left second base for Finley to fiddle with. He devised a round of musical second baseman for Williams to play. Williams listed Gonzalo Marquez, a left-handed first baseman, as the starting second baseman in away games. After Marquez batted in the top half of the inning, Williams sent Dick Green to play second base, Gonzalo having in effect pinch hit for the strong-fielding, weak-hitting Green. Several innings later, Finley had Williams pinch hit for Green and replace him with Dal Maxvill at second. When Maxvill's turn came to bat, Williams sent up a pinch-hitter and replaced Maxvill at second with Ted Kubiak for the remainder of the game.[25] Who said the DH rule simplified strategy? Williams, with Finley's help, could make even the simple complicated.

North, who was quickly catching on to the A's ways, got suspended for throwing his bat at and attacking a pitcher. Campy had sat out a seven-game suspension at the start of the season for throwing his bat at a Detroit pitcher in the '72 playoffs, and North's mentor, Jackson, had rushed the mound in a 1969 game when the pitcher had thrown at him after he hit two homers. But North had his own reasons for going after the Royals' rookie pitcher Doug Bird.

On Friday night, May 18, in the opener of a four-game series against Kansas City at the Oakland Coliseum, North batted in the eighth inning with the A's leading 5–4. Bird threw a low slider. North swung and let slip his bat, which sailed past the pitcher's mound toward the shortstop. North sauntered out to retrieve his bat. The 5-foot 11-inch North stopped at the mound, glared at the 6-foot 4-inch Bird and said, "I remember." Suddenly, North dropped the pitcher with a quick right jab to the head. He punched the fallen Bird several times before the startled umpires and Royal infielders could subdue him.

There had been no play in the game to provoke North's mugging. The broadcasters struggled to make sense of it along with the fans, umps, players, and other witnesses. Afterward, North calmly explained his motive: belated retaliation. Three years earlier, when North and Bird had played against one another in the Midwest League, North came to bat after hitting consecutive homers. Bird threw consecutive fastballs at North's head. North dodged the first pitch. The second one cracked his skull and landed him in the hospital. North hadn't seen Bird until May 18, 1973, in Oakland, but he hadn't forgotten. "I've been waiting for him since," North said.[26]

The umpires ejected North from the game, and Joe Cronin, American League president, suspended North for the remainder of the A's series with the Royals, ostensibly to avoid further violence. Cronin also fined North $100. Finley and Williams appealed the suspension without success. Finley complained that Cronin was picking on the A's unfairly.[27]

The A's missed North, who had earlier in the game driven in the tying run, stolen second, and scored the winning run. Worse, they missed their steady pitching. Through the first two months of the season, Odom lost eight of his first nine decisions and dropped out of the starting rotation. Catfish Hunter didn't win a game until his sixth start. Paul Lindblad struggled in his first two starts. In New York at the end of May, the Yankees beat up Hunter and Vida Blue, one-two. That dropped the world chumps to 23–24, in fifth place, six games behind the White Sox in the American League West.

Joe DiMaggio criticized Jackson on national television. DiMaggio, the Yankees great who had hit for power and consistency, had worked with Jackson in 1968, when Reggie was a rookie and Joe was a hitting coach for the A's. Watching Jackson play in Detroit, DiMaggio, who had hit with power and consistency, suggested that Reggie was going for the tape measure home run instead of the base hit. Indeed, Jackson didn't seem so much to swing his bat as to lash his entire body at the ball. He had connected for some mighty runs, but more often, he missed. The mighty swing corkscrewed him into another strikeout. DiMaggio thought it would be a good idea for Reggie to tone down his swing.[28]

No way, Reggie responded. "I'm not trying to hit the ball out of the park all the time," he said. "I'm very cognizant of getting a run in the first inning. There have been at least ten situations I wasn't even concerned with a hit, much less a home run. All I wanted was a ground ball because that's all it would take to get a run in—just make contact and hit it on the ground. I don't want to change my swing."[29]

The problem wasn't his swing, Reggie said. No, the team had become a victim of its success last year. Reggie complained that it was harder for the A's to win than in the past because they had become marked men. "Other teams are definitely using us as something to shoot at," he said. "Like it means something now to beat Oakland. I don't think we were really prepared for that at the beginning of the season."[30]

In June, the team adjusted, the A's pitchers gained traction, and Oakland finished the month 18–11. There was nothing wrong with Reggie's swing during a 12-game home stand when he homered six times and drove in 17 runs. Hunter once again dominated batters. Blue regained his pinpoint control. Ken Holtzman threw his fastball with his customary accuracy. Paul Lindblad pitched well. On June 28, Blue won his start against the Royals, and the A's moved into first place. That same night in Anaheim, the White Sox' Dick Allen broke his leg in a collision with Angels first baseman Mike Epstein that knocked Chicago out of the division race.

Finley probably credited his uniforms. During June, he had the A's wear their all-green uniforms for the first time, and they won three games in a row. When they lost a game, he switched them to all-yellow uniforms, and the A's won two more games. "The secret here is they (opponents) underrate us," one player quipped. "They don't think we're ballplayers, they think we're bananas."[31]

Reggie's legs, which had been a question mark at the start of the season, had held up through the first three months of the season, but his play had been customarily erratic. While his mouth yapped predictably, his skills sparkled inconsistently. In the second game of the season, he misjudged a fly ball and missed a catch that would have ended the inning. The next batter belted a two-run homer that beat the A's. Then, in late May, he had raced full speed to the wall in Yankee Stadium, snagged a drive headed out of the park, crashed into the fence, and fallen into the seats.[32] In early June, he knocked in five runs in a blowout against the Brewers, but Oakland fans booed him for misplaying three fly balls that yielded two doubles and a single.[33] By the end of June, Reggie was hitting his coveted .300, had slugged a league-leading 16 home runs, and had knocked in 63 runs. But his big swing remained a liability. Often, instead of connecting with a big hit, he chased bad pitches and stranded runners. "He strikes out on pitches over his head and in the dirt," Dave Duncan noted.[34]

After reaching .300, Reggie slumped in early July, going two-for-eighteen in five games, striking out four times and dropping his average to .289. On July 4 against the Angels in Oakland, Reggie dropped a foul ball, his sixth error of the season, and he later missed an attempt to make a diving catch, which opened a three-run inning for the Angels. Williams, a stickler for fundamentals, was upset by Jackson's fielding efforts in the 3–1 loss and let Reggie know. He perhaps kicked when he should have coddled.

Reggie exploded in front of a gaggle of reporters. "You can't play around here and be happy," he said in the clubhouse after the game. "I don't mean the owner. He's fine. But somebody makes a mistake, and the coaches start hollering and kicking water coolers. They act like Babe Ruth, like they never made any mistakes. It ain't me they get on—it's guys like (Ray) Fosse and Dick Green. I don't care what they say to me. They can't do nothing. I'll be here long after they're gone."[35]

Reggie's teammates dressed silently, listening in amusement to his tirade. But the coaches, who also heard his assessment, were not amused. Third-base coach Irv Noren asked rhetorically, "Am I a baby sitter or something?" First-base coach Jerry Adair said, "Tell Jackson I'm sick of seeing him play, too."[36]

Jackson had added, "I like Dick Williams. He knows baseball," but Williams predictably defended his coaches and excoriated his right fielder in the press. "Those other coaches know baseball, too," Williams said. "I suggest to Reggie Jackson that he do the best he can in right field and leave the rest of it up to the coaches and manager. Anything we do is constructive criticism, and if you can't stand the heat, get the hell out of the kitchen!" Then, Williams aimed a blow at the solar plexus of Reggie's ego. "There's some good ballplayers here, but I haven't seen any superstars yet."[37]

After Reggie read Williams's comments in the paper, he erupted again. He blasted Noren and Williams in retaliation. The next day, on the team flight to Baltimore, Jackson walked to Williams's seat, glared at the manager, and said, "Never talk to me again. Just write my name in the lineup." Williams did not respond. Reggie stomped off to his seat.[38]

Finley sent his message to Reggie through the press three days later. The owner and general manager announced that he had renewed the coaching staff's contracts through 1974 and Dick Williams's contract through 1975. *That's what I think of your judgment, Reggie!*

Two weeks after Reggie's outburst and only five days before the All-Star Game, where he was supposed to manage the AL squad, Dick Williams was rushed to the hospital with sharp abdominal pain. The emergency room doctors performed an emergency appendectomy. While Williams recovered in the hospital, Irv Noren replaced the Oakland manager for the A's three-game series against

Cleveland. Hunter, Blue, and Holtzman won their starts, asserting the dominance of the A's pitching corps, and Oakland swept the series. Reggie, not willing to concede credit to his nemesis Noren, pointed instead to his home run in the second game. The homer was his league-leading 21st of the season. It was also pure Reggie: the longest tater hit at Oakland Coliseum. His blast landed in the top row of the right field bleachers, some 470 feet from home plate.[39] He'd show you up any way he could. Look at me!

Hank Aaron poses with **Robert Winborne,** the eighteen-year-old Braves fan who caught the ball Aaron hit for No. 700 and was rewarded $700.

Chapter Nine

"DEAR NIGGER"

Hank Aaron received more mail than anybody else in the country except President Nixon. Thousands of letters and post cards poured into the Braves' offices for him weekly.[1] Some 930,000 in 1973. (Dinah Shore, who had the next heaviest mail load, received 60,000 pieces of mail.)[2] Aaron was the only player in Major League Baseball with a secretary hired to help sort his mail.[3] Many of the letters early in the season were positive. Aaron tried to respond to each of those with an autographed photo. But some of the letters, maybe one in nine, were negative, nasty. The letter writers called him nigger, jigaboo, jungle bunny, super spook, coon, nigger scum. "Go back to Coonsland," they said. And, "Go back to the jungles." And, "Everybody loved Babe Ruth. You will be the most hated man in this country if you break his career home run record."[4] And worse.

At first, Aaron tried to pass off the letters as ignorance, but that became impossible as they piled up. Their vituperative remarks were too pointed, too vehement. There were also too many. This wasn't a solitary, drunk redneck shouting insults from the stands. The hate mail averaged almost 275 letters a day, for every day of 1973. The mail came not only from former slave states but from all over the U.S. As if the Archie Bunkers of the nation had united to embark on a letter-writing campaign. The volume of their hatred overwhelmed Aaron. And for every hate missive he received, he wondered how many people who hadn't written felt like the bigots did, secretly inside, perhaps too timid or socially polished to openly admit their prejudice but privately rooting against him.

White America saw Babe Ruth as one of their own. The Babe and his 714 were part of their culture, already endangered by the times. Many of them didn't want a black man upsetting the balance of tradition. "Encroachment on the Babe's records has come to be regarded as something similar to the defacement of a national tradition," wrote Furman Bisher, sports editor of the *Atlanta Journal.* "In Henry's case, it became exceedingly unde-sirable in some seats of prejudice because here was a black man 'messin' round' with a white man's record that was consid-ered off limits."[5]

The letters burned Aaron inside. He hadn't told any of his teammates about the hate mail. He had not told the press. He had tried to contain the wound they opened without complaining. He learned that from his father, who had worked twenty-nine years in a shipyard without complaining.[6] Something troubling you? Keep it to yourself. But Jackie had urged him to speak out against prejudice. Aaron had learned from him that "when you don't say anything, people think you are satisfied."[7] To remain silent against the onslaught he faced allowed the bigots to continue it with impunity.

The collective hatred finally became too much to bear. On a Saturday morning in early May, when the team was in Philadelphia, Aaron told his friend and teammate, Paul Casanova, about the hate mail. He told Casanova over breakfast about the threats against him and his family. "Cassie, these people are crazy," he said.[8]

Aaron also spoke to the press about the abuse directed toward him because of his race. He had to call out the hatred that sullied America's heart. "I felt this was something I had to get off my chest," he said. "Five years ago, I probably would have walked away from it and said nothing. But now I just feel I have taken all I can."⁹

He could not stomach the status quo, not for himself, not for his people. "All I want is to be treated like a human being," he said. "That's all I ask, that and to be a part of the ball club. Just let me do my job."¹⁰ Weren't all Americans entitled to that under the Constitution—the right to be treated like a human being and do their job? Yet some Americans threatened Aaron's life if he continued doing his job. He had no intention of backing down. "I'm not going to stop because of this," he said. "Put it this way: the more they push me, the more I want the record."¹¹

Aaron's pursuit of Ruth drew out the best and the worst in America, as baseball often will. On May 14, Aaron and the Braves opened a four-game series in Houston. The Astrodome scoreboard welcomed him: "Mr. Aaron, for every one of those bad letters you receive, there are thousands pulling for you. Good luck in your homer quest ... after you leave the Astrodome."¹²

The news about his hate mail made national headlines and inspired a chorus of support from around the country. A New York radio station staged a campaign to stand by Aaron.¹³ A couple from Dayton, Ohio, wrote to tell him they named their baby boy born that summer Aaron, "because of our great respect for you as a ballplayer and as a person."¹⁴ One thousand students from St. Paul, Minnesota, signed a petition on his behalf.¹⁵ Congress introduced a resolution that condemned the "racial slurs and insults" directed at Aaron.¹⁶ Atlanta mayor Sam Massell wrote Aaron an open letter: "You're a hero—Atlanta's hero.... Don't let the bums get you down."¹⁷

Other players voiced their support. Reggie Jackson had read about the abuse directed Aaron's way and heard that the slugger was down.¹⁸ He called Aaron. "I want you to know that all the young black players in the American League realize what the older blacks in the National League have done for us," Jackson said. "You know what I'm trying to say, don't you? Baby, I'm pulling for you."[19]

Aaron's mail picked up significantly, with as many as 3,000 letters arriving each week.[20] The vast majority of writers told Aaron they were cheering for him. A large number came from children, baseball's purest fans. In response, Aaron dedicated his quest "to the kids, black and white, it makes no difference."[21]

One man taped matchsticks to his letter and told Aaron to use them to take care of the negative letters. Aaron didn't burn the hate letters. He saved them. He didn't want to forget, to ignore the way things were. Didn't want to get satisfied.[22] Things still weren't right in America. The outpouring of support showed America's good side. It was heartwarming and uplifting. But it wasn't complete. The warm fuzzies hadn't rooted out the hatred nor eliminated the discrimination. That still prevailed in the United States and in its national pastime. Aaron's mail—the positive and negative letters—revealed a nation still divided over race.

A 1973 *Washington Post* editorial criticized the U.S. government for being capable of sending men to the moon but remaining complicit in racist treatment on earth.[23] Ranger fans in Arlington hurled racial invectives at Minnesota's Rod Carew after he stole home in a June game.[24] The taunting continued in Atlanta. Two men at the Braves' May 24 game tried to bait Aaron into fighting. In June, a man harassed Aaron from the stands: "Hey, jigaboo! How much is two hundred grand in bananas?" and "Hey, Aaron! What are you going to do with all that money you get for hitting them homers? Buy a Cadillac and go on welfare?" Aaron fixed the man with his angry glare.[25]

The most obvious sign of racism's hold on baseball was personified by the man who filled out the lineup card for each team. On all 24 teams in Major League Baseball in 1973, that man was white. Jackie Robinson had cracked the color barrier, but he had not broken it. Twenty-five years after he had proven that blacks could compete on the playing field, the game's white power brokers had not entrusted leadership of a team to a black man. The white owners and general managers hired retired black ballplayers as hitting coaches or to minor league posts, not to manage, not even to coach third base, which required transmitting critical signals and deciding when to send runners home. The prevailing prejudice barred African Americans from positions that called for thinking, decision-making, and leadership.[26]

At the 1972 World Series ten days before his death, Robinson had challenged the status quo and said he wanted to see a black manager.[27] In 1973, Ernie Banks had accidentally fulfilled Robinson's dying wish. An assistant coach for the Cubs, Banks became the first African-American manager in MLB history on May 8 when he took over for Chicago manager Whitey Lockman, who was ejected in the third inning of the Cubs game in San Diego. But the white power brokers still had not trusted an African American with the brains or leadership ability to hire him to manage a big league ball club.

Hank Aaron carried on Jackie's challenge. At a celebration for Aaron on June 2 hosted by the Reverend Jesse Jackson at his Operation PUSH (People United to Save Humanity) headquarters in Chicago, Aaron told a crowd of two thousand supporters that he, too, wanted to see a black manager. "About the only strides we've made is that we've been able to get to coach first base," Aaron said. "When our careers are done and we're no longer needed, then they send us to the back of the bus."[28]

Aaron had spoken out previously about racism in baseball and particularly about the lack of black managers as early as the Fifties. In interviews over the decades, he had expressed his outrage at baseball's glass ceiling. "Unfortunately, no owner has had the guts up to this point to hire a black manager," he said in 1970 after he joined the 3,000-hit club. "In fact, I wouldn't even call it guts; I'd call it common sense....It burns me up a little that there's this kind of— what would you call it?—managerial club, whereby the owners seem to have gotten together and decided that certain men, white men, should be hired and rehired no matter what kind of failures they have been."[29]

No one had paid much attention to Aaron then. He had not yet hit 600 home runs. But in 1973, his pursuit of Ruth's mark gave him a national platform. He clarified in *Ebony* magazine that he did not want to manage because "you end up with too many problems," but that he would like a front office job, say director of player personnel, business manager, or general manager. "Black athletes who know the business should be able to move into the front office," he said.[30]

The racism that confronted him motivated Aaron not only to break Ruth's record but also to squash baseball's discrimination. "If it was Ruth who invented the home run, it was Aaron who found a use for it—a use not his, but society's," Lonnie Wheeler, co-author of Aaron's autobiography, wrote. "In Aaron's possession, the home run record was a public address system that gave volume to a voice nobody had ever listened to."[31]

Aaron appreciated the widespread support from fans, but he knew their good will was not enough to keep him and his family safe. The hate mail he received, some of it signed "KKK," also contained pointed threats. One unsigned letter read: "Retire or die! …You'll be in Montreal June 5–7. Will you die there? You'll be in Shea Stadium July 6–8, and in Philly July 9th to 11th. Then again you'll be in Montreal and St. Louis in August. You will die in one of those games. I'll shoot you in one of them."[32]

Another threatened: "I got orders to do a bad job on you if and when you get 10 from B. Ruth record. A guy in Atlanta and a few in Miami Fla [sic] don't seem to care if they have to take care of your family too."[33]

Someone clipped a photo of Aaron with his eleven-year-old daughter, Dorinda, at a Braves father-child game and sent it to

Aaron with a note: "Daddy, please think about us." Someone stalked Aaron's older daughter, Gaile, a student at Nashville's Fisk University. The FBI dispatched agents disguised as grounds crew and maintenance men around campus to protect her. The bigots called his parents' home in Mobile, Alabama, and told them they would never see their son alive again.[34]

The Atlanta police department assigned one of their officers to protect Aaron. Calvin Wardlaw escorted Aaron to and from the ballpark and made sure he returned safely to his room or home each night. The Braves hired Wardlaw and Lamar Harris, another Atlanta cop, to sit in the outfield seats at home games.[35] The two plainclothes officers watched the crowd for any threatening or dangerous types. Wardlaw carried a brown binoculars case with his badge and a .38 Smith & Wesson tucked inside.[36]

Despite their company, Aaron never felt completely safe. The threats against him and his family flickered constantly in the back of his mind.[37] America was not a safe place for a black man intent on bettering a white champion. Hell, it wasn't safe for anybody controversial. Look what happened to King. To John Kennedy. Robert Kennedy. Someone even shot Andy Warhol, for Christ's sake. After the A's Gene Tenace received a death threat at the 1972 World Series, police had arrested a man with a loaded gun inside the ballpark.[38] "I knew an aroused bigot is capable of anything," Aaron said.[39]

He feared what might happen to his children, a parent's worst nightmare. "My father was worried sick about it," Gaile said. "He flew to Nashville to visit me almost every time he had an off day."[40]

Aaron lived under siege. Instead of parking his car in the players' lot at Atlanta Stadium and walking to the players' entrance, he drove straight into the stadium where the team had arranged a special spot for him.[41] On the road, he registered a room under his name and hotel operators put calls through to the bogus room while he stayed in another registered under a false name. He ate meals delivered by room service and measured hours in soap operas until he could go to the ballpark. He rarely went out, whether at home or on the road. "I was just a man doing something that God had given me the power to do, and I was living like an outcast in my own country," he reflected in his auto-biography. "It should have been the most enjoyable time of my life, and instead it was Hell."[42]

Aaron maintained his reticent and patient composure in public, but he leaked signs of the pressure. He stepped out of the batter's box more frequently. He seemed to grip his Louisville Slugger more tightly. He questioned called strikes. And, while he continued to hit home runs, his batting average sagged well below his lifetime .311 average through 1972. By the end of June, Aaron led the Braves with nine game-winning hits, but he was batting .223, with only 44 hits, almost half of them (20) home runs. Seated on a black plastic chair in the Braves clubhouse before a game, he said in his soft voice, as though apologizing, "Seems that about all I do these days is hit home runs."[43]

Aaron was frustrated with himself. June had almost ended. He was on pace to catch Ruth before the season ended, but he wasn't helping his team win ball games. The Braves had lost 45 games and practically been eliminated already from contention for the division title, mired 18 games behind the division leader. He felt the pressure from fans at home and away to hit a home run with every at bat. They wanted to witness his historic march. But, he claimed, he was not swinging for the fences. Rather, he wanted to get on base or move runners along with base hits.[44]

They just weren't coming. In part because pitchers weren't giving him good pitches. With increasing frequency, they walked him, either intentionally or by pitching too carefully to him. Through his first 40 games, pitchers walked him 28 times. When he did get a pitch he could hit, he had trouble beating the shift teams employed against him. Opposing managers stacked the left side of the field, bunching their outfielders and infielders where the pull-hitting Aaron was most likely to hit the ball. Aaron had difficulty hitting to the gaps in the opposite field because he had adjusted his swing over recent years to accommodate an aching back. He had dropped his hands slightly and started his swing from tighter in on his chest. "The older I've gotten, the closer I've brought the bat in to my body," he said. "That's why I'm pulling the ball more." [45]

"There was a time when I could hit the ball to all fields," he said. "Now, I've got to pull the ball to left or forget it."[46] Other teams had picked up on this, and Braves manager Eddie Matthews figured the shift had probably cost Aaron's average 50 points already that season.[47]

Aaron and the Braves traveled to New York in early July for their final series of the season at Shea Stadium. The fans and the media were waiting when the team bus pulled up. Aaron signed autographs for a group of kids as he walked into the stadium. Five reporters waited for him in the visitors' clubhouse. Another dozen waited outside, near the dugout, along with several cameramen.[48] While crowds in Atlanta remained sparse, they doubled or even tripled in other cities where Aaron played.[49] More than 30,000 would watch each of Aaron's three games at Shea that weekend. The number of autograph seekers and of media also swelled. The closer Aaron got to 700, the more people wanted a piece of him. He arrived at Shea with 21 homers in the season, 694 in his career.

The three-game matchup between the Braves and Mets was a battle of the bottom-feeders. The Braves were in fifth place of the NL's West Division, 15 ½ games out of first. The Mets, ensconced in last place in the NL East, were 12 ½ games behind the division leader. Rumors swirled that the team would fire its manager, Yogi Berra. Willie Mays continued to struggle, batting .185. In the first game on Friday night, he went hitless in the leadoff spot and struck out twice, including his final at bat in the bottom of the ninth with a runner on. For the Braves, Aaron walked once and went oh-for-three, but his team won 2–0.

The next day, Saturday, July 7, both Mays and Aaron rested. The Mets' injury woes continued when outfielders George Theodore and Don Hahn collided chasing a fly ball in the seventh inning. Both were carried from the field on stretchers, Theodore with a dislocated hip and Hahn with bruised ribs and a sprained knee. Mays replaced Hahn in center field. Coming to bat in the eighth inning with two runners on, Mays drilled the first pitch into left field to drive in two runs, then scored the go-ahead run two batters later.

Berra summoned Tug McGraw, last season's star closer, to start the ninth and protect the Mets' one-run lead. Instead, McGraw extended his slump. He gave up a single on his first pitch. Aaron pinch hit and smacked a single on the next pitch. McGraw managed one ground ball out but gave up another single and a walk before Berra relieved him of his misery. When the inning ended, McGraw had given up three runs and lost the game. He had a 6.20 ERA and an 0–4 record.

The hapless Mets lost the third game Sunday 4–2, dropping their record to 32–46. Mays managed two hits, raising his average above .200, but, once again, he failed to deliver in the clutch the way he used to. He struck out in his last at bat with a runner on base.

Aaron was the story of the day. He told reporters when he arrived in New York that he was surprised he had hit as many home runs as he had but that he didn't think he would break Ruth's record in 1973. "I doubt I'll get it this year," he said. "I think I can hit thirty-five (home runs), but I doubt if I'll hit forty-two."[50]

The two homers he slugged on Sunday, Nos. 695 and 696, put him well within reach of Ruth. They also satisfied the 33,017 fans at Shea, who had turned out to watch his last game in New York that season. Aaron's personal home run derby had revived fan interest diminished by the labor wars the past two seasons.

While Orlando Cepeda crusaded for the cause of the designated hitter in the American League with his strong season, Aaron aroused interest nationwide with every long ball he hit that year. They were both succeeding in restoring the game's image and putting fans in the seats. One fan gushed in a letter, speaking as much about Aaron's impact on American society as his contribution to the game: "You are the MESSIAH that has finally arrived."[51]

One of the death threats had mentioned specifically the series at Shea. Aaron had survived that. Three more of the series mentioned remained. The two home runs he hit in New York, moving him 18 homers from Ruth's mark, placed him in the crosshairs of another letter that threatened to kill Aaron at the All-Star Game if he was within 20 homers of Ruth's record by July 24.[52]

Aaron did not back down. He kept knocking them out. His next three round-trippers came at home. No. 697 against Montreal. No. 698 off the Mets' Tug McGraw. No. 699 against the Phillies. The media multiplied. Reporters from national magazines joined the beat writers clamoring for interviews. When Aaron went fishing in Mobile on a day off, three boats full of reporters and photographers from *Newsweek, Time, Ebony,* and other publications hounded him on the water. An NBC-TV crew shooting film for an upcoming prime time special followed him for weeks.[53] The attention focused on Aaron as he neared No. 700 prompted *Newsweek* to call him "the most conspicuous figure in sports."[54]

The most conspicuous, that is, after the one he chased. Even those pundits profiling Aaron couldn't resist writing about Ruth—his adolescence in the orphanage; his legendary appetites for women, drink, and food; his gregarious and outgoing personality; his personal invention: the home run. Aaron always fell short by comparison. "Unlike Aaron, Ruth had an immediate, electric effect on baseball and its fans," *Newsweek* observed in an August feature of Aaron.[55]

Ruth. Seemed everybody had something to tell Aaron about the Babe. How Ruth broke the career mark of 136 in 1921 and reigned as the home run champ for fourteen years while he played. How Ruth changed the game with the long ball, replacing the conventional game plan of eking out runs with singles, stolen bases, and sacrifice flies.[56] How Ruth would surely have hit more home runs if he hadn't spent the first four years of his career primarily as a pitcher, averaging only 137 at bats per year—give him 500 at bats those years, and he would've hit 111 more homers at his career rate of one every 12 at bats; 714 became 815—break that! Ruth would've hit more dingers if he hadn't walked 2,062 times, 700 more times than Aaron was given bases on balls.

The Babe was the Paul Bunyan of the home run. Aaron knew he would never transcend that. He wasn't trying. "The legend of Babe Ruth is indestructible," Aaron said. "It won't matter whether I hit 800 homers—there will never be another Babe Ruth as far as the baseball public is concerned. And some day, some young guy will come along and hit 850 homers, and I'll just be a fellow who hit 750 or whatever total I finish with."[57]

Aaron simply wanted to be recognized for his talents and accomplishments. "I don't want people to forget about Babe Ruth," he said. "I just want to make sure they don't forget about Hank Aaron."[58]

One could hardly mention Aaron's name in 1973 without hearing Ruth's. The prospect of Aaron passing Ruth's monumental mark inevitably led to comparisons and debates over whose 714 homers were the greater accomplishment. The Ruthians contended that the Babe reached 714 in 3,000 fewer at bats than Aaron, slugging a homer on average once every 12 at bats to Aaron's once every 16. In Ruth's prime, from 1920 through 1933, they noted, he hit 637 home runs, an average of 45.5 per 154-game season; Aaron hit more than 45 home runs only once in the 162-game season.

The Babe dominated in a way Aaron didn't. Ruth led the league in on-base percentage ten times (his .474 career mark is second on the all-time list); Aaron never did. Ruth led the league in slugging percentage his first thirteen seasons (his .690 career mark remains the best ever); Aaron led the league four times in slugging percentage (his .555 ranks 27th all-time). Ruth's .342 lifetime batting average eclipsed Aaron's .311 lifetime average. Babe Ruth, his loyalists maintained, was the greatest hitter of all time, bar none.

The Aaron camp countered that his soon-to-be 714 homers were hit under more difficult conditions. Aaron faced bigger, harder-throwing pitchers, many of them fresh relievers in late innings. He played night games when the ball was harder to see. He crisscrossed the country and multiple time zones on late-night flights and played day games after night games. He may not have led the league as often, but year after year—for twenty years straight—he performed consistently, not having a bad season. "Real baseball people understand that the best thing you can have in a sport with a long season is consistency," the syndicated columnist and baseball fan George Will noted. "Henry Aaron, by that measure, is the greatest baseball player ever, period, end of discussion."[59]

Aaron may have benefited from the lighter, thinner bats that players could whip around faster, but the bat's smaller sweet spot required more precision in the swing. Some believed that Aaron also benefited from a livelier ball, but, in fact, the opposite was true. Ruth played almost his entire career in the "live-ball era," which lasted from 1920 to about 1934, when the manufacturers deadened the ball somewhat. Changes to better stitching, binding, and the core revived the ball in the Fifties. "The ball is livelier now than in the late Thirties and Forties but not as lively as in Ruth's years," baseball historian Joe Reichler, a member of the commissioner's staff, told the *Los Angeles Times* in June 1973.[60] Aaron himself pointed out that Ruth never had to face the likes of Bob Gibson, Juan Marichal, and Ferguson Jenkins, because blacks were banned from Major League Baseball in his day. "Ruth may have had it easier for that reason," Aaron wrote in *I Had a Hammer.*

In the end, nostalgia and legend seemed to tip most of the arguments in the Babe's favor. More than half of the letters Aaron received still did not want to see him break Ruth's record. "Of course, you had the man Hank Aaron and the myth Babe Ruth, and then the commercialized image of Babe Ruth," Reverend Jesse Jackson opined. "It was just amazing that the myth of Ruth and this home run number was a kind of white supremacy symbol for many people."[61]

Certainly, Aaron faced pressure Ruth hadn't in the form of hate mail, shouted epithets, and death threats. There was also the invisible but palpable prejudice of apathy and indifference. Aaron felt that as well. Crowds may have doubled in other cities around the league where he played, but Atlanta fans ignored Hammerin' Hank's pursuit en masse. July 21, the day after Aaron hit No. 699, the Braves sold only 16,236 tickets to a Saturday game against the Phillies. Naturally, Aaron wondered if people stayed away because he was black.

Those drawn to Atlanta Stadium by the prospect of Aaron hitting No. 700 clustered in the left-field stands with nets in anticipation. They wanted to witness history but also wanted a chance at the $700 Braves officials had offered as a promotion to the fan who retrieved the historic home run ball.[62]

Aaron singled in the first inning. He batted again in the third inning. Aaron faced the Phillies starter, the left-handed Ken Brett. A solid hitter himself, Brett had garnered headlines and bolstered the National League's argument against the designated hitter the previous month when he homered in four consecutive starts, from June 9 to June 23. Not even Babe Ruth had performed such a feat in his pitching days.[63] Aaron faced Brett with a man on second. He watched two Brett pitches he didn't like, the first a ball, the second a called strike. The second pitch looked high to Aaron. He glanced back at the umpire to let him know. Brett's third pitch was a fastball—

perfect. Aaron lunged and his bat cracked authoritatively against the ball. The crowd recognized the sound instantly and cheered. The roar gained intensity with the trajectory of the ball. Aaron's shot landed five rows into the left-field pavilion. The scoreboard flashed "700."[64]

Aaron rounded the bases in his business-like trot, practiced more than any other living player, his face stoic, elbows jutting behind him. "In one of the great events of history, Hank Aaron has just hit home run No. 700, only the second player in this great game ever to do it," Braves radio announcer Ernie Johnson called.[65]

Rounding third, Aaron smiled slightly, giving the world a peek into his private emotions. He had known as soon as he made contact the ball was gone. The excitement tickled him.[66] Darrell Evans, who scored in front of him, congratulated Aaron at the plate. Photographers on the field snapped excitedly on his walk to the dugout. The rest of his teammates greeted him there on the steps. The crowd had erupted into an ovation when the ball cleared the fence. The 16,000 sounded like a sellout. They continued to stand and cheer after Aaron disappeared into the dugout. He came out twice to tip his cap.[67] When the Braves at bat ended and Hammerin' Hank returned to his position in left field, the pitchers and catchers in the Braves bullpen stood and applauded him.[68]

After the game, which the Braves eventually lost 8–4, media and team officials crowded Aaron in the clubhouse. He sipped champagne in celebration. Photographers stood on folding chairs to snap shots of Aaron holding the home run ball.[69] Eighteen-year-old Robert Winborne, recently graduated from high school, had pounced on the ball after it bounced off the concrete floor.[70] The Braves paid him a pile of 700 silver dollars, and Winborne gave the ball to Aaron. Winborne offered to donate the money to a charity of Aaron's choice. "No, you keep it," Aaron told him.[71]

Aaron had become only the second man in MLB history to hit 700 home runs. Ruth had hit his 700th thirty-nine years and eight days earlier, when Aaron was five months old.[72] Aaron's 700th was a monumental event noted by newspapers, radio reports, and television broadcasts around the country. Aaron received telegrams of congratulations from a hundred people, including National League president Chub Feeney, Jesse Jackson, fans, friends, and a former teammate. Aaron did not hear from commissioner Bowie Kuhn, baseball's primary ambassador.[73]

Kuhn had been absent from Cincinnati three years earlier when Aaron collected his 3,000th hit, a milestone only eight other players had reached at the time. Stan Musial, the only other living member of the 3,000-hit club, had been there. He hopped out of a box seat and hustled onto the field to congratulate Aaron.[74] But Kuhn had not deemed the event worthy of his presence. He had not been in Cincinnati, and he hadn't been in Atlanta for Aaron's 700th homer. Kuhn hadn't even bothered to send a telegram.

Kuhn's defense was that he planned to congratulate Aaron in person at the All-Star Game three days later in Kansas City. That didn't satisfy Aaron. He was compelled to speak up about the perceived injustice. "I believed he would have shown more interest in the record if a white player were involved, and I also believed it was my duty to call attention to discrimination in baseball," Aaron wrote.[75]

The press did not give much credence to Aaron's criticism of the commissioner. *Newsweek* downplayed Aaron's reaction as "minutiae" and called Kuhn's absence of recognition a perceived "petty slight."[76] Had the writer walked in Aaron's spikes, read his mail, lived the daily prejudice, suffered the same indignities, he no doubt would have recognized the validity of Aaron's remarks. As it was, the press's reaction replicated the commissioner's slight.

———————

Going into the All-Star break, Aaron had 63 games left to hit 14 home runs. He planned to play in the All-Star Game on July 24, which meant he had to reckon with a threat from another letter: "If by the all star [sic] game you have come within 20 homers of Babe you will be shot on sight by one of my assassins on July 24, 1973."

Willie Mays and **Hank Aaron** converse at the All-Star Game in Kansas City.

Chapter Ten

THE MIDSUMMER CLASSIC

Charlie Finley phoned Dick Williams at the hospital. Not to wish him a speedy recovery from his emergency appendectomy. No, usually when Finley called his manager, he did so with specific instructions: drop this player in the batting order, shift that player to another position. When a reporter asked him that month who would pitch the next day, Williams glanced at the clubhouse phone, smiled, and said only half-joking, "I don't know. I haven't gotten my telephone call yet."[1] This time was no different. Finley had specific instructions for his manager: Get your ass to Kansas City.

Finley wanted his man in the dugout calling the shots for the American League at the All-Star Game on July 24. The A's owner was proud that his world champions had six players on the team—Reggie Jackson and Bert Campaneris elected as starters by the fans; Catfish Hunter, Rollie Fingers, Ken Holtzman, and Sal Bando selected by Williams, who was supposed to manage the team as the skipper of the defending American League pennant winners. Appendectomy? That was on the 19th, days ago. Charlie talked Williams out of his hospital bed on July 23 and onto a plane headed to the Midsummer Classic.

The MLB All-Star squads had been determined by various means since the original 1933 contest dreamed up by *Chicago Tribune* sports editor Arch Ward. In 1970, commissioner Bowie

Kuhn returned the selection to the fans. They voted for the starting lineups by punching out chads on computer cards. Each squad's manager, the leader of the previous year's pennant winner, picked the starting pitchers and remainder of the players. The commissioner faced criticism for taking the vote away from the participants and even for selling out to the Gillette Company, which underwrote the large cost of printing the ballots. "But I was sure we were right because we were serving the fans," Kuhn wrote in his memoir, *Hardball.* "That was the touchstone, and it was one I would use in future marketing decisions."

The names on the ballot—eight at each position (twenty-four in the outfield) for each league—had been chosen by a committee of general managers, managers, players, writers, broadcasters, and publishers in December so that the millions of ballots could be printed and distributed in time for the following season. The committee operated on the assumption that players would continue to play the same positions in 1973 as they had the previous season. That had Hank Aaron the leading candidate in early returns at first base, a position he hadn't played since 1972.[2]

Another shortcoming of the system occurred when fans voted into the starting lineup favorites who were struggling to hold their position on their own team. Brooks Robinson, for example. By July 24, the Orioles future Hall of Fame third basemen was batting .216 with six home runs and 37 RBIs, yet he received almost 200,000 more votes than the White Sox' Bill Melton, who was batting .299 with 14 homers and 60 RBIs. Had it been up to the players, they would have selected Melton. In a *Sporting News* poll of MLB players, Melton received 83 votes to Robinson's 12.[3]

"The way it's set up now, it's a popularity contest, not a vote to determine the best players," Sal Bando said. Robinson received more than twice as many votes as the A's third baseman, batting .265 with 18 homers and 54 RBIs. The players had cast 26 votes for Bando, more than twice as many as they had for Robinson. "In a case like Brooks's, what are you voting for, anyway?" Bando asked. "A man's career—which in Brooks's case has been great—or his season?"[4]

These errata and discrepancies caused confusion and frustration in voting, but the biggest controversy about the All-Star squad selection focused on the manager's pitching picks. Dick Williams had named his ace, Catfish Hunter, to start. You couldn't argue with that. Hunter's 15–3 record gave him the best winning percentage among major league starters.[5] The AL manager added two more of his own pitchers, Ken Holtzman, whose 2.07 ERA was best among the league's starters, and Rollie Fingers, whose 1.39 ERA was the lowest in the league. Again, justifiable choices. The criticism started with the five other AL pitchers Williams selected. Jim Palmer wasn't among them. The Orioles pitcher had an 11–6 record and 2.86 ERA to date and would win the American League's Cy Young Award that year. Nor was Nolan Ryan of the California Angels among the pitchers the AL skipper chose.

Ryan was a twenty-six-year-old, hard-throwing, often wild pitcher who had not yet refined his curveball nor his control. Batters feared his inaccuracy as much as his velocity. "Ryan's the only guy who put fear in me," Reggie Jackson said. "Not because he could get me out but because he could kill me. Every hitter likes fastballs just like everybody likes ice cream. But you don't like it when someone's stuffing it into you by the gallon. That's how you feel when Nolan Ryan's throwing fastballs by you."[6] As usual, Jackson said what others felt but dared not speak.

Reggie had reason to fear Ryan. After hitting a line drive off Ryan that the Angels center fielder caught, Reggie rounded first base and trotted across the infield toward the bench. He loped across the mound and patted the pitcher on the rump. Ryan didn't like that. The next few games he faced Jackson, the pitcher was "conveniently wild," as Dick Williams put it, and Reggie found himself playing dodgeball with Ryan's heat. Reggie never patted a pitcher on the rump like that again.[7]

Ryan had a breakout season in 1972, winning more games than he lost for the second time in his career, going 19–16 with a 2.24 ERA and an impressive 329 strikeouts, the first right-hander since Bob Feller to fan more than 300 batters in a season. In 1973, Ryan laid the foundation of his legend. His greatness wasn't in his stats—10–11 at the All-Star break with a 3.05 ERA—but in his accomplishments. By July 24, the Ryan Express had pitched the first two no-hitters of his career—the first player to throw a pair of no-hitters in a season before the All-Star break since Johnny Vander Meer in 1938.[8] Ryan's 233 strikeouts led the majors and put him on pace to break Sandy Koufax's single-season record.

On May 15, Ryan had struck out 12 batters on mostly fastballs and no-hit the Kansas City Royals, one of the best-hitting teams in the league. After the game, the Royals Hal MacRae said, "If they had a higher league than the majors, Ryan would be in it ... as a matter of fact, he could be it."[9]

Exactly two months later, on July 15 in Detroit, Ryan struck out 17 Tigers—the most ever in a nine-inning no-hitter—despite (or maybe because) Detroit manager Billy Martin kept yelling at him that the next guy up was going to spoil his no-hitter with a home run. In the ninth, the Tigers first baseman Norm Cash, who had struck out in his previous three at bats, approached the plate shouldering a table leg he had pried off the clubhouse snack table, expressing his futility in facing Ryan. Once plate ump Ron Luciano stopped laughing, he noted Cash's lumber wasn't legal and made him switch to a regulation bat. It didn't help. Cash popped out weakly to left field, and Ryan completed his second no-hitter.[10]

In his next outing, against Baltimore the week before the All-Star Game, Ryan was six outs away from a third no-hitter, when Orioles shortstop Mark Belanger rapped a single to center field. *The Sporting News* columnist Melvin Durslag called Nolan Ryan "the most exciting pitcher in the majors this year."[11] Yet Williams had snubbed him. "He doesn't carry his club," Williams said.

"Bill Singer does." (Williams had picked Singer, Ryan's teammate with the 15–5 record, for the All-Star team.) "Ryan is not even a .500 pitcher."[12]

Williams's omission sparked a near revolution of complaint as well as renewed calls to remedy the All-Star selection system. Commissioner Bowie Kuhn stepped in to remedy the situation. He created an extra spot on each team's roster for an additional player so that Williams could add Ryan to the AL squad. "Luckily for Nolan, the commissioner rode to the rescue, making his most notable announcement since the day last spring when he went on record against wife-swapping," Durslag wrote.[13]

The extra spot on the NL team was designated for Mays. Kuhn's move had been an act of justice in Ryan's case, but it was charity in Mays's. Willie had played in the previous 23 All-Star games, dating back to 1954. He had gotten more hits (including three home runs, three triples, and two doubles), scored more runs and stolen more bases than anyone else in All-Star history. He had also made many spectacular fielding plays, including one in 1955 that robbed Ted Williams of a home run and sent the game into extra innings. Mays's feats had secured his reputation as the greatest all-round performer in All-Star history and prompted Williams to declare, "They invented the All-Star Game for Willie Mays."[14] But in 1973, Mays, with his weakened arm and pathetic batting average, was no All-Star. The fans had cast very, very few votes for him, and the players had not even considered him in their poll. The commissioner's appointment to the team was an honorary gesture fueled by the fumes of nostalgia.

The National League's starting first baseman, Hank Aaron, had begun the season in right field, but Eddie Mathews had moved Aaron to left field in early May. "He simply can't make the throw from right field any more," the Braves manager explained.[15] Aaron admitted that his arm ached and had lost the strength of his youth.[16] For many, Aaron's home run barrage that season had justified his place batting cleanup for the National League, whether at first base or in left field. His pursuit of 714 made him a natural people's choice. After Reds catcher Johnny Bench, Hammerin' Hank received the highest number of votes, 1,362,497.[17]

Two days after hitting No. 700, he upped the controversy at a pregame press conference with his complaint about the commissioner not recognizing his milestone accomplishment with at least a telegram. "I felt let down," Aaron told the assembled media. "I think what I did was good for baseball. I felt like he should have sent me a wire. I'm not agitating him, and I'm perfectly serious. I mean this sincerely. Regardless of how small he thinks it is hitting that home run, it wasn't small to me. I feel he should have acknowledged it somehow. Frankly, it bothers me."[18]

His complaint did not find many sympathetic ears among the attendant press. *The Sporting News* chided Aaron in an editorial for missing the All-Star luncheon, which most players attended: "Since Henry finds oversights difficult to digest, he can't expect one of his own to enhance his chances for additional acclaim."[19]

The designated hitter occupied much of the conversation at the All-Star gathering. Orlando Cepeda had outperformed the other regular DHs in the AL. He had the third highest batting average among them and the most home runs and RBIs. Yet there was no place on the All-Star squad for Cepeda. Back in January, when NL owners had granted AL owners permission to employ the DH experiment, the leagues had agreed that the game would be played by the old rules whenever teams from the two leagues played, most notably in the All-Star Game and the World Series.[20]

It was almost a moot point for the All-Star Game, when pitchers rarely batted anyway. Managers generally opted to use the occasion of the pitcher's at bat to insert a new player into the game as a pinch hitter and utilize another pitcher. It was anticipated that the absence of the DH would favor the NL in the World Series, since AL pitchers would have gone nearly a year without batting. In the nearly 600 games played in the AL before the All-Star break, only two pitchers had batted, the White Sox' Cy Acosta and the A's

Rollie Fingers. Both struck out. *The New York Times* observed, "In the World Series, the American League will be at a disadvantage unless its pitchers take a lot of batting practice over the last two months of the season."[21]

For the most part, fans had responded positively to the designated hitters, who had added offense to the game as expected. But the critics were not silenced by the All-Star break. *The Sporting News* pointed out that a National League pitcher, Steve Blass of the Pirates, was out-hitting all AL DHs with a .455 average (10 hits in 22 at bats). Four more NL pitchers were batting .300 or better, including Philadelphia's Ken Brett, whose four homers would have put him among the top ten designated hitters.

In response to the argument that the DH added value with power, critics countered that was one of the ways the rule dumbed down the game's strategy. With a designated hitter batting in a bunt situation, managers were reluctant to tell power hitters to lay one down. The nine DHs with 200 or more at bats so far had combined for only five sacrifice hits.[22]

National League players remained scornful of the DH. Aaron said he wouldn't want to be relegated to simply a batter. Mays echoed that, after first toying with reporters at the Midsummer Classic. "That's coming into the National League," he said, grinning. "I'm going to play eight more years. With that rule, man, you can play as long as Satchel Paige."

"You mean that, Willie?" one of the gullible reporters asked.

Mays laughed. "I don't know if I could do just that (bat)," he said seriously. "I don't think I'd like it. When I play, if I play again next year, I'd want to play the whole game. When you're a designated hitter, that makes it a one-sided game. Right now, I'd say I wouldn't do it if it comes into our league, but I might change my mind."[23]

Reds manager Sparky Anderson, skipper of the NL squad, firmly denounced the AL experiment. "I don't like it," he told the press in Kansas City. "None of my own pitchers can hit—they average about .050 collectively—but I still think baseball was made for nine athletes, not ten. You can dream up all kinds of ideas to change the game, but we're really dreaming when we reach for ideas to put people into the ballpark."[24]

White Sox manager and AL coach Chuck Tanner, who described himself as the "designated manager" for the recuperating Williams, refused to sing the AL party line. "Amen to what Sparky said," Tanner chimed.[25]

The Sporting News reported that grousing among managers about the designated hitter indicated that if the decision were theirs, they would not renew the experiment for the 1974 season. But Bowie Kuhn reminded managers it was not their decision. In his public relations campaign to restore the game's appeal, and consistent with his *modus operandi*, the commissioner said that fans would ultimately decide the DH's fate: "The final decision is going to be based largely on what the fans want to see."[26] The commissioner's office had not received many letters criticizing the AL's new DH rule, a positive indicator. American League attendance was also up, another factor in the rule's favor. Early returns on the fan vote ran in favor of keeping the DH. If Kuhn was sincere that he would let the fan decide, he was a brave man, given the criticism launched at the fan selection of the All-Star lineups.

By late July, the Watergate scandal had consumed the nation's attention. Americans watched an estimated 1.6 billion hours of daily, live televised broadcasts of the senate Watergate hearings, starting May 17, and another 400 million hours of taped replay on public television during the evening. (The three major networks had initially all broadcast the hearings, but after three weeks, they agreed on a daily rotation of coverage to appease soap opera aficionados and game show diehards upset about missing their regular shows.)[27] On July 24, Americans watched John Ehrlichman testify that President Nixon had considered the September 21, 1971, break-in at the office of Daniel Ellsberg's psychiatrist to be within constitutional limits. Nixon had earlier admitted he had personally approved "the plumbers" to probe the leak of the Pentagon Papers.[28]

The country had also become concerned with the President's finances, focusing on renovations to and taxes paid on his properties in San Clemente, California, and Key Biscayne, Florida. Two weeks earlier, the House government operations subcommittee began investigating federal funds spent on the Nixon homes. By the end of the month, Reverend Robert Drinan, U.S. representative from Massachusetts and the first priest elected as voting member to Congress, would introduce a resolution calling for the impeachment of Nixon.[29]

Also on July 24, a federal judge ordered Nixon's campaign fundraisers to disclose within sixty days a list of people who collectively had contributed more than $23 million before the April 7, 1972, law required all contributors' names be publicized. The ruling had personal implications for George Steinbrenner, one of the secret contributors to the President's 1972 campaign.[30] Before the baseball season ended, Steinbrenner would appear among New York Governor Nelson Rockefeller and comedian Bob Hope in *The New York Times*'s list of the ninety-five largest donors.[31] By then, the Boss would be privately suicidal over the exposure of his wrongdoing but remain publicly defiant about his innocence.[32]

On the day of the All-Star Game, the nation was consumed not only by Watergate but by concerns about shortages of two staples of American life, beef and gas. As they had done in other difficult times, weary Americans turned to baseball for relief; they welcomed the All-Star Game diversion.

Royals owner Ewing Kauffman, thinking the President might need a diversion as well, invited Nixon to attend the game. Nixon instead had dinner at the White House with the visiting Shah of Iran, in town to purchase a dozen F14 supersonic jet fighter-bombers.[33] The President wired his regrets to Kauffman along with his praise for the new Royals Stadium.[34] The scoreboard printed the telegram. Fans booed the signature.[35]

The Royals' new park was impressive. Opened in 1973, it set a new standard for ballparks. While other stadiums built in that era—Busch Stadium in St. Louis, Three Rivers in Pittsburgh, Riverfront in Cincinnati—were multipurpose facilities shared with football teams, Royals Stadium was built for baseball. The others were circular bowls virtually indistinguishable from one another. Royals Stadium did have plastic grass—in step with the Seventies trend—the only American League park with an artificial infield and outfield, but was otherwise virtuous. "Functionally handsome, intimate and bright, Royals Stadium includes a chattily communicative, computerized $2 million scoreboard and a $750,000 'water spectacular' in center field," *Sports Illustrated* gushed.[36]

The city had footed the $75 million construction cost, but Ewing Kauffman (for whom the park was later named after his death) had paid for the scoreboard and "water spectacular."[37] Kauffman, who had founded Marion Laboratories in his mother's basement and grown it into a diversified health care company with sales nearing $1 billion, had endeared himself to the Kansas City community when he bought the Royals as an expansion franchise in 1968, the year after Finley cleared the Athletics out of town.[38]

Kauffman's wife, Muriel, who used to sneak out of her Toronto school as a child to watch the local Triple-A baseball team, had persuaded Ewing to purchase the Royals. She had also come up with the idea for the water spectacular.[39] To give the ballpark its architectural focal point, she commissioned the design of the country's most elaborate water display in right-center field. It stretched 322 feet wide with water cascading over rocks and fountains imported from Italy spraying geysers. Illuminated at night, the dazzling display was unlike anything in any other park at the time, though elements of it have been copied in parks built more recently. The water spectacular was completed just in time for the All-Star Game.[40]

Royals Stadium also had a scoreboard ahead of its time. The twelve-story high scoreboard in straightaway center field employed 16,320 light bulbs to cast images ranging from statistical data to cartoon animations on a 40-by-60-foot screen. The predecessor to today's JumboTron required a team of six men to keep the screen flashing its "chattily communicative" content along with a woman, Hilda Terry, who worked full-time creating the animations. Ewing Kauffman had hired Hilda because he considered her the best man for the job, so to speak.[41]

The Equal Rights Amendment was a hot button issue in '73. In March, Washington had become the thirtieth state to ratify the amendment that would prohibit discrimination based upon sex; ratification by eight more states would make it law. Missouri native Phyllis Schlafly, the conservative's "first lady," led the charge against the ERA that summer, inciting fear that the law would subject women to the draft and allow widowers to receive social security benefits like widows.[42] Missouri had not ratified the amendment, but Muriel Kauffman, a widow herself from her first marriage, did her part to see that women would be treated as equals at the Midsummer Classic.

Until that point, the All-Star festivities had excluded women. The men gathered for cocktails and ate meals together, independent of their wives. "The most frequent complaint was that their wives had always been treated like excess baggage," said Bill Johnston, one of the game's steering committee members. "They had been told to wait in their rooms as the men went off to various parties."[43] The situation reflected that in country clubs, athletic clubs, fraternal organizations, corporate functions, and other gatherings across the country.

Muriel changed that. She included women at the traditional pre-game stag dinner and invited women to attend all other scheduled social events as well. She hosted a wives luncheon the day before the game. There may have been some grumbling from the chauvinist corps, but Muriel, elegant and determined, saw to it that women were not treated as second-class citizens in

Kansas City. "We feel it's time for a definite change," she said.[44] And so it was.

————————

Tuesday, July 24, was soggy in the All-Star city. The heavens formed their own water spectacular. Steady rain canceled batting practice. When it let up, the groundskeepers vacuumed the Astro-Turf and pressed water from the outfield surface.[45] Ewing Kauffman had insisted on the artificial grass for this very purpose when the stadium was built, because it could be dried quicker than natural grass. He knew fans drove great distances from neighboring states to watch the Royals. He didn't want bad weather to spoil their baseball excursions.[46] He certainly didn't want the All-Star Game to be ruined for fans, nor did he want to have to eat the expense of a rainout. His grounds crew had the field ready to start on time.[47]

The cloudy skies didn't deter the fans. The largest crowd ever to watch a baseball game in Kansas City, some 40,849—breaking the record of 39,464 for Opening Day 1973—turned out to Royals Stadium for the Midsummer Classic. An estimated 50 million viewers tuned into NBC's prime time television broadcast.[48] For what had become a TV extravaganza, the network had positioned nine cameras around the park and brought ten mobile units, more than double the four cameras and two mobile units employed for a regular "Game of the Week" broadcast.[49]

Ewing Kauffman threw out the first pitch. Lefty Gomez, the AL starter in the first All-Star Game, and Bill Hallahan, his NL counterpart, also tossed ceremonial pitches. Twenty members from the first All-Star exhibition, including Carl Hubbell, Joe Cronin, Bill Dickey, Jimmy Dykes, Charlie Gehringer, and Wes Ferrell, were on hand to commemorate the 40th anniversary of the game.[50] (The 1973 contest was in fact the 44th All-Star Game, because the leagues had played two games each year from 1959 through 1962.)

The Kansas City faithful booed Dick Williams and the A's players during introductions. Their Royals trailed the Oakland rivals by only 2 ½ games in the AL West Division race, but their boos were interpreted more as enmity toward A's owner Charlie Finley, *persona non grata* in Missouri.[51] Kansas City fans had stood by the Athletics during lean years and felt betrayed when Charlie yanked the team out of town just as it had grown strong. They had not forgiven him nor the players who had gone with him, like Reggie Jackson, a rookie the Athletics' last year in Kansas City.[52]

Finley had worked out his retort in advance. He had arranged for the American League to warm up with one of his orange baseballs.[53]

The fans cheered for the other players, especially heartily for the three Royals representatives: John Mayberry, who replaced the injured Dick Allen at first base; Amos Otis, starting in center field; and reserve infielder Cookie Rojas. The fans gave the honorable Willie Mays a standing ovation for his All-Star legacy, sensing this was the last they would see of him on the field. But the crowd of 40,000-plus saved its heaviest applause for No. 44 of the Atlanta Braves. Aaron, wearing his team uniform like the other players wore theirs, doffed his cap. The cheering intensified. He tipped his cap again. They kept cheering. The future Home Run King was by far the fan favorite of the night. "The salute should allay any doubts he might harbor concerning how the fans feel about his numerous accomplishments," *The Sporting News* observed.[54]

Aaron, ever sensitive to how he was received, felt moved by the salute, especially since it came from an American League city, where he had never played a regular season game. "That was one of the greatest things that's ever happened to me," he said afterward.[55]

Finally, it was time for the game to begin. Hunter opened strong. He retired the side one-two-three in the first. His side was also retired in order in the bottom half. Hunter faced Aaron to start the second. Earlier, Hunter had joked about how he would pitch to

Aaron. "I'm going to throw it right down the middle," he said. "Then, I'm gonna duck."[56]

Hunter induced Aaron to pop out to Campaneris at short to start the second. The next batter, right fielder Billy Williams of the Cubs, lined a shot back through the box. Hunter stabbed at the line drive reflexively with his pitching hand.[57] The ball struck his thumb and caromed through the infield. He made a couple of steps toward it, but seeing the ball was out of his play, grabbed his pitching hand.[58] Dick Williams, still recovering from surgery, shuffled out to check on his injured pitcher. He replaced Hunter with teammate Ken Holtzman.

As the A's ace cradled his broken thumb, Royals general manager Cedric Tallis turned to a companion in his box at Royals Stadium and said, "That might be the season right there."[59]

Reggie Jackson, who had earned a $5,000 bonus in endorsements from a clothing company for making the All-Star team, opened the bottom half of the second with a drive deep to center field.[60] César Cedeño, the NL's center fielder, leaped but could not grab the ball. It bounced off the wall above the 410-feet sign. Reggie pulled into second with a double. Another few feet, and his drive would have been a home run. The Kansas City fans replaced their earlier resentment with partisan applause. Reggie scored on Amos Otis's single to give the AL an early 1–0 lead.

Dick Williams sent Minnesota's Bert Blyleven to the mound to start the third inning. The twenty-two-year-old Twins right-hander had been so nervous before his first All-Star Game that he had developed cold sores and a rash. Toeing the rubber, his mind whirred with anxiety. He walked two of the first three batters, then gave up a single to the Astros' César Cedeño, which scored the NL's first run and tied the game. Watching Hank Aaron step into the batter's box hardly settled the young pitcher's nerves. Blyleven meant to challenge Aaron, but the Braves slugger slapped his high fastball to left field for a single that drove in the go-ahead run.[61]

Trailing 2–1, the AL had a chance to even the score in its half of the third when Jackson batted with runners on first and third. With his last hit coming so close to clearing the fence, Reggie no doubt thought it would be sweet to knock one out of the stadium to put his team ahead with a dramatic three-run homer. Such visions of glory played regularly in his mind, ready to be enacted for the nine television cameras to transmit to the quarter of the country's population tuned in at home. Alas, the big-swinging Jackson grounded out to second to squash the rally and end the inning.

Dick Williams mercifully lifted Blyleven and replaced him with the Angels' Bill Singer to begin the fourth. The Reds' Johnny Bench welcomed Singer to the mound with a leadoff homer that sailed over the left-field seats into a concessions stand, a 450-foot shot that would stand as the longest ball hit at the stadium until Bo Jackson came along.[62]

Singer walked the Cubs' Ron Santo and struck out the next batter. That brought Claude Osteen to the plate and exposed a glitch in the glitzy scoreboard, which flashed the California Angels logo for the Dodgers pitcher.[63] Osteen, the only pitcher to bat in the game, laid down a sacrifice bunt that moved Santo to second. The Reds' Pete Rose dug in. Even though he was not a favorite among the players, the NL's starting third baseman was batting .324. The game's future all-time hits leader had collected his 2,000th hit a month earlier.

Singer's first pitch eluded Carlton Fisk's glove, smacked the Red Sox catcher on the knee and rolled all the way back to the screen. Santo advanced to third. Rose suspected spitball. Fisk confirmed it. Settling back into his crouch, he rubbed his knee and said to Rose, "He (Singer) surprised me more than he did you. He didn't even tell me the damn thing was coming."[64] Singer, long suspected for loading the ball, had been accused of throwing spitballs earlier that season.[65] After the fourth consecutive pitch that Rose suspected was loaded, he turned to the plate umpire and said, "Hey, that's a spitball."[66] The ump let it go. Rose grounded out to third to end the NL half of the inning.

In the AL half of the fourth, the Royals' Amos Otis led off with a single and stole second, giving the locals occasion to cheer, but the .228-hitting Brooks Robinson ended the inning by grounding out to the pitcher. That ended the night for Robinson, who went hitless in two tries.

Bobby Bonds replaced right fielder Billy Williams and came to bat in the fifth with a man on second and two outs. The Giants' star young fielder, who was batting .306 with 25 homers and 64 RBIs, had been far and away the players' top choice for the NL outfield. He had been upset about losing a starting spot to César Cedeño by only 5,231 votes.[67] With a flick of his wrists, Bonds crushed Singer's two-two pitch 410 feet over the left-field fence. The ball almost landed in the waterfall display. Bonds's two-run blast put the National League ahead 5–1.

Nolan Ryan, who hadn't expected to pitch, given Williams's opinion of him, was surprised to start the sixth inning.[68] In typical Ryan fashion, the wild flame-thrower walked the first batter, Santo, and struck out the second, Willie Stargell of the Pirates. Los Angeles outfielder Willie Davis was next. The Dodgers had forgotten to pack their batting helmets, so Davis borrowed Aaron's.[69] There must have been some magic left in that old hat because Davis sent Ryan's two-two pitch over the fence and onto a grassy slope between the waterfall and bullpen in right field. The third homer of the night gave the NL a 7–1 lead.

Jackson came to bat again in the AL's half of the sixth with John Mayberry on second. With all of the home runs being hit, the A's slugger wanted one of his own. Instead, he struck out. The AL went down without adding another run.

Ryan faced Bonds again in the seventh inning. Bonds hit what appeared to be a routine single into the outfield. When center fielder Dave May of the Milwaukee Brewers played the ball casually, Bonds turned on the jets and arrived at second with a standup double, an exciting play that, coupled with his home run, won him praise from his opponents. "Did you get a load of that Bobby Bonds?" Jackson asked reporters afterward. "He's fantastic. What other word could you use for him? He's got to be the best player in the National League."[70]

Ryan, on the other hand, left the game after two innings, having given up two hits and two runs, walked two batters, and struck out two. His last-minute addition counterpart, Willie Mays, pinch hit for Stargell in the top of the eighth inning and faced the Yankees' Sparky Lyle. Mays had hinted at retirement with reporters beforehand, but he was not willing to concede defeat to age. Over the past three weeks, he had raised his batting average over 100 points (to .214) and played adequately in the outfield. In his 24th and final All-Star appearance, Mays struck out. That closed the book on his brilliant All-Star career.

In the AL half of the eighth, Reggie faced the Mets' Tom Seaver with a runner on second. Reggie grounded out meekly to Seaver. Both teams went down in order in the ninth, and the National League sealed the 7–1 victory. The loss was charged to the jittery Blyleven. The Cardinals' Rick Wise, who started for the NL and was its only pitcher to give up a run, was ironically credited with the win. Reggie Jackson, who said he had come to have some fun at the All-Star Game and not to be embarrassed, fell short of his aspirations.[71] "They embarrassed us," Reggie said, unhappy with himself. "That's what they did, plain and simple. They simply embarrassed us."[72]

Manager Dick Williams agreed that his AL squad had been "overmatched." With its victory Tuesday night, the National League had won ten of the last eleven All-Star games, asserting its dominance over the junior circuit. "Those damn National Leaguers are tough," Williams said but then smiled. "Except in the World Series."[73]

The more pressing concern for Williams was Catfish Hunter's thumb. Five days after his emergency appendectomy, Williams was feeling better himself, but he was sick about the injury to his ace. He worried about how it would impact his Oakland team's chance to repeat as World Champions.[74]

————————

A record 54 players appeared in the 44th edition of the All-Star Game, which included another record 13 pitchers and 17 future Hall of Famers. Bobby Bonds, who had gone two-for-two with his homer and double, was deemed the best of them all. After the game, the commissioner presented him with the Most Valuable Player Award. "As of today, he's the best player in America," NL manager Sparky Anderson told the press.

In the clubhouse, Bonds shrugged off Anderson's comment. "I don't know," he told the reporters gathered around him. "There are a lot of great players in this clubhouse. One of them played first base." He looked toward Hank Aaron.[75]

Aaron's third-inning single had proven the difference, putting his team ahead for good. He had also performed well at first base, surprising himself after his failed experiment at that position the previous season.[76] But the reporters were more interested in whether or not he thought he could reach Ruth in '73. Aaron thought he could hit another 14 homers, easy, but he teased them with the suspense. "I do believe I can break the record this year," he said. "But I probably won't play as many games the second half as I did the first half. It will be more likely the first part of next year."[77]

Once showered and dressed, Aaron headed out to the parking lot. He had survived the game without any hint of danger. He had driven in the game-winning run. He carried with him the souvenir of the fans' hearty ovation during the introductions. Yet he also heard taunts thrown across the pavement: "Drop dead—who needs you?" and "We don't want no nigger breaking the Babe's record."[78]

The cheers in his memory could not drown out the angry

prejudice he still faced. So long as he was in America, he remained subject to the nation's racial conflict. It seemed every step of the way that season his path was divided between fans and foes. Such was the road a black man walked in America that summer.

In a familiar scene from 1973, the home plate umpire (John Flaherty) searches Indians pitcher **Gaylord Perry** for illegal substances used to load his famous spitball.

Chapter Eleven

CHEATING

Michael Burke, the former Ringling Brothers boss, may have left the Yankees, but the Steinbrenner circus played on. One June day, at lunch in Tampa, where AmShip had a major shipyard, Steinbrenner told a friend from the chamber of commerce that the Yankees had traded pitcher Mike Kekich, one of the team's wife/life swappers, to the Atlanta Braves for right-handed pitcher Pat Dobson. The chamber friend told one of his friends, a television broadcaster, who contacted Steinbrenner. Since the media was asking about the trade, George apparently thought the team had announced it. "Yes, we've traded Mike Kekich for Pat Dobson," Steinbrenner said in a taped interview. "It's the shot in the arm we need. We needed a left-handed pitcher, and we got one in Dobson."[1]

Reporters called Yankees general manager Lee MacPhail in New York for confirmation. Well, no, we haven't completed that trade yet, MacPhail told them. "We are close to a deal and hope to have an announcement tomorrow." The Braves brass said the same thing: No deal yet.[2]

Oops. Steinbrenner, whom *The New York Times* called the club's "most prolific talker," nearly skewered the deal by announcing it before it was consummated. You would think someone given to engineering a cover-up to throw federal investigators off his trail would practice a bit more discretion in discussing secret team business in public, but not George. "Steinbrenner has said he won't interfere with the daily operation of the club, but like a kid with a new toy, he sometimes can't resist playing with it when he should keep it tucked away in his toy chest," the *Times* observed.[3]

By yapping prematurely to his friend and to the television reporter, the Boss upstaged both Lee MacPhail and Yankees president Gabe Paul and put them in an awkward position. They tried to characterize Steinbrenner's meddling as innocent zeal, but the *Times* foresaw trouble: "Whether Steinbrenner's behavior, which his employees pass off publicly as the innocence of a man new to the business, affects the internal operation of the club remains to be seen."[4] And how! Steinbrenner's effect on the club's internal operations would provide copy that sold papers for more than three decades.

Turned out George had been wrong about the pitcher the Yankees would trade for Dobson. The Boss had named Mike Kekich, but when MacPhail and Paul closed the deal the following day, the Yankees had traded two players to be named later (Dave Cheadle and Al Closter), for Dobson, Frank Tepedino, and Wayne Nordhagen. Kekich, of course, was not happy to hear he had been traded without being informed and told manager Ralph Houk, who was left to clean up the mess George had made. "Now I've got a pitcher upset and that makes me upset," Houk said.[5] Beset by another incidence of the owner's meddling, Houk took a step toward the door himself.

The touch of comic relief George added to his comment stemmed from ignorance. He said, "We needed a left-handed pitcher, and we got one in Dobson." Dobson was right-handed. Best not to take the new owner too seriously when it came to the intricacies of the game.

A day after completing the Dobson deal, Gabe Paul did secure a left-handed pitcher, Sam McDowell, whom the Yankees had pursued since spring training. The Yankees purchased McDowell from the San Francisco Giants for an estimated $100,000. Horace Stoneham, the Giants cash-strapped owner, was happy to have money he could deposit in the bank, and the Yankees were pleased to pay with currency instead of talent. This time, Paul gave away Steinbrenner's money so quickly the owner wasn't able to mess up the deal. "The McDowell deal was concluded and announced in such rapid fashion Thursday that the owner never had a chance to put his two cents in (his $100,000 or so, yes; his two cents, no)," the *Times* reported.[6]

The two trades bolstered the Yankees' pitching corps and boosted their 1973 payroll over the one-million-dollar mark to approximately $1.2 million.[7] Steinbrenner actually paid closer to $150,000 for McDowell, a thirty-year-old pitcher whose better days were already behind him. The pitcher sweepstakes delineated the difference between the club's old ways and its new course. "Under CBS ownership, the Yankees would not have picked up Pat Dobson and Sam McDowell," Dick Young observed in *The Sporting News*. "It took $225,000 to swing both deals."[8]

The fact Steinbrenner was willing to spend so much for McDowell and bankroll such a large payroll, the largest ever in the team's history, showed how badly George wanted to build—even buy—a winning team.[9] Bottom line, he would bumble and bluster his way toward that end.

Mike Kekich eventually did get traded in the flurry. McDowell's arrival put the Yankees roster at twenty-six, one player over the limit. MacPhail sent Kekich to Cleveland for minor league pitcher Lowell Palmer.[10] Shortly after joining the Yankees, McDowell sprained his ankle and missed twelve days. He blamed a department store escalator for the injury.[11] Years later, McDowell admitted a drinking problem that he had concealed from the club. That prompted teammate Dick Radatz to say, "We thought he was just stupid. It turned out he was never sober."[12]

The two new pitchers rallied the Yankees. In June, they moved into first place with an eight-game winning streak, their longest in four years. Cleveland Indians pitcher Gaylord Perry stopped that.

Bill Singer wasn't the only pitcher throwing spitballs that summer. George Steinbrenner suspected Gaylord Perry was also illegally greasing the ball. Singer and Perry weren't the only suspects, but they were the most visible and most successful, particularly Perry, who won the 1972 AL Cy Young Award with a 24–16 record. The thirty-four-year-old right-hander had been accused countless times of doctoring the ball with sweat, grease, or spit but had never been convicted. The Boss was determined to catch the purported cheat when Perry and the Indians came to Yankee Stadium in late June.

Perry had beaten the Yankees 4–2 in Cleveland on June 25 and ended their winning streak. Convinced that Perry was loading the ball, manager Ralph Houk impulsively rushed to the mound in the eighth inning after Perry's first pitch to center fielder Bobby Murcer. Houk tugged off Perry's cap, threw it to the ground and kicked it.[13]

Murcer bunted the next pitch foul down the third baseline. Third base coach Dick Howser picked up the ball and rushed to show umpire Lou DiMuro what he believed was grease smudged on the ball.[14] DiMuro was not convinced. He ejected Howser for his animated and impolite argument.

Later, Houk summoned DiMuro to the mound to search the pitcher. This time, Perry cooperatively removed his hat for inspection. They found nothing.[15]

After the game, Murcer criticized commissioner Bowie Kuhn and American League president Joe Cronin for letting Perry get away with throwing his spitball. "If the league president or Commissioner had any guts, they'd ban the pitch," he said.[16]

The team, it seemed, was starting to behave like its owner, whose behavior *The New York Times* had characterized as "sometimes questionable."[17] For his part, Steinbrenner told the press that he had authorized the installation of two closed-circuit TV cameras to be trained on Perry throughout the Friday, June 29, game at Yankee Stadium.[18] Yankees president Gabe Paul, recently of the Cleveland Indians, had hatched the surveillance plan to catch Perry in the act of doctoring the ball through the slow-motion and stop-action replay of the film. The team invited the league to send an official to watch the film with them.[19]

Steinbrenner approved the plan. If the guy was cheating, The Boss figured he deserved to be caught and punished. He would see to it himself. The irony of Steinbrenner trying to catch a pitcher greasing a baseball while he covered up his illegal contributions to Nixon's campaign was lost on George. Justice would have its day.

The Sporting News columnist Leonard Koppett did not yet know about Steinbrenner's felonious activities, but he wrote presciently and precociously at the time about the connection between Watergate and professional sports. "A central point, made again and again by both the investigators and those testifying, has been that victory at any cost was the motivation in many admitted criminal and unethical acts," Koppett wrote in his July 7, 1973, column. "If the Watergate revelations—regardless of who did what when—truly represent the presence of a flaw in the conscience of many of our 'finest' people, the sports establishment should not shirk its responsibility for its role in helping create the climate of muddy morals. Some heavy soul-searching is in order."

Two days after Steinbrenner said the Yankees would film Perry, Gabe Paul canceled the plan. Although he claimed the team had decided to do so on its own, his statement didn't sound independent. "We're satisfied the American League is conducting a thorough and proper study of the accusations against Perry," Paul said in a carefully worded statement released the day before the June 29 game. "One club should not conduct an examination on its own, and as long as the league is doing a proper job of investigation, we are satisfied."[20]

Friday afternoon, Kuhn met with Murcer, chewed him out for his criticism and fined the Yankees $100,000 -center fielder $250.[21] The commissioner said that Murcer had apologized for his comments. An unrepentant Murcer called a press conference before the game to clarify. "I told him (Kuhn) that we had just lost a tough ballgame, and that a lot of things are said in the locker room that maybe shouldn't be said," Murcer explained. "He told me that I should be a little more discreet in my statements."[22]

Murcer repeated his belief that Perry had been throwing grease-balls and displayed a dab of K-Y lubricating jelly on his fingers to show how hard it was to detect. "Do you see anything?" he asked. "That's the stuff Perry uses."[23]

Meanwhile, the Yankees authorized ABC-TV to film the June 29 game for "Wide World of Sports" to be shown the following day. The commissioner did not intervene. Mega-media personality Howard Cosell and Bobby Bragan, a member of baseball's Playing Rules Committee and an advocate for legalizing the spitball, planned to analyze Perry's performance. The Yankees trounced Perry with a six-run rally in the fourth inning powered by two home runs. One of those came as sweet revenge for Bobby Murcer off his bat. Perry completed the game and lost 7–2. In the fourth, Yankees catcher Thurman Munson twice asked the plate ump to inspect the ball. He found nothing.[24] Nor did Dick Butler, the American League's umpire supervisor who watched Perry from a hiding spot in Yankee Stadium, find evidence of Perry cheating.[25]

But the Yankees were not convinced of Perry's innocence. Fritz Peterson, the Yankees' other wife/life-swapping pitcher, had secretly charted Perry's actions and pitches. He flagged 30 spitters. Peterson believed that Perry dabbed K-Y jelly on the ball where it was stamped with "Reach," the name of the manufacturer. "This makes it difficult to detect since it's on the printed part of the ball," Peterson explained. "Every one of the Yankees believes he throws the spitter."[26]

Peterson had worked undercover for *The New York Times*. He slipped his chart to a *Times* reporter in the Yankees clubhouse after the game. The reporter took the chart to the ABC studios and matched the suspected spitball pitches to Perry's motions before each pitch. Perry performed a variety of rituals before throwing—touching his belt, sliding his fingers across the visor of his cap, reaching behind his ear, rubbing his chest—but he did the same thing before every alleged spitball: the right-hander tugged the inside of his left sleeve with his right hand. Peterson believed that Perry put the K-Y jelly in different places—on his neck, inside his shirt, or in his sideburns—for different games.[27] That night, he seemed to be loading the ball from his left armpit.

The "Wide World of Sports" broadcast showed a shot of Perry reaching under his left arm at least twice, as though Inspector Cosell had caught Perry in the act, but even the replay was ultimately inconclusive. Bragan, billed as a "spitball expert," told three reporters after the game that he couldn't be sure whether or not Perry had cheated. "I think he threw a few spitters, but I couldn't swear to it," he said. Moments later, taping the "WWS" segment, Bragan, prodded by Cosell, swore he saw Perry throw illegal pitches.[28]

The replays also showed certain pitches coming in straight, then suddenly dropping a foot or more—the way a spitball behaved. Peterson noted four spitballs thrown to Munson when he had twice asked the ump to check the ball.[29]

Cleveland objected. Phil Seghi, Gabe Paul's replacement as the Indians general manager, called the commissioner's office to complain, "What Howard Cosell did was conduct a national kangaroo court ... a televised witch-hunt."[30] Others criticized Bragan for letting Cosell browbeat him into his conviction of Perry's guilt.

Steinbrenner may have thought he had vindicated his team by exposing Perry in the "Waterball Affair," as the *Times* dubbed it, but the commissioner remained unconvinced—or gutless, as Murcer would say. Perry would grin and shrug off accusations, but in his autobiography, *Me and the Spitter: An Autobiographical Confession*, released the following spring, he admitted throwing the spitball. Kuhn did not sanction the pitcher.

Steinbrenner had hoped for vindication; instead, Gaylord Perry wiped spit in his face.

The Yankees kept winning and reached the All-Star break still on top of the AL's East Division. They stayed there until early August, when they dropped three of four games in Boston. On August 2, Orlando Cepeda hit his 16th homer of the season, a three-run blast in the Red Sox' 10–0 rout that dropped the Yankees to second place. They would continue to plummet in the standings.

On Wednesday afternoon, August 15, New York trailed the California Angels at Yankee Stadium 3–1. Ralph Houk called on Johnny Callison to pinch hit in the eighth inning. There were two outs and two runners on. The tying run was at first; Callison represented the go-ahead run. The Yankees had sunk to third place but were only two games out of first. Steinbrenner knew a home run could win the game and put the Yankees within one game of first place. Callison, a four-time All-Star, had been a 30-home-run hitter earlier in his career, but the thirty-four-year-old outfielder had faded into a part-time player with a .176 batting average. He hit a ground ball to the second baseman, who flipped the ball to first. Inning over, hope dead. Steinbrenner was not happy with Houk's pinch-hitting selection.

Two days later, Houk sent Callison out to right field late in a losing effort against the Texas Rangers. Steinbrenner, who had traveled to Arlington for the series, didn't like what he saw. He didn't think Callison properly represented the pinstripes. George called Houk that night. Get rid of Callison, the Boss told his manager.

No, Houk said. The former World War II army ranger did not like the owner telling him how to run his team. Houk appealed to Lee MacPhail.

"Better tell Callison," the general manager said.

The next day, Callison was gone.[31]

While in Texas, one of the Yankees—very likely Fritz Peterson—stuffed a hot dog into shortstop Gene Michael's glove. Michael was famous for his aversion to squirming or squishy things. When he stuck his hand in his glove and his finger jammed into the hot dog, Michael yelped and flung the wiener toward the dugout. It soared toward the box seats and landed at Steinbrenner's feet. The Boss disapproved of such shenanigans. He told Houk to find out who was behind the hidden hot dog trick and punish him. Houk shook him off. "He's got to be kidding," he said.[32]

No, Steinbrenner did not have much of a sense of humor. But hot dog capers were the least of his worries as August turned to September. The Boss had thought his $100,000 illegal campaign contribution would ease AmShip's worries, but it had only compounded them. The FBI had opened an investigation of AmShip's bogus bonuses and political contributions. Other companies came clean on their own. American Airlines, Ashland Oil, Braniff Airways, Goodyear Tire and Rubber, Gulf Oil, 3M, and Phillips Petroleum all voluntarily admitted their illegal campaign contributions. None of the executive officers from those companies was indicted on felony charges.[33]

Steinbrenner could have avoided further trouble and faced only misdemeanor charges if he had come clean, too. But that wasn't his style. Honesty and remorse did not seem part of his makeup. He persisted with the cover-up and concocted another means of making illegal political contributions. He reimbursed phony expense accounts with cash that was channeled to designated politicians. In July and August of 1973, Steinbrenner sent $5,650 in illegal contributions to the reelection campaign of senator Dan Inouye (D-Hawaii), a member of the senate Watergate committee.[34] To Inouye's credit, when he found out where the money came from, he gave it back.[35]

Before the FBI interviewed AmShip officers about the bonus scam, Steinbrenner tutored them on how to reply to questions. He wanted them to say the CREEP contributions had been their own idea, a way of saying thanks to the President for his passage of the Maritime Act of 1970, which had been beneficial to the company.[36] AmShip's corporate counsel also coached the employees how to lie about their donations. The loyal employees played it the way the Boss had instructed them to.

But the lie could only last so long. Days later, a grand jury in Washington summoned the eight employees to testify on September 5. That proved the turning point. They had been willing to bluff before the FBI, but they weren't willing to perjure themselves.

Three AmShip officers—Stanley Lepkowski, treasurer; Matthew Clark, director of purchasing; and Robert Bartlome, corporate secretary—met with Steinbrenner to inform him they planned to tell the truth. Steinbrenner lay his head down on the table. "I'm ruined," he cried. "The company is ruined. I might as well jump off a bridge."[37] (Later, he would deny saying he would jump off anything.[38])

On Labor Day 1973, two days before his eight employees were scheduled to testify before the grand jury, Steinbrenner met with a group of his attorneys and advisors. In a motel room near the Cleveland airport, they showed him a sampling of the FBI reports on its AmShip investigation and told him, "You've got a problem."[39]

In a last-ditch effort, Steinbrenner told his once-loyal employees that if they stuck to the company story, that is, his recollection of events, the company would pay their legal fees. However, if they told the truth, they had to pay their own lawyer bills. He tried to convince them to sign statements agreeing to this arrangement. They refused.[40]

Early that week, the *Washington Star-News* ran an article that reporter Jim Polk had been researching for months. It reported: "The Watergate grand jury is probing a secret $100,000 Nixon campaign donation made by officials of a Cleveland ship company while the firm was trying—without success—to win payment of a five million dollar cost overrun on a government contract." Polk had asked Steinbrenner if any of his employees had been given corporate bonuses to be used as political contributions. "Never once have we said, 'Here's a bonus. Give it politically,'" Steinbrenner was quoted as saying. Steinbrenner also denied any connection between the $100,000 campaign contribution and the cost overruns on the OSS *Researcher*, "There was no thought in my mind connected to the *Researcher*—my God, may I be struck down if there was one."[41]

The employees managed to get their testimony delayed by two weeks, but Steinbrenner was unable to avoid the inevitable. In mid-September, with the Yankees struggling to stay above .500 and mired in fourth place, the AmShip employees told the grand jury about the company's bogus bonus plan, the illegal contributions, and Steinbrenner's efforts to cover it up. "I never asked them to lie," Steinbrenner said, but they testified under oath that he had.[42] George, like Nixon, was on his way down. Felony charges loomed.

Steinbrenner and his Yankees weren't the only ones convinced that Gaylord Perry was throwing spitballs that summer. Billy Martin, the Tigers manager, was so certain that Perry was loading the ball while shutting out the Tigers on August 30 that the pugnacious manager ordered his pitchers to throw spitballs the final two innings of the game. "The umpires are making a mockery of the game by not stopping Perry," Martin told reporters afterward. "Everyone knows he does it, but nobody does anything about it. We're going to keep on doing it every time he pitches against us."[43]

That strategy didn't sit well with Joe Cronin, American League president. He suspended Martin for three games. The suspension wasn't good enough for Detroit general manager Jim Campbell, who'd been at loggerheads with his problem-child manager all season. He fired Martin before he served out his three-game suspension.

Martin didn't have time to file for unemployment. Less than a week later, the Rangers fired skipper Whitey Herzog and replaced him with Martin. "I'd fire my mother for the chance to hire Billy Martin," said Rangers owner Bob Short.[44]

The man Michael Burke had recommended to George Steinbrenner was headed to Texas—where he would turn around baseball's worst team and be voted Manager of the Year in 1974—but it wouldn't be long before Billy would join George in New York for their celebrated love-hate affair.

The Yankees finished the season in fourth place, where they had finished the previous year, only worse. In 1972, the team had won more games than it lost. In their first year under their new owner, the Yankees ended the season 80–82, 17 games out of first place. After a promising start, they had lost 37 of their last 58 games. The team had tanked along with Steinbrenner.

Seemed nothing was going right. Following the Yankees' 8–5 loss to Detroit on September 30, the last day of the season, Houk locked the press out of the clubhouse, gathered the players together, and shocked them with his announcement. "I wanted you to be the first to know," he said, his voice breaking and eyes pooling with tears. "I've resigned as manager."[45]

Houk had been a loyal Yankees employee for thirty-five years. He had started with the team in 1947 as a backup catcher to Yogi Berra, managed the team for three years in the early Sixties, served as general manager in '64 and '65 (Berra replaced him as manager), then resumed his managerial post in 1966. He had managed the Yankees for the past eight years and had two more years on his $75,000 contract, but one year under Steinbrenner proved too much for him.

The players were stunned. Houk had been a players' manager, one who'd stood up for them. They had seen the "Fire Houk" and "Good-bye Ralphie" signs in the stands the second half of the season, but hadn't expected him to go on his own. Some of their eyes leaked tears, too.[46]

Steinbrenner had tried to talk Houk out of resigning, but nothing George could say would change Houk's resolve to escape his tyranny. Steinbrenner hadn't fired the man Gabe Paul called "the best manager in baseball," but George had forced him out with his meddling. Steinbrenner would not let him be the field boss that he was accustomed to being. "This year, I thought we had a chance to come back, but it didn't work out," Houk told the media assembled for a brief press conference. "It has been a rough year, so I decided it was probably time for me to go. Maybe someone else can do a better job."[47]

As if Steinbrenner wasn't busy enough with a grand jury on his case, Houk added another item to George's to-do list: find new manager.

The next day, the wrecking ball began its demolition of Yankee Stadium, the first stage of its renovation. The old era crumbled to make way for the next. The city shouldered the expense for the project—which had already mounted from original estimates before it even began—scheduled to take two years, and Steinbrenner would reap the profits from the Yankees' new and improved home. The federal government's case against Steinbrenner also swung at him like a wrecking ball, but he, too, would come back, bigger and better, at others' expense.

Two future Hall of Famers, **Orlando Cepeda** (right) chats with **Luis Aparicio**.

Chapter Twelve

RAH RAH FOR CHA CHA

There may not have been a place on the All-Star team for Orlando Cepeda, but he was playing like an All-Star. His knees, nearly crippled at the start of the season, had grown stronger. He had remained faithful to the conditioning program designed for his knees by the Red Sox trainer, and he had been careful to keep his weight down.[1] Most importantly, Cepeda's swing, which he had claimed was never better when he arrived in Boston, had lived up to his words. His greatest liability and strongest asset won him a place in the hearts of the Fenway crowds and Sox fans throughout New England.

Two weeks after the All-Star Game, Cepeda had the chance to strut his stuff at Royals Stadium. On Wednesday, August 8, Boston's designated hitter slammed four doubles, tying the major league record. The knees carried him safely into second four times, and the swing drove in six runs in the Red Sox' 9–4 win.

Two days later, back in Boston for a series against the Angels, Cepeda hit a two-run homer in the bottom of the second inning to tie the game. It was his 17th of the season and the 375th of his career. That moved Cepeda to 18th on the all-time list, past Rocky Colavito. Cepeda may not have been challenging Ruth, but he was delighting the fans in one of the Babe's old haunts.

Two days after that, on a Sunday afternoon at Fenway, Cepeda doubled in the second inning off California's spitball All-Star Bill

Singer, rapped singles in the third, fifth, and sixth innings, then slugged a solo homer to center field in the seventh. His five-for-five performance lifted his average to .302. His 71 RBIs were second best on the team.

The popularity of the designated hitter had grown in American League cities during the course of the season, but nowhere was the DH more popular than in the person of Orlando Cepeda. "A lot of designated hitters have created excitement in the American League this season, but none more than thirty-six-year-old Orlando Cepeda of the Red Sox," *The Sporting News* reported.[2]

Others performing the same role for other teams, intimately aware of the pressures inherent in the new position, tipped their hat to Cha Cha's success. Frank Howard, the Indians DH, said he would pay his way into the ballpark to see Cepeda play.[3]

After his five-for-five performance, Cepeda talked hitting with a group of sportswriters in the Boston clubhouse. He claimed that he was coming into his prime as a hitter, but that hitting remained a mystery to him. "I don't know how to hit," he said, seemingly defying what they had just witnessed. "Hitting is a personal thing," he explained. "It is not a science to me the way it was to Ted Williams."[4]

While he may not have mastered the science like Teddy Ballgame, Cepeda had made an art of hitting. In the series with the Angels, he had hit one ball into the bleachers behind the Red Sox bullpen in right-center and another into the center-field seats.[5] He had also clubbed many over the Green Monster in left. Unlike Aaron, whose home runs knew just one route—the shortest distance to the left-field seats—Cepeda managed to homer to all fields.

Cepeda was baffling opposing pitchers, proving to be a difficult out. *The Sporting News* offered this scouting report on Boston's right-handed DH: "He lashes outside pitches to right field, and he pulls inside pitches to left. Some managers now believe the best way to pitch him is inside, but then there is the frightful risk of a fly ball into the chummy nets at Fenway."[6] Of course, having played in the National League until 1973, Cepeda had the advantage of being an unknown among his AL opponents, but his ability to hit most pitches frustrated their efforts to learn his weaknesses.

Cha Cha also excelled in the clutch, seemingly hitting best with two strikes on him. He preferred not to swing at the first pitch, wanting first to have a look at the pitcher's stuff. Though that often put him behind in the count, he managed to work it to his advantage. He hit his four doubles in Kansas City and his five hits against the Angels all with two strikes against him. "I hit better when I am behind on the count, after I have seen what the pitcher is throwing," he explained. "I concentrate better."[7]

He was the complete package DH: able to hit for power to all fields, a tough out, and able to handle the pressure, even when he created extra amounts of it. Most importantly, those once wobbly knees had carried him to second for a team-high 21 doubles by mid-August. The fans at Fenway and those watching on televisions flickering throughout New England adored his swing, but they might have loved him best for his knees.

They'd seen how he had strained in his losing effort to beat out a ground ball in the opening series against the Yankees. They knew his history and his pain. So they appreciated him legging out the doubles—even when many of those would have been triples in years past—and they loved him best for the way he hustled out every ground ball, never letting the pain beat him. *Gotta love the heart in that guy.*

The Puerto Rican star was honored for his Hispanic heritage as part of "Latin American Day" at Fenway Park in July, along with eight other players from the Red Sox and Twins, before a game against Minnesota. Also in July, the Puerto Rican Businessmen's Association of Hartford, Connecticut, selected Cepeda as the first recipient of its Roberto Clemente Award.[8] Now that Clemente, beloved in his native Puerto Rico, was gone, Cepeda was the island's reigning star. The Puerto Rican community of New York City honored Baby Bull before a Boston game at Yankee Stadium in September.[9]

But it was in Boston where he became beloved not for his heritage but for his hitting. The city could be hard on its sports figures. The Boston public harbored a fifty-three-year-old resentment against Harry Frazee for selling Babe Ruth to the Yankees. They still begrudged Johnny Pesky for the hesitation on his relay throw in the seventh game of the 1946 series that allowed the Cardinals' Enos Slaughter to score from first and rob them of victory. Hear the boos lobbed at Sparky Lyle when he took the mound for the hated Yankees. But Boston fans also loved a hero, and Cepeda was one for them.

When Cha Cha stepped out of the dugout to swing his bat in the on-deck circle, he looked to the stands. Fans shouted to him. He called back. Joking, bantering. It was a mutual love affair. He was playing out some of the happiest days of his career in Beantown.[10]

The good vibes made him want to play more. He hoped his knees were strong enough to let him play the field again. He told reporters he dreamed "of returning to full-time duty at first base next season."[11] Despite his success in the DH role, he was still not content with the part-time work. The position still carried the stigma of the incomplete player, even for him.

Cepeda's season made a strong case for the success of the DH experiment, which was intended to set off a chain reaction of increased offense, fan interest, attendance, and revenue. Results from around the league bore that out.

Designated hitters easily provided more offense than pitchers, whose natural strength was on the mound, not at the plate. Through the 1973 season, the twelve AL teams used 132 different players in the designated hitter role. Combined, they batted .257, nearly a 90 point improvement on the .169 combined average for pitchers and those who pinch hit for them the previous year.[12] The designated hitters raised the AL's overall batting average 20 points, from .239 in 1972 to .259 in 1973, which bested the NL's overall average of .254 for the first time in ten years.[13]

More hits meant more runs. In 1973 AL games, the two teams averaged 8.55 runs per game compared to 8.31 in the NL. American League teams averaged almost 25 percent more runs per game in '73 than they had the previous season, 8.55 to 6.93.[14]

Home runs in the AL were up to 1,552 from 1,484 in 1971, which makes for a better comparison because teams played fewer games in the strike-shortened '72 season. Again, the designated hitters drove the pace with their power hitting. The designated hitters knocked in a run once every seven times at bat; pitchers had an RBI once every 20 times at bat the previous year. The designated hitters slugged 227 home runs, at a ratio of one every 33 at bats; pitchers homered 48 times, once every 217 at bats in 1972.[15]

The experiment had improved offense, no question. Fans liked that. The Harris poll, taken during the season, showed 62 percent of respondents agreed with the statement: "By allowing a real batter to bat, instead of the pitcher, it means more runs and more action, and that's good."[16] *The Sporting News* conducted its own poll around the All-Star break, figuring that its readers would provide a more knowledgeable view of baseball than the Harris poll's sample of the general population. Fifty-two percent of *The Sporting News*'s readers polled favored the use of the DH, while 48 percent opposed it, not a large majority of support. Fans in American League cities, more likely to have seen the DH in action, did show stronger support for the new rule—57 percent for and 43 percent against—than in NL cities, where 52 percent opposed and 48 percent approved.[17]

The key measure of the fans' interest was revealed at the gate, where attendance showed a strong increase. Attendance at AL games reached an all-time high, with 13,443,016 clicks of the turnstile in 1973, a significant 1.6 million jump from 1971, the last full season. The National League still outdrew the junior circuit by more than three million with an attendance mark of 16,679,175, though that was down 645,682 from 1971.[18] One possible explanation for the NL's drop and the AL's gain could be found in Chicago and New

York, two cities that had teams in each league. The NL teams in Chicago and New York saw a 653,351 drop to the AL teams' 673,873 gain from 1971 to 1973. The addition of the DH in the AL no doubt factored in the figures from those two cities, where both NL teams were involved in division races until the end of the season, but neither AL team was.

Major league attendance overall set a record mark, topping 30 million for the first time. The AL accounted for most of the rise. That suggested that the DH experiment had helped fans get over the bitter feeling they had about baseball's labor relations at the outset of the season. Nine teams playing better than .500 ball and two tight division races at the All-Star break also contributed to the AL's increased attendance. The two five-team division races halfway through the season created "an unprecedented state which is having a beneficial effect on the gate."[19] The new ballpark in Kansas City alone nearly doubled the Royals' attendance, up by 637,685 in 1973 from 707,656 in 1972. But the designated hitter was widely seen as the primary factor generating more interest and increased attendance throughout the league.[20]

Fans also liked seeing their favorite stars play an extra season or more. The new DH rule extended not only Orlando Cepeda's career; it added years to the careers of many players. The eight top designated hitters of the rule's inaugural season—Cepeda, Tommy Davis (Orioles), Tony Oliva (Twins), Frank Robinson (Angels), Deron Johnson (A's), Rico Carty (Rangers), Jim Ray Hart (Yankees), and Ollie Brown (Brewers)—were all aging players, many recovering from injuries, fit to bat but not to field, the early definition of the DH.[21] All except Oliva had enjoyed success in the National League. Their reputations alone drew fans to see them in the AL, often for the first time. This had not been one of the stated objectives of the experiment, but it proved a popular side effect for the fans and lured them through the turnstiles.

Bowie Kuhn had said he would let the fans decide the fate of the DH experiment. By that, the commissioner meant if they responded by turning out in larger numbers, they would have their designated hitter. He wanted them to put their money where their opinion was, and they did. Each additional click of the turnstile deposited extra revenue in the owners' pockets. What had started out as a three-year experiment had proven such a success that the owners voted after just one season to make the rule permanent.[22]

A's owner Charlie Finley's lobbying for the new rule is widely credited for its eventual adoption. He found a measure of vindication in the decision. "At first, they thought I was nuts," Finley said. "But after continuously harping, I finally woke them up."[23] Yet the AL owners' vote remained far from the final word on the designated hitter.

The National League, content with its status quo, still wanted nothing to do with Finley's permanent pinch hitter. Chub Feeney, NL president, said he had observed "no real interest" in the DH among NL owners.[24] He credited the AL's improved attendance to close division races, not the designated hitter. Opposition among NL owners to the designated hitter was so absolute that they rejected their AL counterparts' request to use the DH in All-Star and World Series games played in AL parks.[25]

Thirty-five years later, the leagues remain divided, the DH being the only rule on which they cannot agree. The rule also polarizes fans, managers, and players. "I screwed up the game of baseball," Ron Blomberg said thirty years after he made history as the game's first designated hitter. "Baseball needed a jolt of offense for attendance, so they decided on the DH. I never thought it would last this long."[26]

Some say Blomberg's right—he screwed up the game. Others say he's wrong. The argument usually pivots on the way the DH has—or hasn't—diminished the game's strategy. That was Feeney's main objection in 1973. "I like the strategy and the fans do, too," Feeney said. "And I think the DH rule takes some of that away. It deprives them of thinking along with the managers."[27] He still speaks for many fans, managers, and players today.

But not all. "Everyone in the world disagrees with me, including some managers, but I think managing in the American League is much more difficult for that very reason (having the designated hitter)," said Jim Leyland, who has won pennants as a manager in both leagues and skippered the Detroit Tigers in 2007. "In the National League, my situation is dictated for me. If I'm behind in the game, I've got to pinch hit. I've got to take my pitcher out. In the American League, you have to zero in. You have to know exactly when to take them out of there. In the National League, that's done for you."[28]

The venerable Bill James backed him up. In *The Bill James Historical Baseball Abstract*, he demonstrated mathematically how the use of the DH actually increased the use of strategy.

Carl Yastrzemski and others had initially feared that the DH rule would endanger hitters by allowing pitchers to freely throw at their heads, unchecked by any fear of retribution. Minnesota Twins manager Frank Quilici believed the rule had the opposite effect, giving umpires the chance to better police the game and protect batters with warnings for suspected chin music. "The DH took away the fear of retribution by a pitcher who knowingly threw at a hitter and allowed the umpire to control the game instead of the unwritten rule in baseball that left it up to the players to decide when action should be taken," Quilici said after he retired in 1975.[29]

An economist and a mathematician from the University of the South in Sewanee, Tennessee, presented a paper at the Joint Mathematics Meeting in January 2004 that backed Yastrzemski's claim. They called the DH a "moral hazard," an economics term referring to "the idea that someone insured against risk is more likely to engage in risky behavior." The pair, Charles Bradbury and Doug Drinen, figured pitchers who did not have to answer at the plate for their actions were more likely to throw at opposing batters. After a detailed analysis of eight MLB seasons, Bradbury and Drinen determined that the DH rule "increases the likelihood that any batter will be hit during a plate appearance between 11 and 17 percent."[30]

While batters worried about the moral hazard posed by the DH rule, fans continued to worry about the rule's impact on the integrity of the game's records, particularly among pitchers. They focused on Nolan Ryan.

The California Angels flamethrower finished the season with two no-hitters, though he nearly racked up four. In addition to the no-hit bid spoiled in the seventh by the Orioles' Mark Belanger in his first start after Ryan no-hit the Tigers, Ryan had another no-hit game spoiled by the scorer, though no one realized the fact until it was too late to protest.

Against the Yankees on August 29, 1973, Ryan struck out ten, walked three, and retired the final 15 batters in order. The only "hit" he allowed came in the first inning when Yankees catcher Thurman Munson hit a popup to shallow center. The Angels shortstop and second baseman gave chase. Both called for it. At the last instant, both backed off, and the ball dropped between them. The official scorer credited Munson with a hit, though if the play had occurred in the later innings of Ryan's no-hit bid, the scorer would probably have given one of the infielders an error, following the traditional practice of requiring a clean hit to break up a no-hitter. That simple twist of timing kept Ryan from becoming the only pitcher in history to throw three no-hitters in a single season.

Ryan's near-miss may have inspired heartbreak, but his pitching moment that provided the test case for the DH's impact on pitching records occurred with Ryan's final pitch of the 1973 season. On Thursday, September 27, he faced the Minnesota Twins first baseman Rich Reese in the top of the 11th inning. Ryan had already struck out 15 batters that day, tying Sandy Koufax's single-season record of 382 strikeouts set in 1965. With a runner on second, two outs, and two strikes on Reese, Ryan threw an inside fastball by Reese for strike three and strikeout No. 383 on the season, a new record.

The Angels won the game in their half, giving Ryan his 21st win of the season against 16 losses for a team that was last in the American League in hitting, runs batted in, and home runs and that had lost more games than it won. The last-minute All-Star addition bested two more Koufax records that season. The Dodger great had struck out 10 or more batters 21 times in 1965; Ryan struck out 10 or more 23 times in '73. Koufax set the modern record (since 1900) with 699 strikeouts in consecutive seasons; Ryan struck out 712 in 1972–1973.[31]

Initially, it was thought that the new rule might reduce a pitcher's numbers because the DH meant he faced tougher competition, a lineup of nine valid batters without the gimme out of the pitcher at the plate. By that measure, Ryan's 383 strikeouts came against more difficult conditions than Koufax's 382 in 1965, when he fanned the pitcher 53 times. Ryan had fanned pitchers 42 times in 1972, when he led the majors with 329 strikeouts, but struck out designated hitters only 30 times in 1973. The DH was a tougher out, but Ryan had still struck him out 30 times. In that regard, the DH rule had boosted the quality of the mark Ryan set.

The biggest boon to pitchers from the DH rule was that it allowed them to stay in games longer—instead of being lifted for a pinch hitter—and determine the outcome of the game. Ryan completed 26 of his 39 starts in 1973, throwing 326 innings, up from 20 complete games and 280 innings the previous year. Koufax pitched 27 complete games and 335.7 innings in 1965. Ryan's strikeout record was deemed a legitimate besting of Koufax's mark. "He (Ryan) might have struck out 400 (batters) if he was facing pitchers instead of designated hitters," *The Sporting News* surmised.[32] Ryan vindicated pitching records in the DH era.

By allowing a pitcher to stay in a game longer, the DH rule, originally intended to boost offense, had, ironically, produced a record number of 20-game winners (12) in the AL. In 1971, the last full season, 537 AL pitchers had completed their starts; in 1973,

614 did.[33] "Beyond doubt, the DH enabled many a pitcher to remain on the job and win instead of bowing out for a pinch hitter," *The Sporting News* observed in a year-end editorial. "That's the only logical conclusion to be drawn from the AL's twelve 20-game-victory hurlers, the highest total for one majors since the National produced 17 in 1889."[34]

Some pitchers remained adamant that the rule change favored the hitters, but there was no denying pitchers had also benefited from the change. The rule may have taken away an easy out and denied pitchers the chance to help their own cause at the plate, but it certainly allowed them to focus on their primary task, pitching, without having to worry about their turn at bat.

As the commissioner well knew, there was no pleasing all of the people, whether they were pitchers, managers, fans, or players. After only one season, the DH had become as certain in the American League as death and taxes in the United States.

———————

The long season caught up with Cepeda in September, when he turned thirty-six. He pulled a muscle in his leg and had to sit out several games.[35] He seemed to have lost his home run strength, clouting only one tater all month. Prior to coming to Boston, he had stolen 141 bases, but he didn't steal a single base all season. He also managed no triples. Certainly, in days of better knees, he would have stretched many of his 25 doubles into triples. With his current, worn-out knees, he ignominiously led the league in the number of double plays he grounded into (24), unable to beat relay throws to first. "If I could run, I'd be in the Kentucky Derby," Cha Cha joked.[36]

Still, worn-out knees and all, the Red Sox DH managed to finish the season with some impressive numbers. The man who had thought his career over the previous winter had batted 550 times in 142 games. His final home run, a three-run blast on September 26 that gave the Red Sox a 3–2 win over the Indians, was his 20th homer of the season and 378th of his career. His 15 game-winning hits led the Red Sox and tied him for fifth-most in the AL, seventh-best in majors. His 25 doubles had tied him with Yastrzemski for the team lead. Cepeda's 15 game-winning hits were tops among designated hitters. His 20 homers and 86 RBIs were both second-best among designated hitters. He scored 51 runs himself.

Cepeda was named the Outstanding Designated Hitter of the year, the first recipient of the annual award established by the Manchester, New Hampshire, *Union-Leader* in cooperation with the American League. A seven-person committee of broadcasters, writers, and Hall of Famers selected Cepeda ahead of Tommy Davis and Tony Oliva. "Orlando Cepeda, whose career was revived by the American League's designated hitter rule, has been named the outstanding practitioner of the substitute batting art in the 1973 season," *The Sporting News* announced.[37]

His numbers and the award seemed to confirm what *The Sporting News* had reported earlier about his successful debut as a designated hitter: "He will definitely fill the same role in 1974."[38] But it was not to be.

The Red Sox had finished second in the AL East division, a disappointing eight games behind the Baltimore Orioles, who had pulled away after the All-Star break. Boston fired manager Eddie Kasko on the last day of the season. His replacement, Darrell Johnson, was not a strong Cepeda supporter, the way Kasko had been. Johnson had come up the managerial ranks through the Red Sox minor league system. He had seen talent there that he wanted to bring to the big leagues. The thirty-six-year-old Cepeda, short-stop Luis Aparicio, a month shy of forty, and pitcher Bobby Bolin, thirty-five, stood in the way of Johnson's youth movement.[39] The new manager released the aging trio near the close of spring training the following season.

Cha Cha's fans complained, but they could not win him back his DH spot. Neither his success nor his popular standing could guarantee Orlando Cepeda a job. His precarious position on the team mirrored that of the designated hitter's place in the game. It was destined to delight some, to antagonize others, but never to rally united support.

Hank Aaron watches one of his patented home runs clear the left-field fence.

Chapter Thirteen

LOVE ATLANTA STYLE

A 162-game schedule wears down a thirty-nine-year-old man. Six months of red eye flights across time zones, long bus rides to hotels and stadiums, empty beds in rented rooms. Seven months—if you count spring training—of the daily drill at the ballpark: taking batting practice, playing a game, running the bases, chasing fly balls. That drains a man's stamina. The arms slacken, the legs stiffen. The bat grows heavier, the distance between bases widens. The older the player, the heavier the bat, the farther the bases. After nineteen seasons of the same, you can appreciate how tired Hank Aaron would have been in ordinary times.

But 1973 was no ordinary season. Add to the grind the media circus swirling about him, the steady stream of hate mail choking his mailbox, the extra precautions to protect against threats—the police chaperone packing heat, decoy hotel rooms that didn't always work, room service meals eaten alone. Then, factor in the pressure he felt every time he stepped into the batter's box knowing that the fans in the park and Americans across the country were watching, expecting him to do what he had done more times than any other man in history—save one—hit a home run.

Yes, returning to the Braves after the All-Star Game, Aaron was tired. It didn't help that he played for a lousy team. After 102 games, Atlanta was 45–57, a hopeless 19 games out of first place. There was the added discouragement of knowing that sixty games remained in a losing campaign. No wonder he had told reporters in Kansas City that he would play fewer games the final two months of the season. He had to limit himself if he were to survive.

Aaron had been pacing himself already, but coming back from the break, he planned to rest more deliberately. His knee ached, a souvenir of a home-plate collision three years earlier. He wore a brace to support it, but that didn't take away the pain. He had to have it drained regularly.[1] His back ached, so bad sometimes that he had to sit out. Other times, the pain kept him from hitting outside pitches with any power.[2] "I can't play every day anymore," he said. "It's not that you get tired, but your body just doesn't come back as fast as it did."[3]

He played about two out of every three games, resting the second game of doubleheaders, day games following night games, and games after long flights to the West Coast.[4] Braves manager Eddie Mathews trusted his former teammate's judgment and let Aaron decide when he was fit to play.[5]

The rest may have helped his body survive the season's physical rigors, but the relentless mental pressure of his home run pursuit weighed upon him. He had developed a cyst on his abdomen that caused him to miss a few games on a road trip in late June. He had the cyst removed and returned to action the next day.[6] Exhausted, he slept more. Sometimes, he lay down in his hotel room at 9 p.m. and slept twelve hours.[7]

Other nights, he lay down but couldn't sleep. "I was beginning to wear down," Aaron recalled in his autobiography. "It was always hard to keep up your energy level through the muggy summer in Atlanta. On top of that, I wasn't getting much rest. As much as I tried to fight off my anxieties and fears, they hounded me at night in lonely hotel rooms."[8]

He started going to the ballpark a couple of hours early. He stretched out on a cot in the trainer's room and tried to steal some shut-eye before his teammates and the reporters showed up. The trainer's room, off limits to the media, provided a brief sanctuary. Soon as he stepped into the clubhouse, the writers and photographers would be there, lying in wait for him.[9] On good days, he managed to doze.

Time was his biggest foe. Collected into years, it had broken down others' bodies. He saw it in contemporaries like Willie Mays, and Aaron felt the years breaking down his body, too. Time was also running out on the season. Sixty games. That was enough to hit 14 homers. That is, if he played every game. Which he knew he wouldn't. Yet for every game he rested, there went four or more at bats, four chances to hit another home run. Each lost chance added pressure to the reduced number of chances he did have at the plate. The question was, Would he be able to play enough games to reach Ruth before time expired on the season?

Aaron wanted to do it for the fans, especially the young ones. He knew he let them down when he didn't play, especially those who came to Atlanta Stadium or ballparks on the road specifically to see him make a piece of history only to discover he wasn't in the lineup. Sure, he might pinch hit, but that reduced their chances of seeing him hit a home run. "I realize I've disappointed some fans by not playing every game, especially recently, but the name of the game is to win, and I refuse to make a fool of myself," Aaron said late in the season. "I've helped the team and myself by not playing every day. I don't care where the team is in the standings. I can't let one hit that means something to Henry Aaron stand in the team's way. I feel loose and confident because I've gotten my rest."[10]

Aaron knew he didn't have to catch Ruth in 1973. Barring injury or some freak occurrence during the off-season, he could resume the pursuit next season. But he sure would welcome the relief from getting it done.

Aaron enjoyed a brief respite on August 6, declared "Hank Aaron Day" in Wisconsin, where the Braves played an exhibition against the Milwaukee Brewers. The game was for fun, the way it was meant to be played, and an occasion to honor the Braves slugger in the city where his major league career had started.

He was doubly honored that day in Cooperstown by one of his old teammates. Warren Spahn, the former Braves pitcher, was being inducted into the National Baseball Hall of Fame along with Monte Irvin, George Kelly, and Mickey Welch. "Henry Aaron is the greatest athlete I've ever seen in my life," Spahn said.[11]

Aaron was touched by Spahn's comment and the crowd that had turned out on "Hank Aaron Day," more than double the number that had shown up at Atlanta Stadium for "Hank Aaron Poster Day" earlier in the season. Problem was, Aaron's back had been acting up that week. He had played in only two of the Braves' last five games. Of course, Aaron would not think of not playing. Mathews solution was to write his name in the designated hitter slot, where Aaron could at least rest from the fielding duties. Since they were playing the game at the Brewers home field, then an American League site, Mathews thought it legitimate to play by their rules. Not so. The National League rules specifically prohibited the use of the DH, even in exhibition games.[12] That's how strongly the NL owners opposed the junior circuit's gimmick.

Braves officials tried to secure special permission from NL president Chub Feeney, but in those days before cell phones, they were unable to reach him at the Cooperstown ceremonies. The head of the umpire crew scheduled to work the game decided to ignore the rule and permitted Mathews to use Aaron as a designated hitter.[13] Though Aaron had previously stated that he would not want to be a designated hitter, his placement in the role that game foreshadowed how he would play out the last two years of his career as Milwaukee's DH.

It would be a good fit. The Wisconsin people remembered and still revered Aaron from the Braves days based in Milwaukee and Aaron's earlier days with their Eau Claire affiliate. More than 33,000 fans from the dairy state gave him a standing ovation when he was introduced before the game. They continued to cheer for more than two minutes. "I'm so happy to have played before so many wonderful fans," Aaron told them.[14]

Once the game started, they kept cheering for him. He did not disappoint them. He brought them to their feet over and over. In the sixth inning, he drove a fastball over the outfield fence, one of his patented Hank Aaron home runs. They rose and cheered. They cheered while he trotted around the bases and even after he disappeared into the dugout. He stepped out to tip his hat. His eyes glistened with tears.[15]

Too bad the homer didn't count toward his overall total. But it was good for the warm feeling it brought the Milwaukee fans and Aaron in return. Two days later, he resumed the regular season grind.

After Aaron had hit his 700th home run on July 21 and hurdled the 700-mark, he felt he had almost arrived at his destination. He hadn't reached the summit yet, but he could see it from where he stood. Then, he stumbled. He didn't hit a home run for over a week. Seemed 701 lurked even farther in the distance than 714. It took him ten days to reach No. 701. He didn't hit another home run for two weeks. "The whole situation took something out of me," Aaron said. "I think I let up for a little while after that, and suddenly I stopped hitting home runs."[16]

Pitchers were throwing more carefully to Aaron. The closer he crept to the record, the fewer good pitches he saw. Earlier in the season, commissioner Bowie Kuhn became alarmed at the idea pitchers might groove pitches to the Braves slugger when he read an AP story that quoted Mets pitcher Tug McGraw, among others, saying he would throw Aaron his best pitch and "hope like hell he hits it." Most took the screwball's comment for what it was, a joke. Not Kuhn. The commissioner fired off a warning letter that promised suspension for any player who "intentionally fails to give his best effort." Aaron was insulted by Kuhn's reaction, which he took to mean the commissioner didn't think Aaron would be hitting so many home runs if pitchers showed him their best stuff.[17]

Aaron saw the commissioner's reaction as an incendiary slight that fueled criticism of what he was accomplishing. "The commissioner overreacted," Aaron told reporters. "He threw another log on the fire to stir up people who've already said I've played a thousand more games than the Babe. The commissioner shouldn't have said it. He touched off a lot of unpleasant things."[18]

Kuhn's overreaction and Aaron's reaction to it thickened the bad blood between the commissioner and the future Home Run King. After slugging two homers in a game at Shea Stadium several days later, Aaron said pointedly, "I hope the commissioner was watching. Neither pitch was down the middle."[19]

Nobody was grooving pitches to Aaron after the All-Star break during his drought when he couldn't buy a home run. "Hell, I don't even see good pitches in batting practice anymore," Aaron joked.[20]

On August 16, the Braves played the Cubs at Wrigley Field in an afternoon game (the only kind played at Wrigley in those days before light standards towered over the ivy-laced brick walls). Aaron had started little more than half of the Braves games since hitting No. 700.[21] The counter on his home run drought had reached sixteen days. He was hitting the ball, just not over the fence. No. 714 had almost slipped out of sight, visible only as a dark silhouette among the clouds.

The Reverend Jesse Jackson, a strong supporter of Aaron's home run crusade and African-American campaign, had staged a "Hank Aaron Day" in Chicago. He had introduced the future Home Run King to a group of children before the game. The way Jackson tells the story, Hammerin' Hank promised them he would hit a home run that day. The preacher and the group of kids he had brought to the game watched excitedly from the bleachers. Aaron hit a line drive single to left field in his first at bat, hit a line drive the left fielder caught in his next, and grounded out to third. He came to bat again in the eighth inning and walked. The Braves staged a nine-run rally that inning, and Aaron batted again. This time, Jackson remembered Hammerin'

Hank "gave a high sign" to kids in the Wrigley bleachers. They screamed back. He waved to us. Did you see that? He waved to us. This is it![22]

Aaron worked the count to two and two, then saw a fastball he liked. He drove it over the left fielder's head, over the left-field fence and over Waveland Avenue—420 feet. The way Jackson told it, Hammerin' Hank was the Babe reincarnate, calling his shot in Chicago for the children, just like he'd promised.[23] The preacher's story elevated Aaron to the status of an omnipotent deity—right up there where many regarded the legendary Ruth—able to manipulate outcomes, control his destiny, and rewrite history.

If only it were that easy. Reaching No. 702 certainly hadn't been. What pleased Aaron was the solid feeling when he connected with the pitch. He hit that ball harder than he had hit any other in the past three weeks.[24] The way he'd connected had to be a sign of good things to come.

The kids in the bleachers cheered happily for him. So did the rest of the Wrigley crowd. It was the only home run the Cubs fans would see Aaron slug in Chicago all season. They applauded him heartily in his home run trot. That pleased Aaron, too. "It gives you a little bit of a tickle around the heart when they give you those great ovations here," he said.[25]

He hit No. 703 the next day in Montreal. The following day, Aaron punched out No. 704. When it rained, it poured. Three homers in three days washed away the drought. With thirty-six games remaining, the clouds had cleared from the summit, and 714 was again within sight—depending, of course, on how many of those games he played.

More important to Aaron in the moment was the number of extra-base hits he had racked up with his last home run. The 1,378th extra-base hit of his career moved him past Stan Musial into first place on the all-time extra-base hit list. That mark demonstrated he was more than a one-dimensional hitter, a fulfillment of his struggle to establish himself as one of the greatest hitters of all-time. "Getting that many extra-base hits means even more to me than 714 or 715 home runs," Aaron said.[26]

The Braves were mathematically eliminated from the division race by early September, though they had in fact been out of it since the season began. They never reached .500 after peaking the first week at 3–3 and never rose above fourth place. One bright spot had been knuckleballer Phil Niekro's no-hitter against the San Diego Padres on August 5, the first in Atlanta Braves history. Otherwise, the Braves had given the Atlanta fans little to cheer. By September, the only suspense left in their season was measured in home runs.

The Braves had the chance to become the first team in history to have three players hit 40 homers or more in a season. In addition to Aaron, who needed 41 to reach Ruth, third baseman Darrell Evans, who had played with Aaron in the All-Star Game, and his roommate, second baseman Davey Johnson, had both been clouting home runs at a healthy pace. Evans had hit only 19 home runs in 1972, his first full major league season, and Johnson had never hit more than 18 in any of his eight previous seasons, but 40 seemed within reach for all three as they entered the final month of the 1973 season.

While sportswriters toyed with that possibility, the overwhelming majority of their interest focused on Aaron's race to 41. The media frenzy had peaked in July around his 700th home run, then tapered slightly after the All-Star Game.[27] It was the quiet before the storm.

The media tornado hit Aaron with full force in September. The front page of *The New York Times* tracked his daily progress with a graphic showing the number of his latest home run inside a baseball. Famous prognosticator Jimmy the Greek gave Aaron 3–1 odds to reach 714 before the month ran out.[28] NBC interrupted its scheduled programming to show footage of Aaron hitting each homer that moved him closer to the monumental mark.[29]

The two magic numbers at the start of the month stood at 8 and 27: 8 homers to tie Ruth and 27 games left to do it.

Reporters swarmed him before and after games. The Braves traveling secretary, Donald Davidson, fielded over one hundred interview requests in a single city on the road. Aaron had to give two press conferences a day to accommodate the legion of reporters. In Los Angeles, the Braves pulled their team bus onto the field after the game and boarded in front of the visitors dugout to avoid the crowds. The NBC television crew following the chase had shot 12 miles of film for its special on Aaron scheduled to run in October.[30] *The New Yorker's* Roger Angell described the swarm as "a hovering daily horde of newsmen, network camera crews, photographers, publicity flacks, souvenir hunters, advertising moguls, league officials, and other assorted All-American irritants and distracters."[31]

Fans wanted a piece of him, too. Aaron stopped into a coffee shop, and by the time he had paid his bill, twenty-five people waited outside for his autograph. Stadiums hired additional ushers and security guards to monitor fans in the outfield seats and break up any scuffles over Aaron's home run balls. Three overly enthusiastic teenagers in Los Angeles pounded the door of his decoy hotel room with bats one night when the Braves were in town.[32] The mail continued to pour in, most of it supportive, but still sprinkled with messages spewing hate.

Every time Aaron came to bat in September, the plate umpire stopped the game. The batboy ran to the plate with a handful of baseballs that the Braves equipment manager had marked with infrared numbers, so that if Aaron hit one out, the Braves, who continued to award cash prizes for the balls, could avoid counterfeit claims.[33] The umpire called for the game ball from the pitcher and tossed him one of the marked balls. After Aaron's at bat—if he hadn't hit a home run—the ump again exchanged balls with the pitcher and returned the marked balls to the batboy.[34] The routine underscored the expectation Aaron already felt with every at bat to knock out another homer.

Aaron maintained his grace under the pressure. He was cordial with the reporters that surrounded him on his way to the batting cage, into the clubhouse—wherever he went. He answered their questions, mostly the same ones, courteously. "Pressure, what pressure?" he repeated like a refrain.

But sometimes the media presence became too overbearing for Aaron, a man of Herculean patience. When his patience gave out, he taunted the reporters by walking onto the field and crossing the foul lines into the territory forbidden to the press. He walked inside the foul line down to the outfield wall and along the warning track, knowing they watched every step.[35]

That not so subtle taunting revealed a little crack in the public façade. An intensely private person and naturally reticent, Aaron didn't want to let on how much the pressure bothered him, but it did. Oh, Lord, did it. He lay awake at night in his hotel room, feeling like a prisoner, scared for his life and his children's, exhausted by the long season. About the only other way he admitted to the overwhelming pressure was to say that next year, 1974, when he would be able to put some distance between himself and the Babe's 714 mark, would be his last. Enough already. Otherwise, in his characteristic understatement, he called the last ten days of the season "hectic."[36]

Which wasn't to say the attention was all bad. He had labored so long in the overlooked cities of Milwaukee and Atlanta that he was pleased to finally receive the recognition his achievements deserved. "The truth is that Henry sincerely appreciates the attention," said the Atlanta Braves PR director, Bob Hope (no relation to the comedian and Nixon campaign contributor). "He'll come into the office when we're at home and spend considerable time going over all the new clips we have on him. It's rewarding to watch because you can see the glow come over him."[37]

Of course, Hope didn't read Aaron's hate mail nor spend nights when the anxiety tossed and turned him in his bed. He could see only what it looked like from the outside. Neither Hope nor anybody else had any idea what it was truly like to be Hank Aaron in September 1973.

———————————

Atlanta alone maintained its indifference to what Aaron did—until the end. On September 10, Aaron hit No. 710, but fewer than 2,900 people in Atlanta Stadium watched him.

The magic numbers were down to 4 (homers) and 16 (games). Possible. Quite possible. But then Aaron hit another dry spell. He didn't hit a home run for a week.

On September 17, up against the season's opening "Monday Night Football" broadcast (the New York Jets versus the Green Bay Packers), he poked out No. 711 before the smallest crowd in Braves history. This time, the crowd was so pathetically small that one hot dog vendor could have served them all. Bowie Kuhn was one of the 1,362 in the stands, part of his conciliatory crusade with Aaron. The previous month, the commissioner had made a surprise visit to St. Louis to watch Aaron, but Aaron didn't think the gesture erased Kuhn's earlier transgressions. In Atlanta, Kuhn asked Aaron to throw out the opening pitch for the first game of the World Series, another stab at repairing their strained relationship. Aaron accepted, but the reconciliation remained incomplete. The tension between them would carry over into the next season.

Aaron was further disturbed by Atlanta's indifference. The ocean of vacant blue seats in the nearly empty stadium that night over-whelmed him. "That was a pretty strong statement of what Atlanta thought of me and my record," he observed.[38]

Five days later, Aaron hit No. 712 in Houston on the Braves' last road trip of the season. The magic numbers were down to two and six. Two to tie, three to pass the Babe outright. Six games, that was maybe 24 at bats. He was averaging a homer about once every nine at bats. Two were not only possible, they were probable.

Aaron didn't play the final road game in Houston. The magic numbers changed to two and five, and the odds lengthened.

Meanwhile, his teammate, Davey Johnson, had already slugged 43 homers for the season. Darrell Evans stood poised at 39 homers along with Aaron.

The Braves returned to Atlanta for the final five games of the season, three against the Dodgers and two more against the Astros. In the first game against the Dodgers, on Tuesday, September 25, Aaron hit a ball deep to center field. The solid crack of his bat brought the crowd of little more than 10,000 to life. They watched the 400-foot flight of the ball with anticipation, but it fell short of the fence into the glove of the Dodgers All-Star center fielder Willie Davis at the warning track.[39] Aaron finished the day oh-for-four in the Braves 5–1 loss. The magic numbers: two and four.

Rain delayed the next night's game. Fewer than 6,000 fans braved the wet weather. By the time it was over, Aaron had batted six times. He hit a long ball to the left-field wall (caught for a sacrifice fly) in the first inning, singled in the second, walked in the seventh, but otherwise made three outs, including the last one of the game when the first baseman caught his foul pop-up. The Braves lost 9–8. Darrell Evans hit his fortieth home run of the season. Aaron remained stuck at thirty-nine and 712.

Rain again delayed the start of Thursday night's game. The journalists jumped at the chance to talk more with their quarry. More than a hundred reporters, including George Plimpton from *Sports Illustrated*, stuffed into the Braves clubhouse and lobbed questions at Aaron. Georgia governor Jimmy Carter popped in to say hello and wish Aaron well. After an hour, Braves chairman Bill Bartholomay and chief umpire Tom Gorman, along with the two managers, summoned Aaron for his assessment of the field's playability. It was extremely unusual to ask a player to weigh in on whether or not to play a game. But the truth was the game didn't matter—both of the teams were out of the division race—except for the chance it gave Aaron to move closer to Ruth. If the game was canceled, they would not be able to make it up because the Dodgers were scheduled to play the next day in another city. So the officials let Aaron make the call.[40]

Aaron looked at the field slopped by rain. If they didn't play, he gave up four, five, maybe even six chances like the night before, to tie and catch Ruth. At the same time, it could be dangerous to play under those conditions. "The field was unplayable, but the managers were worried about my record," Aaron said. He told the officials, "You can't sacrifice twenty players just to satisfy one."[41] Game called. Magic numbers: two and two.

Friday was an off day. Aaron had nothing but time. To think. He'd played in only 118 games so far, including pinch-hitting appearances. Only 385 at bats. What if he had played just three more games, squeezed in another 12 at bats, would that have been enough to have put him at 714 by now? Or, what if he had managed another five? Just five more games, fewer than one more a month—he probably would have passed the Babe already. He could have sat out one of these last two. Rested easy. Instead, he was sweating out the final two games against the Houston Astros.

September 29, the Braves sold 17,836 tickets to their last Saturday night game of the season. Aaron figured he had to hit a home run that day to give himself the chance at least to tie Ruth before the season ended.[42] Yes, he felt the pressure Saturday night. He singled and walked in his first two at bats. He stepped into the batter's box again in the fifth inning, with two runners on, the Braves leading 2–0. The fans greeted him with a standing ovation. Southpaw Jerry Reuss was on the mound for the Astros. He threw a slow curve. Aaron saw it well. He swung. Wood met horsehide with a confident CRACK! The ball sailed over the fence in deep left-center field.[43] Say goodbye to No. 713.

His father and mother were there to see it. They lent their voices to the thunderous chorus that cheered Aaron around the bases. The applause continued well after he had ducked into the dugout. His teammates ushered him out to take a curtain call. He tipped his cap. He waved. His family and fans cheered mightily.[44]

Aaron had one more chance that night. He singled. The three hits raised his average to .297. His goal to bat .300 for the season had seemed impossible in June, when his batting average sagged in the low .200s. But he had batted .354 since June 15, and suddenly .300 for the season was within reach.[45] "As far as I was concerned, that would be my biggest accomplishment for the season, because it was what I had set out to do early on," Aaron reflected.[46] Stir in some more pressure for Sunday's final game.

No. 713 had also been No. 40 on the season. The Braves had made history, the first team to have three 40-home run hitters in a single season. Aaron sat at the post-game press conference alongside his record-setting teammates, Davey Johnson and Darrel Evans. Aaron wanted to spread around the glory, but all of the questions came at him. "Look, I wanted to share this with these guys," Aaron finally said. "If nobody is interested in that, then the press conference is over." He stood up and walked out.[47]

Before he left, he had finally admitted to the pressure he felt that day. "You can't imagine the pressure, knowing that even if you get a single with the bases loaded, you've disappointed the people," he told the large gathering of reporters. "Tomorrow is going to be the test I've been waiting for all these years. If I get a pitch to hit, then the world will know if I'm a good hitter. If I don't hit it tomorrow, it's going to be a long, cold winter."[48]

Finally, Atlanta got it. Within half an hour of their hometown hero's 713th home run, fans started to line up outside the ticket windows to buy tickets for the Braves final game of the season the following day. This was their last chance to see Hank Aaron make history that year. The Braves kept the windows open until midnight. They reopened the next morning to a line of waiting ticket buyers. By gametime Sunday afternoon, 40,517 had plunked down their cash to see what Aaron would do in his final four or so at bats of the season. Aaron's last chance to catch the Babe in 1973 drew a record crowd—14,000 more fans than at any other Braves game that season.

Aaron badly wanted at least to tie the record that day. He and Billye planned to marry in November. He wanted to be able to focus on that, not to have the almost-record, an oh-so-close moment hanging over him all winter. Roberto Clemente had died after the 1972 season and his 3,000th hit. What if something happened to Aaron and he couldn't get past 713? What would the bigots say then? He couldn't bear the thought of satisfying them and of letting his people down. "I hated the idea of coming so close and not making it," he recalled. "Sounded too much like failure to suit me."[49]

Dave Roberts took the hill for the Astros on a cool and wet Sunday afternoon, September 30. He had thrown the pitch a week earlier that Aaron smacked over the fence for No. 712. Roberts's teammates had started teasing him before the game, calling him "714." They taped the number above his locker. He had no intention of grooving Aaron a pitch on the last day of the season.[50]

Aaron had pulled an inside slider from Roberts for No. 712. He didn't expect another slider or inside pitch. Roberts surprised him during his first at bat Sunday with an inside pitch. Aaron lunged at it and pulled the ball foul. After that, he saw nothing but off-speed pitches around the edges of the plate. No home run bait.[51]

Aaron singled his first at bat and singled again in his second. That put his average at an even .300 for the season. His third at bat, he singled again. Rain had fallen off and on during the afternoon. The skies even thundered. The umpire wiped home plate with a rag, but he wouldn't consider calling the game. Not with history on the line and so many fans there to witness it.[52]

In the bottom of the eighth inning, Aaron came to the plate for his fourth and final at bat of the season, still one home run shy of the Babe. Hammerin' Hank faced Don Wilson, who had replaced Roberts. Wilson had made Aaron look bad in the past with a cut fastball that dodged his bat.[53] The 40,517 watched the drama unfold with tense excitement.

Wilson came inside with a fastball. Aaron popped a blooper to the second baseman. It was a weak out, hardly the stuff expected to explode off the future Home Run King's bat. The out provided a feeble climax to the season. Aaron had not been nervous, but he felt disappointed to have the season's pursuit end this way.[54] He felt he had let down the fans.

There he was, stalled at 713. That's how the season would end, how he would have to endure the long, cold winter. Knowing he had come so close, so tantalizingly close—just one away! Close enough to be tormented by the thought that if the one he hit in the exhibition in Milwaukee had counted ... or if the umpire hadn't taken that one away in St. Louis back in 1965 ... or if he would've played another game or two ... or if rain hadn't canceled the game Thursday night—he would've reached 714 instead of hanging one short of Ruth all winter. The thought that he had finished with a .301 average brought some—but not complete—consolation.

The clouds spit rain when Aaron jogged out to his position for the top of the ninth inning. The fans in left field stood and welcomed him with their applause. The fans behind third base stood and joined them with their cheers. The fans behind home plate, right field, and throughout the upper decks rose and clapped. The entire body of 40,517 showered him with a heartfelt, resounding ovation.[55]

Their gesture caught Aaron off-guard. He thought he had disappointed them with his squib popup. At first, he didn't know what to do. He posed with his hands on his knees and stared toward the plate, waiting for the inning to begin.[56] The rain beaded on the brim of his cap. The cheers continued, swelling to a crescendo.[57] Slowly, the cheers sank in.

He rose up, smiled and waved back. He took off his wet hat and held it up like a torch, a beacon of hope to the people now applauding him. He turned a full circle, smiling at the fans in every section. The applause persisted, minute after minute, going on five minutes. They cheered and cheered for Hank Aaron. The ovation gave his opponents goosebumps. It put lumps in the throats of jaded sportswriters in the press box.[58] Aaron couldn't believe that they were cheering for him like this in Atlanta, Georgia.[59]

The spontaneous applause cascading down upon him didn't take away the hate mail, the death threats, the shouted insults. It didn't erase the commissioner's slights. He still had to wait out the winter at 713. But for the moment, it felt good. This reward was his. For that moment, with 40,000-plus on their feet cheering him, Hank Aaron, a black man in the deep South, he felt the respect he was due. On that singular and soggy Sunday afternoon, Atlanta's love swelled within him.[60]

Billy North (left) with his mentor, **Reggie Jackson**, in the A's clubhouse during the 1973 season.

Chapter Fourteen

WRASSLIN' ANOTHER DIVISION TITLE

When Catfish Hunter grabbed at Billy Williams's line drive in the All-Star Game, he broke his thumb. X-rays revealed a hairline fracture below the first knuckle on his pitching hand. The league's best pitcher would miss a month. The A's felt the hurt immediately. They lost the first three games after the All-Star break. Their first place lead—2 ½ games over the Royals at the break—shortened to half a game. "Catfish Hunter's gone and Oakland's down the drain," gloated Amos Otis, the Royals All-Star outfielder.[1]

On July 30, the Texas Rangers' Jim Bibby added insult to injury. The imposing right-hander tamed the rowdy and wrasslin' gang with a no-hit, 6–0 shutout in Oakland. The loss—at home—let Kansas City slip even with the A's, tied for first place.

Finley, never one to sit by idly in a crisis—real or imagined—got busy. Famous for working the phones, he culled his sources for castoffs or unwanteds that could give the A's the extra oomph they needed in the final two months of the season. Ever skilled at finding reserve cavalry, he added three players to the roster the day after Bibby's no-hitter. Welcome Jesus Alou, a reliable-hitting utility outfielder purchased from the Astros and the third Alou brother to play for the Athletics (older brothers Felipe and Matty played for the Yankees in 1973 until September, when Steinbrenner sent Felipe to Montreal and Matty to St. Louis);

Vic Davalillo, a reliable-fielding outfielder and pinch hitter purchased from the Pirates; and Mike Andrews, a second baseman and designated hitter formerly of the White Sox.

Mike Andrews was a curious case. When the second baseman read in the newspaper that White Sox general manager Stu Holcomb didn't think he could hit, field, or throw anymore, Andrews asked the team for his release. The Sox granted it, seeing no reason not to, given his supposed lost abilities.[2] At the time, Andrews had been playing the season without a contract. Under the rules of the reserve clause, if a player and team couldn't agree on terms of a contract, the player was obligated to play for the team under the terms of his contract from the previous year. Marvin Miller, Players Association executive director, understood that to mean for one season only. Had Andrews finished the 1973 season playing without a contract for the White Sox, he may have become the first player to test Miller's interpretation of the reserve clause duration. Baseball would have to wait another two years for Andy Messersmith and Dave McNally to bust open the gates to free agency.

As it was, Andrews became a free agent immediately upon his release the week before the All-Star Game. He had not sparked any bidding wars as a second baseman whose arm was reportedly shot and a designated hitter with a .201 average. Matter of fact, hardly anyone had noticed his availability until Charlie O, always on the lookout for specialists, had signed Andrews to pinch hit.[3]

The twenty-nine-year-old Andrews had played seven major league seasons with the Red Sox and White Sox. He'd been an All-Star in 1969 when he batted .293 for the season. But he had fallen on tough times with a case of throwing yips. Seemed whenever he had an instant to think about a throw—which second baseman often have—he couldn't make the throw.[4] When Andrews arrived in Oakland, he pronounced himself physically sound. "I know a lot of people have been talking about how poorly I threw the ball in some games this year," Andrews said.

"Hell, that was a mental thing. I had some shoulder problems before, but the arm feels fine now. I hope I can help here. I'm only thirty. Can I be washed up?"[5]

Dick Williams wasn't convinced. Earlier that season when the A's played a series in Chicago, Williams had watched one of Andrews's infield throws fade before it reached first base. The official scorer had awarded the batter a hit "because Andrews had done the best he could."[6] His throwing troubles—whether rooted in his mind or arm—seemed real enough for Williams to keep him off the field.

But in early August, regular second basemen Dick Green and Ted Kubiak weren't hitting. Williams, still looking for a solution at second, gave Andrews another chance there for three games. Andrews had difficulty throwing the ball to first. End of audition. Williams relegated Andrews to a spot-hitting role and said, "He won't start at second base any more because we just can't afford it."[7] Andrews was done at second for the regular season, but he would play a critical role there in the World Series.

———

On August 7, Oakland split a doubleheader in Detroit. The Tigers blanked the A's in the second game, 2–0. The top of the order—Bert Campaneris, Billy North, and Sal Bando—all struck out in the A's half of the ninth to end the game. Their star pitcher remained injured, out of action. The new reserves weren't delivering. The A's weren't winning at the rate the Royals were. Oakland dropped to second place. The strain proved too much for Charlie O.

Working late in his Chicago office that night, Finley felt chest pains. Familiar chest pains. Like the heart attack he'd suffered a year earlier, when Blue had held out. Here came another. Only stronger. The next morning, he decided he better have his heart checked. He walked into the Passavant Pavilion of Northwestern University Hospital on his own.[8] He stayed twelve days. "It wasn't a severe heart attack," he told the press. "It was a mild one. But some people don't walk away from a heart attack, regardless of its severity. I'm lucky, I guess."[9]

The doctors wanted Charlie O. to take it easy. They prescribed rest, no work. They banned him from using the telephone. They might as well have banned him from breathing. Soon, he was sneaking away from his hospital bed to call Williams and other employees.[10]

Five days after Finley's heart attack, on Sunday, August 12, the A's played a day game at Yankee Stadium. They had lost three of their last four games and remained in second place, two games behind the Royals. At the top of the seventh inning, down 11–5, the A's appeared headed for another loss. With their turn to bat, Williams walked through the dugout and told his starters, "Okay, one more at bat, then I'm putting in the other guys."[11]

Top of the seventh, Reggie Jackson dug in for what he thought would be his last at bat of the day. He faced Sam McDowell, one of Steinbrenner's recent acquisitions. Jackson had homered off McDowell in the first inning and singled in the fourth, but the Yankees leftie had whiffed the A's big swinger in the sixth. The A's had two runners on base, two outs. The situation was ripe for a Reggie moment.

Reggie may have been the mouth in the clubhouse and often the heart of the team's dysfunction—witness his temper tantrum over the coaching in July—but he was also The Man. He was the guy the A's wanted at the plate in the clutch. He not only led the league in home runs and RBIs; he led the majors in game-winning hits. "If you wanted to win a game with a bat, Reggie was your man," A's catcher Ray Fosse said. "Reggie loved the big stage, the opportunity to have the bat in hand."[12]

Here was Reggie's opportunity. There was no stage bigger than Yankee Stadium. He smacked a single to right field that scored one runner and moved the other to third. It also knocked McDowell out of the game.

Sparky Lyle, McDowell's replacement, walked designated hitter Deron Johnson to load the bases. First baseman Gene Tenace doubled to left, driving in Billy North and Jackson and moving Johnson to third. Finley's find, left fielder Jesus Alou, singled to score Johnson and Tenace. Catcher Fosse singled. Sparky Lyle exited, replaced by Tom Buskey. Williams pinch hit another Finley find, Vic Davalillo, for the inconsistent-hitting Dick Green, who had led off the inning with a walk and scored on Reggie's single. Davalillo hit a ground ball that the second baseman booted. Davalillo reached on the error, and Alou scored. Billy North finally made the third out, but by then the A's six-run rally had tied the game 11–11.

Next time up, Jackson walked, then scored on Deron Johnson's single. Johnson scored on Gene Tenace's sacrifice fly. The Yankees added a run on designated hitter Jim Ray Hart's solo homer in the bottom of the ninth, but the A's held on to win 13–12.

Five A's players had multiple hits that day, but none outshone Reggie. He was three-for-four, with a home run, three RBIs, and three runs scored. The day capped off a huge series in New York for Jackson. During his three-game performance, he had slugged three homers, knocked in eight runs, and scored seven himself. He declared that he loved playing in New York. "There's something about playing in this city that means excitement," he said in the visitors clubhouse at Yankee Stadium. "It brings out the best."[13]

George Steinbrenner couldn't help but notice Reggie's stellar performance. He wanted Jackson playing for his team, not against it. Once the advent of free agency allowed the Yankees owner to pursue his vision of Jackson in pinstripes, Reggie declared at his first press conference as a Yankee, "I did not come to New York to be a star. I brought my star with me."[14] He had hung that star in the green and gold with performances like his mid-August display at Yankee Stadium.

Finley was released from the hospital on August 20 with a handful of medications and doctor's orders not to strain his heart. He returned to his home in La Porte, Indiana, pale and thin.[15] His team, on the other hand, looked robust. The seventh-inning six-run rally had proven the turning point in their season. The come-from-behind victory had been the second in a nine-game winning streak that extended through the day of Finley's hospital release. The streak had moved the A's back into first place, where they enjoyed a three-game lead.

Catfish Hunter returned on August 24 and, without missing a beat, defeated the Yankees at Oakland 5–1. The next day, Vida Blue blanked New York 2–0. The day after that, Ken Holtzman shut out the pinstripes 1–0. The A's pitching corps, which had faltered early in the season, appeared as good as predicted preseason to lead them to a third straight division title. The late August sweep of the Yankees padded the A's lead in the AL West to five games.

The A's returned to Kansas City the last day of August for a three-game series. The crowd of 36,242 hadn't forgotten May 18, when Billy North had mugged pitcher Doug Bird on the mound. In the Friday night opener, the Kansas City crowd booed the A's center fielder every chance they could. That charged his juices. With the score tied in the ninth, North again faced Bird, who had come on in relief. North singled. The speedy North stole second off Bird, then scampered to third when the catcher's throw skipped into the outfield. North taunted Bird with a big lead at third. When he tried to return to the bag, Kurt Bevacqua, the Royals third baseman, shoved him away. Startled, North tried again to touch the base, but Bevacqua shoved him again. North jumped him, fists flailing at the third baseman's head. The dugouts emptied, and teammates untangled the combatants. Bevacqua stumbled to his feet. Armchair judges scored it a unanimous decision for North. The umpires ejected both players, but the fight riled the brawlin' A's to victory.[16]

North, who gave new meaning to the term "designated hitter," mixed it up again in the next series in Anaheim. In the fourth game of the series, North came to bat in the eighth after smacking two singles and scoring a run. The Angels reliever, Dick Lange, dropped North to the dirt with a fastball over his head. North bunted the next pitch to the first base side of the mound, daring Lange to field the ball and step into his path. Lange held up, and Angels first baseman Mike Epstein, formerly of the A's, scooped up the ball and tagged North so hard that he jarred the ball out of his mitt. North reached first safely, then turned and called Epstein a "big goon." The heavyweight first baseman prepared to crush North, but Reggie Jackson, who had fought Epstein in the A's clubhouse the year before, rushed from the dugout and blocked his nemesis from his friend.[17] Thanks to Reggie, North escaped demolition.

Earlier in the series against the Angels, Deron Johnson, the A's conventional designated hitter, unwittingly attached an asterisk to Nolan Ryan's season strikeout record. Making a rare start at first base for the September 3 game, Johnson hit a pop fly that the second baseman caught for an out. But the third base umpire ruled that he had called time before Ryan's pitch when he spotted a ball errantly thrown out of the Angels bullpen. Johnson returned to the plate and the three-and-two count. Ryan fanned him on the next pitch. Had he not been given a second chance to strike out Johnson, Ryan would've ended the season tied with Koufax's record or had to try to break it on the last day of the season on only three days' rest. Thanks to the ump, that wasn't necessary.[18]

Reggie entered September on pace for his $100,000 season. He had belted 31 home runs and driven in 106 runs—both totals already exceeding his goals with a month left in the season. His batting average, .298, was two points off the .300 mark he had set for himself, though it had surged as high as .307 in mid-August. His home run and RBI totals both led the league. Reggie was playing even better than he thought he could.

Reggie had that rare combination in a big man of power and speed. By September 1, he had stolen more than 20 bases and scored over 90 runs. He was fast for a man of any size. But his large frame strained his muscles. On September 8, a Saturday afternoon game in Arlington, he pulled his left hamstring running out a ground ball. That was the hamstring he had ruptured in the playoffs last season, the injury that had denied him the chance to play in the '72 World Series. This time, the wounded leg forced him out of the lineup for two weeks.

That hurt. Reggie desperately wanted to be the best. And he was. He led the American League in the two power categories, homers and RBIs, but the Pirates' Willie Stargell led the majors. Reggie's hamstring remained tender, but he thought he could still swing the bat, either as the designated hitter or as a pinch hitter. The extra at bats would keep him in the race for the power titles. He asked to play. Williams refused to put him in the lineup.[19] Reggie helplessly watched Stargell pull away from him. That bruised his pride.

Once again, Reggie was pissed at his manager. Yet his anger was misplaced. Williams wanted to let Reggie play, but Finley forbade his manager from putting his superstar in action that would unnecessarily risk worsening his injury. They needed Jackson healthy for the postseason. The A's owner was still recovering from his heart attack. Charlie O. rode in a wheelchair and carried a bottle of yellow heart pills everywhere.[20] He lacked some of his bluster but none of his will. *No way will Reggie play before I say so.*[21]

This wasn't the first time that the A's owner had played doctor with one of Reggie's injuries. When Jackson had jammed his thumb his rookie year, the team physician initially told reporters before the game that the injury would prevent Jackson from playing that day. Finley talked to the team doc and phoned the manager in the dugout. Suddenly, Jackson was pronounced fit to play.[22] It wouldn't be the last time Charlie O. manipulated medical reports on players.

The A's owner was famous for his megalomania. Writers who followed the team couldn't understand why Williams let Finley work him like a marionette. Williams's success gave him options.

He could manage another team. In fact, at the start of the season, the Angels general manager asked Finley for permission to speak with Williams, but Finley denied it.[23] *He's my manager. Stay away from him.*

Okay, so Williams had options if he could get around Finley, who had just renewed his contract in July after Reggie's tantrum against the coaching staff. But that still didn't explain why the manager took the blame for Finley's decisions, unless it was to spite him in a twisted way. "He takes all kinds of crap from Charlie and seldom complains," said Ron Bergman, the *Oakland Tribune* writer who traveled with the team. "He has to carry out a lot of orders. He puts up with a lot of interference.... He wants to prove he can win in spite of Finley, I think."[24]

This time, Finley had nearly pushed Williams to the breaking point. The owner had put his manager in a position that antagonized his fragile superstar, jeopardizing his delicate relationship with Jackson. Williams knew how carefully he needed to treat Reggie and that if he alienated him, he might lose his production, so necessary to the defending world champions' chances of repeating. The situation required a desperate measure. Williams invited Reggie over to his apartment for dinner.

Dick Williams was not one of the guys. He was not a manager who hung out with his players. He was definitely not the type to invite them into his home. But with less than two weeks before the playoffs, he felt the urgent need "to explain the situation and pacify" his temperamental superstar.[25]

Reggie was grateful for Williams's patience and magnanimity. "He could have ripped me for blowing up at him and his coaches, but he didn't," Reggie said. "He could take it out on me in a lot of little ways, but he doesn't."[26]

Williams told Reggie that he wanted to let him play, but the owner had forbidden it. The A's manager confided in Reggie, Joe Rudi, and Sal Bando that he'd had enough of Finley's controlling ways. Williams did not say so explicitly, but he hinted strongly that he wanted to work for someone else. Jackson, Rudi, and Bando realized these might be their last few weeks playing for him.[27]

Tennis upstaged baseball's division races on Thursday night, September 20, with its "Battle of the Sexes." Bobby Riggs, a fifty-five-year-old former Wimbledon champion and self-confessed "male chauvinist pig," had challenged Billie Jean King, the reigning women's Wimbledon champ, to a tennis match. Riggs had beaten the top-ranked Margaret Court in straight sets four months earlier on Mother's Day and promised to put King in her place. ABC-TV had its top announcers, the "Monday Night Football" tandem of Howard Cosell and Frank Gifford, call the match for 40 million viewers across the nation. In the most-hyped and most-watched tennis match of its day, the fairer sex prevailed.[28] Billie Jean King won respect for women's athletics with her 6–4, 6–3, 6–3 undressing of Riggs. The Equal Rights Amendment may have stalled, but Title IX, the law passed a year earlier to guarantee women equal opportunities in school sports, gained prominence that Thursday night.

Back at the ballpark, Reggie Jackson finally returned to the lineup on Saturday afternoon, September 22, in Chicago. He played right field and batted fourth, going two-for-five and knocking in a run. His leg looked strong enough running out a double. Perhaps he would be fit for the playoffs.

The following day, the A's clinched the division title with a 10–5 victory over the White Sox. Vida Blue notched the win, his 20th of the season. After struggling in 1972, his contentious holdout season, Blue had returned to his Cy Young/MVP form of 1971, when he was 24–8. In '73, he had improved his breaking ball and his ability to work the edges of the plate. The result was a 20–9 record for himself and another division title for the team.[29]

Ken Holtzman, who'd never won 20 games in any of his seven seasons, finally reached the watershed mark. He finished the season at 21–13. Catfish, despite missing a month with his broken thumb, went 6–2 after his return and finished 21–5. Once again, he led the majors in winning percentage. Going into the playoffs, the A's pitching displayed its dominance, looking every bit as good as Williams and Finley had said it was—good enough to win another World Series.

Finley, who'd attended the game in his wheelchair, phoned Williams downstairs in the clubhouse to congratulate him, a feeble conciliatory gesture.[30] Charlie had attended the two games at Comiskey to test his heart, seeing if it was strong enough to endure the strain of the playoffs.[31] It appeared to have passed the test.

Reggie, two-for-four on the day, poured the champagne. The A's had clinched their third straight AL West title, but the celebration was subdued. "The players sat on their stools in the clubhouse drinking champagne and looking like customers in a workingman's bar," *Oakland Tribune*'s Ron Bergman reported.[32] Their goals were bigger than another division title; they wanted nothing less than to repeat as world champions.

Yet they knew the difficulty of plucking that goal from its lofty perch. Three days earlier in Arlington, they had lost their feisty center fielder. Billy North twisted his ankle when he tripped over first base on September 20 and tore ligaments. At the time, he led the league in stolen bases (53). The A's leadoff hitter was batting .289 and had scored 98 runs. Finley's off-season acquisition had proven a key contributor to the A's success in '73. "Bill North in center field helped us win our division a week earlier than we might have hoped," Jackson said. "He can catch, throw, hit, run, everything. He's a competitor, he can really shake up the opposition."[33]

The team doctor examined North's ankle but initially refused to issue a statement for reporters. The trainer said they were working under explicit orders from Mr. Finley that no statements could be released until the owner approved them.[34] Eventually, the team admitted that North's injury would keep him out of action until after the playoffs and World Series had finished. The hole in center field at the start of the season that North had filled gaped open once again, a large question mark. "We'll make do with what we've got," Williams said. "We won without Jackson last year, remember?"[35]

Well, they had won the World Series without Jackson, but not the division playoffs. He had played a critical part in winning the league championship, injuring his hamstring while scoring the tying run in the final game. Williams could replace North with Angel Mangual, who had lost the center field job last year and batted only .224 in sparse action this season. Or, Williams could switch Reggie to center as he had done in times of need before, but Reggie's hamstring still wasn't 100 percent. His gimpy legs, another question at the start of the season, had reasserted themselves.

The thermometer decided the issue. Reggie came down with a fever and sore throat the weekend before the playoffs. That prompted Williams and Finley to go with Mangual. When told on Wednesday that he would be starting in center field in the division opener on Saturday, Mangual asked to be traded. "I want to be away from here, anywhere," he said. "I'll do the best I can, but this place is too crazy for me. Why kill your mind with so much trouble?"[36] Ah, the A's remained one big happy family.

Jackson himself remained a question mark. He had put up terrific numbers for the season. He led the league with 18 game-winning hits. He also led the league in home runs and RBIs, though the Pirates' Stargell had finished higher in both categories. After spending time above .300 in August, Reggie slumped in the final weeks and fell to .293, seven points below the $100,000 mark he had set for himself. He had also managed only one home run in the final month of the season. He'd finished with good numbers but who knew how much Finley deemed those numbers were worth? Reggie knew a strong performance in the postseason would give him more leverage negotiating his contract for next season. He also knew he could take Finley to arbitration this time if his offer wasn't enough.

More immediately, the A's needed to know if Reggie could deliver again in the playoffs and ultimately in the World Series. The big stage would be his biggest test. They needed their big man at his best to win another championship.

A tearful **Say Hey Kid** says goodbye to America on "Willie Mays Night" at Shea Stadium, September 26, 1973.

Chapter Fifteen

SAY GOODBYE TO AMERICA

On July 31, the week after the All-Star Game, Willie Mays and the Mets lost a game at Shea Stadium to the Pittsburgh Pirates, 4–1. *The New York Times* observed that the Pirates—who out-hit, out-pitched, and out-fielded the Mets—played "like a team in a pennant race," and the Mets played "like a team in last place."[1] The Mets fourth straight loss dropped the team to 13 games below .500, dead last in the NL East, 10 ½ games behind the division-leading St. Louis Cardinals. The Mets had spent the entire month at the bottom of the division. Murray Chass ended his game recap with a sarcastic jab, "Mets fans are beginning to wonder if the Mets are going to make it past last place."[2]

Mays, back from his ceremonial yet flaccid pinch-hitting appearance in Kansas City, started in center field and batted in the leadoff spot on July 31. He went oh-for-four and made two throws from the outfield that lacked his trademark zip. One toss to home plate was off the mark and allowed a run to score. Worse, the long heaves strained his right shoulder, the one that had put him on the disabled list two months earlier. He sat out the next two games. Willie appeared finished as the Mets center fielder.

With only two months left in the season, the Mets seemed destined for a dismal finish. An inordinate number of injuries, the inability to score runs for their pitching ace, Tom Seaver, the mysterious disappearance of their star reliever Tug McGraw's skills, and the slow fade of the game's greatest player, Mr. Mays, had all but buried the New York Metropolitan Baseball Club.

The keen baseball eye of Roger Angell fingered Mays as the heart of the Mets' troubles. He wrote in the July issue of *The New Yorker* that the Mets suffered "from a plain dearth of talent," which included the geriatric Mays. "One of their problems, it must be admitted, is Willie Mays, who has so far resisted the clear evidence that he should retire," Angell wrote. "He plays sporadically, whenever he is well and rested, and gives his best, but his batting reflexes are gone, and so is his arm."[3]

Seeing Mays strain to make a throw that bounced off the mark—like that one on July 31—pained those who knew how Willie once could throw. They couldn't help but contrast him with his former self. His best throw, by his own memory, came in his first season. The twenty-year-old Willie stretched to grab a line drive on the run, turned in one motion, and heaved the ball from deep right-center to the plate on the fly to nail Billy Cox, the runner who'd tagged up at third, by ten feet. "It was the most perfectest throw I ever made," Willie said.[4]

Those who watched it agreed. "Once, he could do everything, and he could do it better than anyone else with joyous grace," Arthur Daley wrote in his *New York Times* column in 1973. "It hurt to see him floundering like an ordinary ballplayer in his final year with the Mets."[5]

The no-longer-young man's arm now hurt and his knees ached. Much as it pained him to play—and pained those who watched him—Mays and his fans had trouble letting go. They preferred to revel in the happy yesterdays rather than face the harsh facts of today. "Those skills had faded beyond recognition until the vast army of Mays admirers found themselves trying to blot the present with memories of the glorious past," Daley observed.[6]

Mays had played in 150 or more games for a record thirteen consecutive seasons, but he hadn't played more than 140 games in any season since 1968. In 1973, he would appear in only sixty-six games. "He has hung on tenaciously long past the normal retirement age and every so often there is a spark of the old greatness," *The Sporting News* observed midseason.[7] But those sparks were becoming increasingly rare.

In July, Mays admitted to himself what others like Angell had been saying all season. The time had come for him to call his career quits. The decision to abandon the game that had given him his identity, his status, his livelihood, and his lifeblood did not come easily for Mays. He privately told the Mets management that he would retire at the end of the season but asked that the team not announce the news until September.[8]

Mays hinted to reporters that his play in center field embarrassed himself and the team. "I can catch the fly balls and I can run," Mays told writers on August 3. "But I can't throw. I can throw, but I can't throw hard."[9] After resting his sore shoulder for two games, Willie returned to the lineup—at first base. He had played 11 games at first the previous season, but he did not feel at home there. He still used his outfielder's glove instead of a first baseman's mitt. But he seemed resigned to his place. "I can play first base and do more for the club," he said. "That's the only position I can play right now."[10]

Other Mets followers had placed the team's poor showing that season on manager Yogi Berra. Yogi had skippered the Yankees to a pennant title in 1964, but the Hall of Fame catcher was having more trouble coaxing success out of the crosstown team. His critics complained that his tactics were unimaginative and his leadership was uninspired.[11] Tom Seaver, the Mets superstar pitcher, faulted Berra for assuming his players wanted to win as badly as he did rather than putting the fear of losing in them like his predecessor Gil Hodges had.[12]

Yogi had replaced Hodges after a heart attack felled the forty-seven-year-old Mets manager at the golf course on Easter Sunday 1973. Hodges was a strategist; Yogi wasn't. As the team sank in the standings, the players grumbled comparisons. Gallows humor transformed one complaint into a clubhouse joke among the players:

Q: What is the difference between Gil Hodges and Berra?

A: Three innings.

See, in the third inning, Hodges was thinking about what he would be doing in the sixth; in the sixth inning, Yogi was thinking about what he should have done in the third.[13]

All summer, the rumor mill churned with talk of Berra being fired. One unfounded report said Billy Martin would replace Yogi.[14] That would have given history a different twist, Martin the Met, but he had a rendezvous with destiny as a Yankee under Steinbrenner's employ. When asked about his jeopardized job status, Berra simply replied, "I don't know nothin' about nothin.'"[15]

As the Watergate hearings and tax return investigations turned up new dirt on the President, Mets reliever Tug McGraw wondered aloud in the clubhouse who would get fired first that summer, Yogi or Nixon?[16]

In response to the rumors, Donald Grant, the Mets chairman of the board, said he would not fire Yogi "unless public opinion demands it." So the *New York Post* polled public opinion. For three days, the paper ran a ballot with photos of Berra, Grant, and general manager Bob Scheffing. Turned out public opinion thought Scheffing should be first to go. The majority of fans blamed the general manager for weakening the team with bad trades. Witness the one that sent Nolan Ryan to the Angels. They blamed chairman Grant next for bad deals and his stinginess. Only 15 percent faulted Berra. They thought he had done the best he could with the players he had available; they did not think he was to blame for the team's injuries or the bad trades.[17] Grant apparently decided public opinion was not the best guide for his management decisions. He didn't let anybody go that summer.

The tension between Berra and Mays—evident during spring

training when Willie had gone to his San Francisco-area home without the manager's permission and missed a team workout—persisted. Some days when Mays saw Berra had written his name on the lineup card, he told the manager, *Nope, not today. The body's not up for it.* And Yogi penciled another player into Mays's spot. "I play when I can play," Mays explained to reporters. "Where I play and where I bat is up to Yogi."[18]

Some faulted the manager, saying he was too easygoing, which let the players take advantage of him in ways that Hodges never would have tolerated. That caused a breakdown in his authority and a letdown in their performance.[19] Others faulted Mays, who had butted heads with Giants managers. "His dealings at times with managers and even owners were disappointing," Bob Broeg wrote that summer in his *Sporting News* column.[20] Some Mets teammates thought Mays undermined the manager. They complained privately that he had become a liability.[21]

Both had their part in the strain between them, but, ultimately, tension with a player became the manager's problem. "He (Yogi) seemed incapable of achieving a détente with the team's resident immortal, the increasingly crotchety Willie Mays," *Sports Illustrated* reported.[22]

In Mays's return to first base, he hit an infield chopper and bunted safely, going two-for-four. He handled 12 throws at first without error. He also scored twice in the Mets 5–1 win over the Pirates. The next night, Mays, again playing first base, struck out twice but homered in the seventh. His three-run homer—the 659th of his twenty-two-year career—put the game out of reach, securing the Mets 7–3 win over the first-place Cardinals. It was one of those rare sparks left in Willie's bat, which showed it still could, with a single swing, seal a victory for his team.

Wins proved rare for the team that long summer. The Mets lost the next three games to the Cardinals and fell 11 ½ games behind the division leaders. That was the farthest out of first they had been all season. With fifty-four games to play, the Mets were

48–60, 12 games under .500, and seemed all but eliminated from the division race.

––––––––––––––––

The Mets slide had coincided with reliever Tug McGraw's slump, which dated back to early May. On May 4, McGraw had come into a game in Houston with the bases loaded in the eighth and walked three batters to squander a three-run lead in a game the Mets eventually lost. Two nights later, he entered in the sixth with two Houston runners on and a four-run lead. He gave up a double and a home run that tied the game, walked the next batter, threw a wild pitch that allowed the runner to advance, and finally managed an out on a foul ball. He allowed a single to the leadoff batter in the seventh before Yogi mercifully yanked him. But the damage was done. That runner scored. McGraw was tagged with the loss, the team's fifth in a row, and the Mets dropped below .500 for the first time that season.

Houston haunted McGraw. He worried about walking batters. He aimed his pitches instead of throwing hard. Batters hit him instead. He lost his concentration. He lost his timing. He lost his confidence. Finally, he lost his temper, hurling objects in the clubhouse and kicking balls on the field. He continued to blow leads and lose games.[23]

Sport magazine profiled McGraw in its June 1973 issue. The copy, obviously written and edited before his slump began, claimed "he just may be the best relief pitcher in baseball." The irony rang as an accusation. The best. Maybe he once was the best, but no more. Not this June. No, sir.

Not July, either. In Montreal, McGraw entered a game with a one-run lead, and gave up three walks, four hits—including two home runs, one of them a grand slam—and seven runs. The Mets lost 19–8.

Two weeks later, Yogi tried to snap McGraw out of the slump with a surprise start against the Braves. In six innings, McGraw hit a batter, walked four, served up three gopher balls—including Hank Aaron's 698th career home run—and surrendered seven runs. At the plate himself, he struck out twice. Starting wasn't the cure for McGraw.

Mays and the Mets, however, pulled off a mini-miracle in Atlanta. After McGraw had put them in the hole 7–1, the Mets scored five runs in a ninth-inning rally to pull within one run, 7–6. With two on, two out, and the game on the line, Berra sent his best clutch hitter to the plate. Willie punched a single deep to right field that scored the tying and go-ahead runs. Yogi had put his faith in the Willie of old, and Mays delivered the game-winning hit. The Mets continued to lose, but that night in Atlanta they showed their mojo hadn't evaporated completely.

After the Expos shelled him, McGraw had quipped, "I got that out of my system."[24] But he hadn't. The slump lingered deep into August. He had no feel for the ball. He felt paranoid—the baseball gods had conspired against him getting batters out. On the mound, he wanted to drop to his knees and implore, "Shit, I don't know what to do!"[25]

Neither did Yogi. In the past, McGraw had been his first choice out of the bullpen, but his top reliever had become a liability. McGraw, who had posted an ERA of 1.70 over the past two seasons combined, watched his 1973 ERA balloon over 6.00. Even when he pitched well, he couldn't win. He threw four innings of strong relief against the Giants on August 11, but in the 13th, he hit a batter, saw another reach base on an error, then gave up a single to All-Star MVP Bobby Bonds, and McGraw had lost his fifth game of the year without winning any. "If you ain't got a bullpen, you ain't got nothin,'" Berra said.[26]

On August 17, Willie Mays connected for the 660th home run of his career. Batting third and playing first base, Mays hit the first pitch he saw in the fourth inning over the Shea Stadium fence in deep right-center. It would be the last home run he hit. He had slugged his first homer twenty-two years earlier, a memorable blast at the Polo Grounds. That day, May 28, 1951, when he was a twenty-year-old with a bright future, seemed so far away.

Mays's solo blast on August 17, 1973, wasn't enough for the Mets. The Reds won on a pinch-hit home run of their own in the 10th. The loss dropped the Mets to a new low: 13 games under .500.

The newspapers derided the hapless Mets. In mid-August, Yogi clipped one article that accused the players of simply going through the motions and carried it around the clubhouse. He waved the article under his players' noses and said, "You stink. It says so right here in the paper. It says you guys don't wanna play no more."[27] Berra figured his players had enough pride left in them to want to show up the naysayers.[28]

Yogi had been telling reporters all summer that his team hadn't made its move yet.[29] The Mets may have been 13 games under .500, but they were only 7 ½ games out of first place. They had been as far as 11 ½ back on August 5 after losing both games of a double-header to the Cardinals. All they needed, he figured, was a hot streak, but if they didn't catch fire soon, their season would extinguish with them in the ashes.

Slowly, things seemed to start turning in their favor. On Saturday, August 18, shortstop Buddy Harrelson, the linchpin of the Mets infield, returned to action after missing over two weeks with a broken breastbone. It had been his second time that season on the disabled list. In the Mets' injury-riddled season, they had eight times placed players on the DL, a record.[30] Cleon Jones (sore feet, sprained wrist); Rusty Staub (separated shoulder, chipped wrist); Buddy Harrelson (broken wrist, cracked sternum); Jerry Grote (broken arm); John Milner (pulled hamstring); Jon Matlack (fractured skull); George Theodore (dislocated hip); and Willie Mays (sore shoulder) were among the casualties, and that didn't register the assorted sprains, pulls, and bruises that sidelined others throughout the season.[31]

The Mets celebrated the return of the healthy Harrelson with a 12–1 thumping of the Reds. The Mets beat them again the next day, and Yogi saw his team on the move. Though still 12 games under .500 at 54–66, they were only 6 ½ out of first place. "Everybody in our division had some kind of streak except us, and I had my whole team back," Berra said. "I felt if we could go on a little streak, we could make a move."[32]

Three days later, Tug McGraw snapped out of his slump. On Wednesday, August 22, he entered the game in the eighth inning with the Mets trailing the Dodgers at Shea 3–2. McGraw put down the Dodgers in order. He did it again in the ninth, registering three strikeouts in two innings. He'd found his concentration, his timing, and his confidence. This was the Tug of old.

He had done his part—kept his team in the game rather than putting them out of it like he had done too many times the previous three months—but the Mets still trailed by a run in the bottom of the ninth. Left fielder Cleon Jones led off with a single. McGraw came to the plate. Berra showed enough confidence in his pitcher's resurgence to keep him in the game in case it went to extra innings rather than pinch hit for him. McGraw moved Jones to second with a sacrifice bunt. Three singles later, the Mets pulled ahead 4–3. McGraw had won his first game of the season.

A week later, the Mets swept a series against the San Diego Padres. Their 3–0 win on Wednesday, August 29, pulled them out of the cellar, into fifth place, only 5 ½ games back. "I been tellin' you," Berra told reporters after the game, "in this division anything can happen. We're the only club that hasn't had a hot streak. Maybe we're gonna have one now, but remember, it's never over until it's over."[33]

With the retelling, that phrase morphed into "It ain't over 'til it's over," one of the most famous Yogi-isms, even becoming the title of an authorized collection of his sayings. While it may be true, in Yogi's words, "I never really said everything I said," the sentiment of his "it ain't over" proclamation would prove prophetic—though not immediately.

The Mets rise out of last place was short-lived. The next day, Tom Seaver pitched another one of his gems, shutting down the

Cardinals for nine innings. Yet once again, the Mets failed to score runs for him. It was the fourth time that season that the Mets had been shut out when Seaver pitched. Despite his 200-plus strikeouts and 1.70 ERA, he was only 15–8. The Mets had supported him with a total of only seven runs in his eight losses. If the Mets would have given him two more runs per game, Seaver would have won 20 games by the end of August.

But that was one of those would've, could've, should've scenarios. Those could mess with your head if you let them. Seaver couldn't afford that. The reality was, with one day left in August and only thirty games left in the season, the Mets were back in last place, where they had been almost continuously for the past two months. They had made some small steps forward, but they didn't have much to show for it.

Yet no team had been able to pull away in the NL East. At the end of August, all six teams remained in contention. Only six games separated the last-place Phillies from the first-place Cardinals. McGraw won again on August 31—the day after he turned twenty-nine—defeating St. Louis 6–4 in ten innings. The Mets slipped into fifth place, only 5 ½ games back. Even old man Willie Mays started to believe it wasn't over yet.

Writer Charlie Einstein, who had already written one book chronicling Mays's career and would write three more, talked to Mays on the phone at the end of August. "It's coming true," Einstein said. "First place is there and nobody wants it."

"I know," Willie said. "We've got a chance."[34]

If only they could believe it.

Sport magazine had entitled its June profile of Tug McGraw "The screwball behind the screwball." McGraw threw a wicked scroogie. The leftie's best pitch broke in on left-handed batters and away from right-handers—like a curve going the wrong way. The pitch fit his personality.

He shagged flies behind his back during batting practice. He told kids while being interviewed on national television that they should practice signing autographs on baseballs by wrapping a piece of paper around an orange: "That way, when you get to the majors, you'll be ready."[35] He drove a 1954 Buick, which he said he liked "because it plays old music."[36] In the years of strict hair restrictions, he showed up at spring training with a mustache and General Custer hair, which manager Gil Hodges promptly made him shave and trim, respectively.[37] McGraw was the kind of guy who would do anything for a laugh, teammate Ed Kranepool said.[38]

One time, on "Camera Day" at Shea Stadium, when the fans were allowed on the field before the game, McGraw pulled on Mays's No. 24, blackened his face, and strode onto the field to sign autographs and be photographed. "No problem," Willie said. "McGraw is McGraw."[39]

So, just as the team fell and rose with its star reliever's slump and resurgence, it seemed fitting that their resident screwball provided their mantra.

One day in July, when the Mets were mired in last place, Donald Grant, the Mets chairman of the board, decided rather than yield to public opinion and fire his general manager or step aside himself, he would give the team a pep talk. It was an unusual move, especially from a Wall Street man like Grant, more at home in a bank than on a ballfield. The players gathered in the clubhouse after batting practice to listen to the chairman. "I just thought I should talk to them to try to get their chins off the ground," Grant said.[40]

The man in the pinstripe suit told the players that there was still a lot of time left in the season, that they shouldn't give up, that if they believed in themselves, they could come back.[41] "I believe that when you guys get healthy, there'll still be time left for you to get healthy on the field and win this thing," Grant said.[42]

The chairman finished his speech and turned to walk out of the door. Tug McGraw jumped up from his locker stool and shouted,

"You gotta believe! You guys, you gotta believe!" Grant, who was still within earshot by the trainer's room, turned and came back into the room. McGraw looked at him and said, "You're right, Mr. Grant. You gotta believe."[43] Grant gave McGraw a disapproving look and walked out.[44]

McGraw ran around the clubhouse from one player to another, lifting their heads by their hair and shouting maniacally, like a Southern preacher, "You gotta be-lieve!" His teammates thought he was crazy. Some laughed. Others worried that he had just insulted the chairman of the board by mocking him.[45]

One of those worried was McGraw's roommate, first baseman Ed Kranepool. "Tug," he said. "You've got to be crazy. You'll be gone tomorrow."[46]

Kranepool urged McGraw to explain to the chairman that he meant no harm. McGraw phoned Grant upstairs and assured him that he would never, in any way, mock him, and he was sorry if that was the impression he gave. He said he was simply trying to inspire the team. The chairman bought it and thanked McGraw for calling to apologize.[47]

It started as a joke. You gotta believe. Right. They were playing like a last-place team. Believe in what? Bad luck? Rotten breaks? They were too far down, too beaten up to believe. The players bantered around McGraw's phrase sarcastically.

After McGraw broke out of his slump with the victory August 22, he slapped his glove against his thigh coming off the mound and ran into the clubhouse, screaming, "YOU GOTTA BELIEVE!"[48] He had feared he would finish the season oh-for-1973, but he had just captured his first win, and he started to believe himself.

In 17 appearances starting from that day, McGraw figured in 16 Mets victories, winning four games and saving 12. McGraw slapping his glove against his thigh coming off the mound after a win became a familiar sight. As their comeback gained traction, McGraw's teammates started to take his words to heart. "You gotta believe!" they shouted at one another to lift and remind themselves. McGraw's rant became their war cry.

———————

In Montreal on Sunday, September 9, Willie Mays, playing first base, chased a foul pop toward the Mets dugout in the first inning. His eye on the ball, the long-time center fielder didn't realize how close he was to the dugout. He slammed into the dugout railing chest-high. The collision knocked the wind out of him. He took two minutes to catch his breath but returned to and completed the game. However, he did not show up for the Mets' next game in Philadelphia on September 11. For the second time in 1973, Willie had gone AWOL.

Mays wanted to have his bruised chest examined. He asked Yogi Berra for permission to return to New York on the 10th, an off day, to see the doctor. Okay, Berra said, meet us in Philadelphia on the 11th. When Mays missed the game and reporters asked Berra, "Where's Willie?" all Yogi could say was, "I don't know." That embarrassed Yogi.[49]

While the Mets played the Phillies, Mays was home at his Riverdale apartment, waiting for the doctor to call. Peter LaMotte, MD, the Mets' physician, had examined Willie's chest in New York on the Mets off day. Dr. LaMotte told Willie to call him if his ribs were still sore the next day, the 11th. They were, so Willie called and left a message. By game time, the doctor had not received the message, and Willie missed the game.[50]

Mays's teammates weren't happy with his vanishing act. Many resented the special treatment he received, the way the Mets brass protected him. Mays's place also challenged Berra, a source of tension between manager and player. "His somewhat privileged status was regarded by many observers as an irritation to manager Yogi Berra and his (Mays's) teammates," the *Times* noted.[51]

Willie surprised Berra and his teammates the next day, September 12, when he showed up forty-five minutes before the game. The flurry of phone calls from Mets officials and reporters checking on his status had alerted Mays of the brouhaha his unexcused absence had caused. He drove down to Philadelphia for that night's game.[52]

His teammates greeted him with barbed jokes when he walked into the clubhouse:

"Hey, the kidnappers let you go? Who paid the ransom?"

"The weather's nice in Tahoe now, isn't it?"

"What did you shoot today?"[53]

Berra did not fine Mays. The next day, he wrote Mays's name on the lineup card at first base. After Willie took some swings in batting practice, he told Berra he was too sore to play. LaMotte, the doctor, confirmed that Mays had cracked two ribs when he crashed into the railing in Montreal. Berra scratched out Mays and wrote in John Milner at first base. Milner was a twenty-three-year-old "outfielder who couldn't throw" whom Berra had moved to first in 1973.[54]

"John (Milner) has been swinging the bat real good, and I didn't think I could swing it as well as he has," Mays told reporters later. "I probably could play, but I might be able to help later on down the line."[55]

Willie was right about Milner—his replacement got a hit and scored a run in the Mets 12-inning, 4–2 victory over the Phillies— but it remained to be seen whether or not Mays himself would be able to help the team down the stretch.

———

The Mets had stormed into September. Behind McGraw's reversal of fortune, they started winning games, beating teams that mattered—St. Louis, Montreal, Chicago, Philadelphia—and gained ground on their division foes. McGraw's August 31 victory over the Cardinals had set them off on a 12–5 run that put them in fourth place. By then, Philadelphia had dropped out of the race, but Pittsburgh, Montreal, St. Louis, Chicago, and New York remained in contention.

On Monday, September 17, the Mets opened a crucial five-game series with the Pirates only 2 ½ games behind the current division leaders. Tom Seaver started the first game in Pittsburgh, but in a rare poor start, he was knocked out in the third inning. The Pirates ran away with a 10–3 win. "And lying trampled in the ashes of the uprising that wound up at 10–3 long after Seaver had departed, might have been the Mets' pennant hopes," Murray Chass wrote in his *New York Times* game summary.[56] "The loss … dropped the Mets 3 ½ games from the top of the Eastern Division. The deficit isn't necessarily insurmountable, but a victory in what was expected to be a 'sure thing' with Seaver pitching tonight was almost a must if the Mets hoped to take three or four of the five games."

The next night, the Pirates led 4–1 in the ninth inning and appeared to have the door closed on another victory. "The 4 ½ game deficit that would result in another few minutes would, in reality, be insurmountable," Murray Chass wrote. "And certainly would cost Berra his job," Chass added.[57]

But the Mets refused to die. They staged a ten-batter, five-run rally in their half of the ninth, capped off by a two-run single by Willie Mays's replacement in center field, Don Hahn, that scored the go-ahead runs. Berra sent 15 batters to the plate, but not Willie, whose ribs remained tender and wrapped. He stayed on the bench.

In one of his questionable pitcher selections, Berra sent Bob Apodaca, who had been hurriedly summoned from the minors to replace the injured Harry Parker only the day before, to the hill to protect the Mets' lead. The move puzzled even Bob Prince, the voice of the Pirates, calling the game on KDKA–AM. "It's hard to imagine a tougher spot for a rookie to make his major league debut," Prince said. "The twenty-three-year-old Bob Apodaca, A-P-O-D-A-C-A, takes over the pitching for the seventh inning."[58]

Apodaca walked the first two batters he faced, putting the tying runs on base. Berra replaced the rookie with Buzz Capra, who had given up a home run to the second batter he faced the night before.

Berra had to call in Capra because he "had mystifyingly brought in Tug McGraw earlier in the game with the team behind, 4–1," Chass reported in the *Times*.[59] McGraw had left the game for a pinch hitter.

Capra gave up a sacrifice bunt and an infielder's choice ground ball that scored a run to bring the Pirates to within one of the Mets' lead. Capra walked the next two batters, one, Willie Stargell, on purpose, the other, Richie Zisk, by accident. Capra faced Manny Sanguillen with the bases loaded, two outs, and a fragile one-run lead. He threw two balls, a called strike, and another ball. Sanguillen finally swung at the next pitch and lifted a short fly to left field that Cleon Jones raced in to grab for the final out.

McGraw, who pitched two scoreless innings of relief, picked up the win, but it was the ninth inning that was the story of the season. Facing nearly certain defeat—again—the Mets could have packed it in, gone through the motions and gone home. But they stayed and fought—again. They rallied to victory—again. They moved within 2 ½ games of the division leaders—again. They kept alive their pennant hopes—again. The Mets season pivoted on that inning. "Every Met, from that evening on, claimed that this was the inning that did it all," Roger Angell wrote.[60]

They believed. It wasn't over.

The series shifted to Shea for the final three games. Wednesday night, September 19, the Mets won again, 7–3, behind the strength of two home runs from left fielder Cleon Jones. Earlier in the season, Jones had complained about his sore feet and a sprained wrist. Teammates had grumbled that he didn't always give 100 percent.[61] Nobody was complaining now, with Jones getting hot both at the plate and in the field, slugging homers and diving for fly balls. Tug McGraw, whom *The New York Times*'s Joseph Durso called "the whirling dervish of the bullpen," picked up the save. With four victories and nine saves in his last thirteen appearances, McGraw became "the central figure in their (the Mets) rousing revival."[62] The win put the Mets within 1 ½ games of the Pirates' division lead.

Thursday night, September 20, the Mets continued their relentless resistance to elimination. Three times in the late innings, they came from behind to tie the game—in the sixth, the eighth, and the ninth. In the 13th, it looked like the Pirates would once again take the lead—and perhaps the game—when Pittsburgh center fielder Dave Augustine launched a shot over Cleon Jones's head. As the ball soared toward the left-field fence, it looked certain to be a two-run homer that would score Richie Zisk from first base. Jones, not ready to give up on it, gave chase.

Then, in a moment that suggested God wore orange and blue, the ball fell an inch short of clearing the fence, struck the top of the wooden plank just above the 5 in the 358 sign, and—instead of bouncing over the fence—leaped back into Jones's waiting glove. Surprised by his fortune, Jones turned and threw to the cutoff man, Wayne Garrett. The Mets' regular third baseman, Garrett had moved to short late in the game to replace Buddy Harrelson. The third baseman wasn't used to handling relay throws—and he needed a perfect one to nail Zisk, who'd been running with the pitch. Once again, an orange and blue God winked, and Garrett's throw bounced cleanly into catcher Ron Hodges's glove. Hodges tagged out the sliding Zisk to complete the miraculous play.[63]

Bob Prince was dumfounded that the ball had bounced the way it had with the wind blowing out. He hinted that the Mets had angels on their side in the outfield. "This is the wackiest, doggone baseball season any of us have ever seen," the voice of the Pirates told his listeners. "It may be 1969 all over again for the Mets, but I'm gonna figure that somebody's going to get mad enough at them to whack 'em. Pittsburgh or St. Louis or somebody. They're not going to win this darn thing, in the NL East because I don't like to see that kind of stuff."[64]

Instead of being down by two runs, the Mets retired the Pirates with a chance to win the ball game in their half of the inning, which, of course, they did. Ron Hodges, called up from Double A earlier in the season when the Mets had already gone through three catchers and were desperate for someone behind the plate, proved the hero of the "four-hour thriller." The Longines clock above the outfield scoreboard showed nearly midnight when Hodges came to bat with two on and one out. He singled to drive home the winning run. The Mets had stolen within half a game of the Pirates' division lead with one game to go in the series.

When the ball bounced back from the fence into Jones's glove, the entire momentum of the game and the division race bounced from the Pirates to the Mets. Running out to take the cutoff throw—just in case the ball somehow didn't clear the fence— Wayne Garrett watched it ricochet right into Jones's glove and thought, *This is our year. No way we can lose now.* He had seen a lot of balls strike Shea's left-field fence but never seen one bounce like that.[65] It wasn't over. You gotta believe.

Friday night, September 21, Tom Seaver pitched the fifth and final game of the series. For once, the Mets supported him with a generous dose of runs—ten—which was far more than Seaver, who held the Pirates to two runs, needed. The Mets fourth straight victory over Pittsburgh improved their record to 77–77 on the season and moved them ahead of the Pirates. That made the Mets the first team in the history of the game to reach .500 and take first place on the same date in September.[66]

The largest crowd of the season so far, 51,381, turned out to celebrate the occasion. They cheered steadily throughout the game, gleefully tossed paper airplanes, danced in the aisles—even on top of the dugout—and chanted, "We're No. 1!" for the team that had been No. 6 most of the summer.[67] With the game in hand, the organist played "You're the Top!" and the outfield scoreboard beamed "Look Who's No. 1!"[68] The crowd cheered and danced in delight. The Mets had won them back. They believed!

Berra believed, sort of. "We've been hot since the 17th of August (when Willie hit his 660th career home run), but it's still wide open," he told the reporters crowded into his clubhouse office afterward. Five teams remained within 2 ½ games of the Mets division lead with eight games left in their season. "We won't know until it's over."[69] This time, a cautionary note replaced the earlier optimistic tone of his "It ain't over 'til it's over."

———————

Willie Mays did not play in the Pittsburgh series. He nursed his tender ribs on the bench. Yogi started John Milner at first and used young Don Hahn and Dave Schneck—a .199 career hitter in 143 games from 1972–74—in center field. In the five-game series, Yogi summoned pinch hitters fourteen times but never called on No. 24. Mays stayed on the bench throughout the Mets dramatic five-day surge from fourth place to first. He had only six at bats all month.

But Willie did make news during the series. On September 20, before the Mets' dramatic 13-inning victory, he stood in front of a group of reporters and photographers packed into the Diamond Club at Shea Stadium, wearing a tie and green-checked sport coat, and announced the end of his twenty-two-year career. "I'm not just getting out of baseball because I'm hurt," he said. "I just feel that the people of America shouldn't have to see a guy play who can't produce.

"At forty-two, you can't play the way you could at twenty. I've got to face facts"—meaning his .211 batting average, only 44 hits in 209 at bats that season—"I've been in a lot of slumps and come out of them, but now I'm running out of time."[70]

The Mets brass flanked Mays: chairman Donald Grant, general manager Bob Scheffing, and manager Yogi Berra. Turned out that Willie—and none of the three candidates for release in the *New York Post* poll—was the first to go. Mays declared that Mets management had not forced his retirement. "It was my decision alone," he said.[71]

Willie remained dry-eyed during the press conference. "I thought I'd be crying right now, but so many people love me that I don't hurt too bad," he said. "Maybe I'll cry tomorrow."[72]

Tomorrow came five days hence, on September 25. Willie had arranged with Grant to hold his retirement party that night at Shea, before the game against the Montreal Expos.[73] Mays had initially resisted the idea of a ceremony, not wanting to take away from the team's division title quest.[74] He thought maybe he could ride quietly off into the sunset, but Grant knew fans wouldn't stand for that. A record crowd of 53,603 people showed up to bid farewell on "Willie Mays Night," a cool evening that warmed the hearts of Willie's public.

New York's love affair with Willie Mays dated back to the first major league home run he hit in the city on May 28, 1951. After being called up by the Giants, Mays had gone oh-for-twelve in his first three games in Philadelphia. In his Polo Grounds debut, he faced Braves Hall of Fame pitcher Warren Spahn and connected for his first big league hit—a Ruthian clout that landed on top of the left-field roof. The New York Giants fans leapt to their feet, cheering exuberantly. One fan who was at the Polo Grounds that evening recalled, "The electricity, the tingle, the fun of Willie Mays began then."[75]

The 50,000-plus fans at "Willie Mays Night" on September 25, 1973, felt the tingle all over again. They waved signs that read, "A Giant Among Mets," "Say Hey Belongs to Shea," "Willie, We'll Never Forget You." The outfield scoreboard declared, "So Long, Yes" on one side of a large "24," and on the other, "Goodbye, Never."[76]

During the hour-long ceremony, friends showered No. 24 with gifts ranging from golf clubs to a trip around the world. Giants owner Horace Stoneham gave him a Mercedes Benz. Chrysler Corporation presented him with two cars, one for himself and one for his wife, Mae. Willie's friends also gave her a full-length, white mink coat.[77]

Former teammates and baseball greats turned out to honor Mays. They included former New York Giants Bobby Thomson and Dusty Rhodes; rival Brooklyn Dodgers Joe Black, Pee Wee Reese, and Duke Snider; Cardinals great Stan Musial; Mr. Cub, Ernie Banks; and Yankee Clipper Joe DiMaggio, Mays's boyhood idol. The All-Star lineup reminisced about Mays's legendary feats and testified to his greatness while he brushed his eyes with a white handkerchief.[78]

Finally, it was Willie's turn at the microphone. New York mayor John Lindsay introduced Mays. Over 50,000 New Yorkers roared their love. Willie stood at home plate, waiting by the idle microphone. The "thundering ovation" lasted six minutes.[79]

The emotion absent at his press conference now overwhelmed Mays. He had not written out a speech; he spoke what he felt at the moment.[80] "This is a sad day for me," he told the crowd, his voice choking. "It is a new experience for me to have you cheer for me and not be able to do anything about it."[81]

He thanked various people who had presented him with gifts and paid him compliments. His words echoed back at him. He addressed his teammates, "Forgive me. It's my night, but it's your night, too. I hope you go on to win the flag for the New York people."[82]

Then, to the New York people, he continued, "There always comes a time for someone to get out. I look at the kids over here, the way they're playing, the way they're fighting for themselves, and it tells me one thing: 'Willie, say goodbye to America.'"[83]

There, the words were out. It was finished. He could no longer deny the time had come for him to step aside, to stop casting his shadow upon their success. It was time to let them shine on their own. He said goodbye.

Willie stepped from the microphone and let the tears flow. He wiped the back of his hand across his eyes. His wife Mae and his son Michael hugged him. Baseball was all he had ever known.[84]

In the game that followed, Willie took his customary spot on the bench toward the back of the dugout. Yogi walked past. "I may need you tomorrow," the manager said.

"Fine with me," Mays replied.[85]

But Willie did not break out of his spectator role that night, nor the next day, nor in any of the Mets remaining regular season games. He would have to wait for the playoffs to dab the finishing touches on this twenty-two-year career.

Following Mays's retirement tribute, Cleon Jones provided an inspired performance. The left fielder slugged a home run in the sixth inning and made a running, backhanded catch in deep left-center that saved two runs the following frame. "When I saw Willie crying, I felt bad," Jones told reporters after the game. "It was a sad day for us all. All I wanted to do was to get out there and play the game."[86]

The game ended with McGraw slapping his thigh, recording his 11th save in the past 15 games. The Mets 2–1 victory—their seventh straight—put them a game and a half ahead of the Pirates with five games left to play.

Just when it looked like they were about to cruise to a happy ending to their remarkable season, the Mets stumbled. They lost the next day to Montreal. Their lead dwindled to half a game.

On September 30, which had been the day the season was scheduled to end, five teams remained in contention for the NL East title. There were more than twenty different ways the race could play out, including the unbelievable possibility that the Mets, Pirates, Cardinals, Cubs, and Expos would all finish 80–82 in a five-way tie.[87]

The Mets still had four games left, two doubleheaders against the Cubs, the final two being make-up games from earlier rain-outs. The Mets split the first doubleheader, leaving them 81–79 and a game up on the Pirates, who would play a make-up game against the San Diego Padres on October 1. If the Pirates won and the Mets lost both games of their final doubleheader, the two teams would finish the season tied and have to settle the division with a playoff game. However, the Mets could clinch the title outright by winning one of their two games scheduled for Monday, October 1.

Yogi named his ace to start the first game of the doubleheader. Some of his players questioned the decision to pitch Seaver. "He got us here, but he's got to be tired," shortstop Buddy Harrelson said. "If he doesn't make it, I've got to sympathize with him."[88]

Monday afternoon, Cleon Jones gave his pitcher an early lead with a second-inning home run—his seventh homer in eleven days—but Seaver looked tired. His arm lacked the strength to hurl his fastball, so he relied on his curve and slider. By the fifth, his team had given him a 5–0 lead, but he did not make that look safe the way he was throwing. The Cubs answered with a pair of runs in their half of the fifth. The Mets scored a run in the seventh, but the Cubs came right back in their next at bat. Seaver allowed a single to the leadoff batter, then served up a gopher ball to the next. The two-run homer cut the Mets lead to 6–4.

Berra decided Seaver had had enough. He walked slowly to the mound, took the ball from Seaver, and replaced him with Tug McGraw. The Mets' title fortunes settled onto McGraw's shoulders. Fitting, given the way they had fallen and risen all season with McGraw's performance. McGraw came on with a light rain and heavy pressure, but he was "all jacked up and believing like hell."[89]

He put the Cubs down in order the next two innings, striking out three of the six batters he faced. In the ninth, McGraw, still protecting a two-run lead, gave up a single to the leadoff batter. He struck out the next. The next batter hit a soft line drive that the Mets' first baseman John Milner nabbed. McGraw rushed toward first, "screaming like a banshee," for Milner to step on the bag to double up the runner.[90] Milner did. Mets won.

The Mets tumbled up a flight of stairs to the visitors clubhouse at Wrigley for their postgame celebration, which was initially restrained by the thought of having to go out and play another game. But the umpires decided it was too wet to play—not to mention, unnecessary, since the Mets had already clinched the division outright—and the team began their title celebration in earnest. McGraw described the scene in his autobiography, *Screwball,* "We stopped being restrained and began pouring it on, hollering and screaming and wondering what all the people who'd counted us out of the human race a couple of months earlier must have been thinking."

The moment was particularly sweet because of how unexpected it was. The Mets had clinched the division with a .509 winning percentage, the lowest ever to win a division or a pennant. They had wallowed 13 games under .500 at one point. They had been 11 ½ games out of first. They had spent nearly the entire summer in last. They had placed eight men on the disabled list. They didn't have a single .300 hitter nor 20-game winner among them. Nobody on the team had come close to driving in 100 runs. Yet they had played .675 ball since August 31, winning 21 of their last 29 games, and here they were, division champs, headed to the playoffs. It all seemed so improbable, yet it tasted oh so sweet.

Tug McGraw jumped up on an equipment trunk, clutching a bottle of champagne, and kept screaming, "You gotta believe! You Gotta Be-lieve! YOU GOTTA BELIEVE!" His teammates shouted it back at him.[91] They believed. Oh yes, the gods be praised, they believed.

The Mets celebration was the antithesis of the subdued scene in the A's clubhouse when they had clinched their division title. Both teams had enjoyed extraordinary seasons under quite different circumstances. Now, fate summoned them to one end, which would leave room for only one team's champagne-soaked celebration.

———————

Willie almost missed it. After "Willie Mays Night," he was ready to pack his bags and head back to his California home with Mae. He had retired. He had given the press conference, gone through the retirement ceremony, accepted the gifts, acknowledged the fans, and said his goodbyes. Now it was time to take his aching body home.

Not so fast. Mrs. Joan Payson, the Mets owner, phoned him at his Riverdale apartment. She didn't want him to leave before the season ended. "You can't go home now, Willie," she said.[92] So he stayed to see how it would all play out.

Instead of Willie going home, Mae flew to Chicago for the final weekend. After the Mets' victory Monday afternoon, she ushered Willie out of the clubhouse and back to the hotel. They had a private celebration in their room. Willie drank two glasses of champagne and "was zonkered."[93] The old man slept.

Cincinnati's **Pete Rose** attacks New York shortstop **Buddy Harrelson** in the third game of the National League pennant playoff.

Chapter Sixteen

PENNANT FEVER

Yogi Berra and Richard Nixon had survived the summer, but autumn initiated a heightened level of scrutiny for both men. In October, an embattled President Nixon remained defiant about investigations into his finances and burglaries. The President defended his extravagant expenditures—$10 million in federal funds—on improvements to his personal properties in California and Florida, while his friend Bebe Rebozo testified before the Senate Watergate Committee that he had received a $100,000 cash contribution from Howard Hughes on Nixon's behalf. Nixon's vice president, Spiro T. Agnew, faced a possible grand jury indictment in Baltimore and impeachment proceedings by the House of Representatives.

Meanwhile, on Saturday, October 6, the American League and National League began their pennant playoffs. At 1 p.m., Eastern Time, the Oakland Athletics played the Baltimore Orioles, followed by the New York Mets versus the Cincinnati Reds at 4 p.m. The two league championships foreshadowed the World Series. The way each pennant winner played showed what it would bring to the Fall Classic.

Excitement for the Mets in New York seemed directly proportional to disgust for the Nixon Administration—Metsomania had taken hold of "Met City," as *The New York Times* took to calling the

Big Apple. Inebriated by their belief in the amazing Mets, the Metsomaniacs transformed Shea Stadium into a hostile environment for the opposition. In the riotous end, they even turned on themselves. Their newly retired hero, Willie Mays, remained in uniform and performed an unexpected role.

The Mets' amazing finish in September placed them in a situation calling for another amazing feat. They faced the defending NL pennant-winner, the Cincinnati Reds, who had also completed an astonishing season. Eleven games behind the Dodgers in July, the Reds won 70 percent of their games the last three months to take the division by 3 ½ games. Their 99–63 record was the best in the major leagues that year.

The Big Red Machine featured three future Hall of Famers plus the all-time hits leader. In 1973, Pete Rose rapped 230 hits, more than any of the other 600 batters in both leagues and more than any other switch-hitter ever. He had won his third batting title with a .338 average, and he would be named the NL's MVP for the season. Joe Morgan, a future Hall of Fame second baseman, scored 116 runs and knocked in 82. Catcher Johnny Bench, another future Hall of Famer, hadn't put up the same numbers from his 1972 MVP season, but he still drove in 104 runs and had a sharpshooter arm behind the plate. First baseman Tony Perez, who rounded out the future Cooperstown enshrinees, had knocked in 101 runs and batted .314. Shortstop Dave Concepción had been selected to the All-Star team, along with pitcher Jack Billingham. In addition, the Reds had some strong young players, including rookie outfielder Ken Griffey Sr., who made his MLB debut on August 25 with two hits. The Reds had beaten the Mets 8 out of 12 times during the regular season. Cincinnati liked its chances of breezing by the Mets to another World Series berth.

The best-three-out-of-five series opened in Cincinnati, drawing a record playoff crowd of 53,431 Reds fans to Riverfront Stadium. Cincinnati loved its Reds with a fanaticism on par with Green Bay's affection for the Packers.[1] The Reds enjoyed paralleled success.

As had become his custom for big games, Yogi Berra picked his ace, Tom Seaver, to start. The problem was Terrific Tom's shoulder. He had finished the season 19–10, with a .208 ERA and 251 strike-outs—good enough to win him the Cy Young Award that season—but 18 complete games and 290 innings had strained his arm. His shoulder had been sore throughout the final month, and he had not been able to overpower hitters the way he usually did with his fastball, which he relied on heavily. The Mets' team doctor, Peter LaMotte, gave Seaver a shot of Butazolidin to treat the inflamed shoulder before the first playoff game, and Seaver told Yogi on Saturday his arm felt good.[2]

Seaver gave himself an early lead in the top of the second inning when he hit a long double to the left center field wall that drove in a run. He protected the slim 1–0 lead by striking out more than a third of the batters he faced. The fading sunlight and long shadows made it more difficult for batters to see the ball, but his fastball was also on that day. Every time the powerful Reds hitters started a rally, Seaver squelched it with a strikeout. Through the seventh inning, Seaver had struck out 12, and the Mets clung to the one-run lead.

Seaver's big delivery of his fastball had been a thing of beauty that afternoon. "The way Tom throws it (fastball) past a hitter—with his powerful body dropping low and driving forward at the instant of delivery—is one of the ornaments of modern baseball," Roger Angell observed with his equally admirable prose.[3]

Seaver started the eighth with another strikeout, his 13th, setting the NL playoff record. Pete Rose came to bat with one out. Rose was the spark plug of the Big Red Machine. Mr. Hustle had grown up in Cincy. The fans cheered his approach to the plate. He was one of them, and they revered him. "Rose has reached such eminence in Cincinnati, which is his hometown, that he gets ovations for everything but sneezing," *Sports Illustrated* noted.[4]

Rose's 230 hits that season gave him a career total of 2,152, en route to his 4,256. Of those 4,256, only 160 were home runs; of his 230 that season, he hit only five home runs. The thirty-two-year-old was a punch hitter, able to punch balls into gaps, not a power hitter, but, every so often, he managed to lift one over the fence. That's what he did with the 2–1 fastball Seaver threw him—poked it over the right-field fence. Seaver threw a good pitch, but Rose made a better swing. The MVP trumped the Cy Young Award-winner. Rose's home run deepened the hometown's affection for him. They cheered him warmly.

In the ninth inning, Pedro Borbon, the Reds' reliable reliever, took over the pitching duties. Borbon had appeared in eighty games that season and been a big part of the Reds' strong second half, winning nine games and saving seven since July 4. The Dominican pitcher was as renowned for his firecracker personality as he was for his fastball. "He is a shot of juice if things get dull," *Sports Illustrated* forecast in its playoff preview.[5]

Borbon came in with a runner on first and promptly retired the side, ending any hopes of a Mets rally. The score remained tied 1–1, headed into the bottom of the ninth inning.

Seaver induced Tony Perez, the first batter, to ground out, short to first. Johnny Bench stepped in to try his luck. It proved good. Bench sent an inside Seaver fastball over the left-field fence for a walkoff home run. The Reds had won the opener 2–1.

Once again, the Mets had failed to support Seaver with any runs. He had provided their only productive offense that day, driving in their lone run with his double. The day had shown that good pitching wasn't enough to win a pennant; the Mets would have to come through with their bats if they wanted to advance to the World Series.

Cincinnatians loved their Reds so much that even more of them, 54,041, turned out at Riverside Stadium on Sunday, breaking the previous day's record, but they found little to cheer. Mets pitcher Jon Matlack, the 1972 NL Rookie of the Year, followed Seaver's gem with one of his own. The twenty-three-year-old pitched the best game of his life, a two-hit shutout. The Mets offense did its part. Right fielder Rusty Staub homered in the fourth inning, and

New York managed a typical Mets rally in the ninth—two walks and five singles—that produced four runs. The Mets' 5–0 victory evened the playoffs at a game apiece.

The two teams traveled to Met City to decide the series. On Tuesday, October 9, the Metsomaniacs outdid themselves— 53,967 filled Shea Stadium for the afternoon game, over three hundred more than had turned out for "Willie Mays Night." "YOU GOTTA BELIEVE" banners complemented the red, white, and blue bunting decorating the box seats. This was the Mets' first postseason game at Shea since October 16, 1969, when the miraculous Mets had won the World Series. That day as today, Jerry Koosman pitched. And pitched well, keeping the powerful Reds bats in check.

Rusty Staub tickled the already juiced crowd with a first-inning home run over the Manufacturers Hanover sign in center field.[6] The Mets batted around in the second inning, scoring five runs on four hits and two walks. One of those hits was another Staub home run. The Metsomaniacs were loving this. The Reds scored two runs off Koosman in the third, but so what? The Mets scored one themselves in the third and added two more in the fourth to build a 9–2 lead. Believe it!

Pete Rose refused to. Rose singled with one out in the fifth inning. Joe Morgan followed with a ground ball wide of first base, a perfect double-play ball. Mets first baseman John Milner grabbed the grounder and threw to shortstop Buddy Harrelson, covering second. Harrelson caught the ball, stepped on the bag, and threw back to first to complete the double play, 3–6–3. But Rose's hard slide took down Harrelson.

Rose had a reputation for this type of rough play. Three years earlier, he had surprised nearly everyone in the 1970 All-Star Game when he bowled over Ray Fosse to score and separated the catcher's shoulder. Critics maligned Rose for injuring another player unnecessarily in what many viewed as a ceremonial event. His fans defended the play as another example of Mr. Hustle, the consummate competitor they admired. "I'm no damn little girl out there," Rose told reporters after his slide on Harrelson. "I'm supposed to give the fans their money's worth and try to bust up double plays—and shortstops. I'll be honest, I was trying to knock him into left field. I play to win."[7]

Harrelson came up angry. The Reds had played that way against them all year. A takeout slide like Rose's in June had broken his wrist. This time, Rose's elbow had smacked his head.[8] The 146-pound shortstop scrambled to his feet swearing at the 200-pound runner. The heavyweight Rose went after the welterweight Harrelson. The Mets infield rushed over, the benches cleared, and the bullpen emptied. Rose claimed that the Mets third baseman Wayne Garret and pitcher Matlack punched him while he was on the ground.[9] Tug McGraw raced in from the bullpen, a hundred yards across the outfield grass, and wrestled Rose off Harrelson,[10] who bled from a cut above his left eyebrow.[11]

When the bullpen emptied, the Reds firecracker, Pedro Borbon, squared off against Mets pitcher Buzz Capra. Borbon decked Capra with a punch to the face. Mets bullpen catcher Duffy Dyer cold-cocked Borbon in return and dropped him. When Borbon stumbled to his feet, he placed a cap on his head.[12] Someone pointed out that it was a Mets cap—not his, but Capra's. Borbon yanked the cap off his head and bit it, tearing out a hunk of cloth with his teeth.[13]

The umpires finally restored order on the field after the five-minute free-for-all, but they could not calm the Metsomaniacs. The fights had riled the 53,967 Mets loyalists. Fans may have loved Rose in Cincinnati, but they suddenly hated him in New York. When he went out to his position in left field, the Metsomaniacs rained down a barrage of insults and an artillery of garbage. Rose flung at least two items back into the stands, which only inflamed the attack upon him.[14] One fan's errant toss of a beer can struck Reds relief pitcher Gary Nolan in the bullpen. With the Mets' Felix Millan at bat and two outs, a whisky bottle sailed out of the stands and nearly clocked Rose.[15]

The Reds left fielder called time out and headed toward the dugout. Manager Sparky Anderson came out to meet him on the field. Rose told him about the whisky missile. That was all Anderson needed to hear. He called his players in and escorted them off the field. He refused to resume play until the umpires had tamed the crowd.[16]

Chub Feeney, NL president, left his box seat and hustled onto the field to consult with the six-man umpire crew. The umpires suggested Rose move to center field, but Anderson didn't think that was the solution. Feeney had opted not to kick Rose and Harrelson out of the game after the brawl—which would have protected Rose—because he didn't want to take out two major fan attractions. Instead, the NL president decided to fine them each $1,000.[17]

After talking to the umps, Feeney walked over to the Mets dugout and told Yogi Berra that New York would have to forfeit the game if the crowd did not calm down. The public address system implored the fans to behave and repeated the forfeit warning.[18] Feeney suggested that Yogi and Willie Mays speak to the crowd in the left field seats. The NL president said he would go out there himself, but they would probably just throw things at him, too.[19] "He chose Willie Mays as designated peacemaker and asked Berra to serve as a Henry Kissinger in knickers," Red Smith wrote in *The New York Times*.[20]

Mays and Berra walked out to left field, joined by Cleon Jones, the Mets left fielder; Tom Seaver, the pitching ace; and Rusty Staub, the hero of the day with his two home runs. Seeing Willie walk across the outfield grass, the Metsomaniacs erupted into a cheer. "They hadn't seen Willie in quite a while and they were happy to see him," Jones said.[21]

Mays gave the fans the peace sign. They cheered back at him.[22] "Look at the scoreboard," Mays yelled to the fans. "We're ahead. Let 'em play this game."[23]

"Keep quiet," Berra added. "Let them beat us. We're ahead 9–2."[24]

It took more than ten minutes to rein in the crowd and a nine-man grounds crew to clean up the littered outfield. Police dotted the left field foul line and inhabited the left field grandstand porch, but no more incidents erupted.[25]

Play finally resumed, rather anticlimactically. Koosman completed the game. The Mets escaped a forfeit and won 9–2 to take a two-to-one lead in the playoff series.

Another 50,000-plus Metsomaniacs enlivened Shea Stadium the next afternoon, Tuesday, October 9. They unfurled a new crop of banners to accompany the "You Gotta Believe" standards: "Rose is a weed," "This Rose smells," and "Rose is a pansy" greeted the Reds left fielder when he showed up for another day's work.[26] Rose's teammate Johnny Bench saw it as a good thing. "The best thing you can do is get Pete Rose mad," he said.[27]

The Metsomaniacs booed Rose lustily whenever they saw him or heard his name announced.[28] They chanted obscene jibes.[29] From the left-field seats, fans heckled Rose mercilessly. Rose grounded out in the first inning, much to the satisfaction of the Mets fans. He singled in the fourth. Tony Perez hit a double play ball to second. Rose bore down on Harrelson, waiting to turn the play. Here we go again! Rose slid hard toward Harrelson on the right side of the bag. Harrelson managed to leap over him and complete the double play without incident but with an advantage in the grudge match. *Take that, Rose! You stink!*

The Mets scored a run in the third; the Reds matched it in the seventh. The game stretched into extra innings, tied at one apiece.

In the tenth, the Reds loaded the bases. Tony Perez blasted a ball deep to right field. The Mets right fielder Rusty Staub raced back, reached over his head, snared the ball—and crashed into the wooden wall. The impact threw him onto his back. He clenched the ball in his glove for the final out of the inning. Staub stayed in the game, but he had wrenched his throwing shoulder—another Mets injury that would work against them later.[30]

In the top of the twelfth, Rose batted with one out. The crowd booed. The count went to two balls, two strikes. He swung at the next pitch, tipped it, but catcher Jerry Grote couldn't hang onto the third strike. Rather than walking back to the dugout, Rose stayed at the plate for a second chance. He lifted the next pitch into the right-field seats for a home run.[31]

Rose ran around the bases with his right fist thrust triumphantly in the air. When he reached home, he jumped on the plate to add an exclamation point.[32] *Smell that, New York!* The fans in left field applauded him with eggs and apples, but "nothing solid," he said.[33] The cap-chomping Pedro Borbon retired the Mets in order, and Rose's home run stood up. Pete Rose had evened the series at two games apiece.

The playoff came down to the fifth and final game on a beautiful, clear autumn afternoon, Wednesday, October 10. At stake was $14,000 in prize money per player for the winning team against an $8,000 share for the losers. Most importantly, the winners would advance to the World Series.

Another 50,000-plus Metsomaniacs stormed Shea Stadium. Throughout Met City, those who couldn't make it to the ballpark gathered around television sets and radios to follow the action. The National Broadcasting Corporation apologized to baseball fans for interrupting its coverage of the game in the early innings to announce the resignation of Vice President Spiro T. Agnew. The network ended its report with the upbeat, "And now back to the ball game."[34]

Game five was a rematch of game one, Tom Seaver versus Jack Billingham. The Reds' Cy Young Award candidate had won 19 games and led the league with seven shutouts. Billingham had retired 16 consecutive Mets in the first game before being lifted for a pinch hitter in the eighth inning. He seemed the stronger of the two pitchers on Wednesday. The soreness had returned to Seaver's shoulder. Without his fastball, Seaver wasn't ringing up the strikeouts the way he had in the first game.[35]

The Mets jumped to a two-run lead when Ed Kranepool, who replaced the injured Rusty Staub in right field, drove in two runners with a sharp single. Pete Rose doubled off Seaver in the fifth then scored to tie the game at two-all.

The Mets rallied in the fifth. With two runners on and a 3–2 lead, Yogi decided to pinch hit for Ed Kranepool, even though Kranepool had driven in the Mets first two runs. For the first time in over a month, Berra asked Willie Mays to bat. Willie happily obliged. Watching the game from his customary spot at the back of the bench, Willie had hoped for the chance to contribute in a clutch situation.[36]

Mays had been forgotten in the Mets lineup. He had not contributed to the division title. He had not played in the pennant playoff. Here was his chance.

When Mays walked to the plate, the Metsomaniacs at Shea went wild. They stood and cheered. Willie had not played since cracking his ribs against the dugout railing in Montreal on September 9. He had not had a hit since August 29. But they didn't care. They loved Willie and knew what he was capable of. This was the sort of dramatic moment that heroes were created for. Arthur Daley reported, "The crowd went bananas," and Red Smith observed that their "ovation brought a lump to the throat."[37]

Reds manager Sparky Anderson brought in Clay Carroll to pitch to Mays. When Willie saw the right-hander come in, he felt confident he would hit the ball somewhere.[38] The Metsomaniacs roared their encouragement. The crowd gathered on the Fifth Avenue sidewalk outside a Sony showroom at 56th Street tensely watched the eighteen television sets tuned to the game.[39]

Eager to deliver, Mays swung at the first pitch. He overswung and hit a Baltimore chop, a high bouncer in front of the plate. Carroll, the pitcher, could only wait for the ball to fall and throw— too late—to home. By then, Willie was safe at first and another run had scored.

"It was the shortest heroic blow in memory," Roger Angell reported. "But, as Mays suggested after the game, box scores do not record the distance of hits, or their luck."[40] Nor did the Metsomaniacs care about the distance or luck of Mays's hit. They only cared that Willie the Magnificent had added an insurance run. Inside Shea and outside the Sony showroom and all across Met City, they cheered heartily.

The Mets rally continued. Mays scored on Buddy Harrelson's single. By the time the fifth inning ended, the Mets led 7–2.

Mays stayed in the game in center field, where he recorded one putout. He grounded out to the pitcher to end the sixth inning and flew out to right to end the eighth. But no matter. The Mets added three more runs to give Seaver a 10–2 lead. Happy fans lit firecrackers that echoed against the stadium walls.[41]

By the time Seaver took the mound in the bottom of the ninth, the Metsomaniacs at Shea were so riled with delight that they abandoned their seats and poured into the lower aisles—bulls in the chute, poised to explode with excitement onto the field once the game finally ended. They chanted with anticipation. "There was some enormous urgency visible here—a yearning for the field itself, a need to belong to this event in a deeper way," Roger Angell wrote.[42]

Not even Seaver walking a batter and giving up a single subdued their enthusiasm. The Mets still led 10–2. With one out and two on and Pete Rose at the plate, the crush of fans snapped a temporary fence behind the Mets dugout, and they seeped onto the edge of the field. The umpires stopped play. Once again, the Metsomaniacs threatened to spoil the game for the Mets. Seaver walked off the mound and shouted at the fans to get off the field.[43]

The fans retreated—temporarily. Play resumed, Seaver walked Rose to load the bases, and Yogi Berra strolled out to the mound. He took the ball from Seaver, patted him on the back, and called for McGraw.[44] Thus repeated a familiar line from the script of their success: exit Tom, enter Tug.

The crush of fans in the lower section had become more riotous mob than happy crowd. The Cincinnati Reds' wives feared for their safety. They were ushered out of their box seats through the Reds dugout.[45] The Mets had hired 340 city police officers and private security guards to maintain law and order. They proved insufficient.[46]

When McGraw set down the final two Reds batters to end the game and claim the NL pennant for the Mets, the celebration reverberated throughout Met City. "Sirens went off on Fifth Avenue," the *Times* reported. "Bus drivers on Queens Boulevard blew their horns. Tabloids were shredded and dropped from East Side apartment windows. Victory beer flowed at the Avenue U Bar in Sheepshead Bay and at New York University's Loeb Student Center."[47]

At Shea, the Metsomaniacs exploded onto the field. The fans—most of them young men, no doubt a few beers in their bellies and probably other chemicals animating their bloodstreams—rushed for the green, knocking down anyone in their way. The scribes called it "pandemonium," but not even John Milton could have imagined such a scene when he originated that word. "It was frightening in a way, and so was the enormous horde let loose by the final out, and the sight of Reds and Mets alike (Tug McGraw from the mound, Pete Rose from the base path) running and dodging, as if for their lives, through hundreds upon hundreds of grasping hands, past hundreds of passionate, shouting faces," Angell wrote.[48]

Given the way the series had been played, Rose had reason to fear for his life. He "darted through hundreds of surging fans, cutting from side to side and finding holes better than O. J. Simpson ever has," Murray Chass wrote in *The New York Times*.[49] Rose's teammates brandished bats to protect him.[50]

A young man grabbed at Willie Mays. Another reached for him from behind. Mays clutched his hat and fought them off, headed for the safety of the Mets bullpen in right field. He realized they just wanted a souvenir, but he didn't want to part with his lucky cap. In a newspaper photo, the moment looked more like he was being mugged on the street than congratulated by reveling fans.[51]

Papers and streamers swirled above the field in the late afternoon. Fans clawed up the bases and home plate as well as large chunks of the infield and outfield turf. They tore away sections of the fence. A red flare exploded. The scrabble kicked up a large dust cloud that hovered in the air. Some fans perched on friends' shoulders. Many thrust their fingers in the air and cried, "We're No. 1!" Fights broke out.

With the swarm of fans edging toward violence amidst the haze, the infield scene resembled the setting of a rock concert rather than the denouement of a baseball game. The boisterous fans enacted a new brand of victory celebration. "This sort of riotous unleashing has almost grown into an institution in our sports in recent years," Angell wrote.[52] The culture had infiltrated the sport, forever leaving its mark. Innocence of days gone by had given way to destruction. Viewed through one lens, the scene on the field was a metaphor for the legacy of the Sixties: American society disintegrated into pandemonium.

The melee resulted in thousands of dollars of damage to the field and in many bodily injuries. Staff in the Shea Stadium first aid center treated thirty people. Five more required hospital care, including a young man trampled while trying to illegally steal second base.[53]

Within the bowels of Shea, the Reds locked the door to their clubhouse and played out their variation on the destruction theme. Frustrated players sought relief from the agony of defeat by smashing chairs and pounding bats against lockers.[54]

Across the way, champagne flowed inside the Mets clubhouse for what *Time* magazine called a miracle "worthy of a week at Lourdes."[55] Winning pitcher Tom Seaver stood on top of a platform for a TV interview. He spotted McGraw across the clubhouse and shouted, "You gotta be-lieve!"[56]

While teammates around him shampooed one another with champagne, Willie Mays, who had done little of late other than calm bottle-chucking fans, talked about his solitary hit. "I wanted to do something for this team," he said. "They (his teammates) have taken care of me all year. I mean, they didn't bother me about playing. You always want to play, but when you get older . . ."[57]

Ah, when you get older, it becomes so much more difficult to live up to the legend you once were. The past becomes a torment with memories of glorious deeds no longer repeatable. The heroic deeds came now—when they came—in short and lucky chops. Willie knew, better than anyone. Fitting that his grand career would play out amidst the pageantry and scale of the World Series, yet he realized that mega event could become a final chance to tip his cap with more heroics or an occasion of shame that exposed him for what he no longer was.

———————

The Oakland A's four-hour flight to Baltimore, where they would open the AL pennant playoff against the Orioles, gave Reggie Jackson plenty of time to think. In addition to his $100,000-season goals, Reggie had set another goal for the 1973 season: to make it to the World Series. Last year, he had fallen short. His team had made it—even won it—but without him. That hurt even more.

In 1972, his season had ended in the fifth and deciding game of the AL pennant playoff against Detroit. As part of a double steal in the second inning, Reggie had broken for home. The Detroit catcher blocked the plate. Reggie slid and crashed into the catcher. His right foot reached the plate safely, but his left leg twisted underneath him. The slide tore his hamstring. He departed the field on a stretcher.[58]

The A's won the game 2–1, and Reggie celebrated the pennant victory leaning on crutches and swilling champagne with owner Charlie Finley. But Jackson's smile quickly evaporated. Reggie remembered the injury as the unhappiest moment of his life. He cried on the bus back to the hotel and on the plane to Cincinnati, where the World Series opened.[59]

Introduced with the team before play began, Jackson limped out on his crutches, wearing a sport coat, striped slacks, and fashionable boots instead of the Fort Knox gold uniform and kangaroo whites of his teammates. He sat on the bench in the A's dugout. Reporters and the TV cameras still sought him out, but the attention only reminded him that he couldn't play.[60] Alongside his teammates, he felt like an outsider with his crutches and street clothes.

Reggie lost his appetite during the Series. He couldn't sleep.[61] He cried alone in his room at night.[62] The situation seemed impossible for him. He would either suffer defeat with his teammates or watch them win without being part of the party. In the end, they won, and he suffered. "I must admit, it hurt me a little when the A's were able to win without me," he wrote in his diary, *Season with a Superstar*. "I was happy for the team but sad for me."

The A's had become world champions without him. They hadn't needed him. That was a blow to his ego. So 1972 had become a painful memory he wanted to erase with his success in 1973. This year, he determined to play in the World Series.

There, he could indulge the gluttony of his ego. For him, baseball was about more than the money. He had already made millions in real estate by the early Seventies. Baseball offered the fame and fans, the glory and adoration he craved. Nobody applauded a real estate closing. Reggie had wanted to have a one hundred grand season for the status that afforded him. "I want to be a $100,000 ballplayer," he said. "It's not the money I'm after, it's the image."[63]

Image, baby. Reggie excelled at creating that for himself. The right image brought the adulation he craved. The World Series gave him a canvas large enough to paint his portrait before millions.

He'd had his $100,000 season, but that wasn't enough. "I want to be the big man in the league," he said. "I want to be the Most Valuable Player. I want respect. Not the respect of the writers or fans. That, too. But the respect of the players I respect. What players think when they think of Joe DiMaggio or Ted Williams or Willie Mays or Henry Aaron, that's what I want them to think when they think of Reggie Jackson."[64]

He was on his way. The numbers he had put up in the regular season, even with his September injury and slump, would make him the unanimous choice as the league's Most Valuable Player when the Baseball Writers Association of America voted in November. That put him in the elite company of Hank Greenberg, Al Rosen, Mickey Mantle, Frank Robinson and Denny McLain, the only other five to be unanimous AL MVP selections in the past fifty-two years.[65]

Reggie hoped the injury—aggravating the hamstring he had torn in the '72 pennant playoff—would not trouble him in the post-season. His leg felt good. If it could stay that way, he could have a good playoff and watch his dream unfold in the World Series.

But first, Reggie and the A's had to get past the Baltimore Orioles. When he and his teammates took their seats on the Boeing 707 headed across the country, they were given a thick scouting report on the AL East champs. Finley's scouts had assembled a volume that included manager Dick Williams's analysis into volumes that were stapled and mimeographed for each A's player—Charlie's required reading for them.[66]

They read how every batter swung, what he swung at, where he was most likely to hit the ball, and when he might bunt for a base hit with two out. In the days before videotape analysis and computer program breakdowns, this was the most complete study of another team used in baseball.[67] It put the A's at the forefront of breaking down the game, right where they would be thirty years later with their Moneyball approach.

Reggie and the boys already knew that the Orioles, with starters Jim Palmer, Mike Cuellar, and Dave McNally, were the only team in the majors that could match them in pitching strength. They knew that the Orioles were strong fielders with an infield anchored by Brooks Robinson. No matter what the All-Star question mark hit, he was an incomparable fielder—in 1973, Robinson won the 14th of his 16 consecutive Gold Gloves. They knew the Orioles were fast and stealthy—that season they became the first team in baseball history to have eight players steal ten or more bases. The Birds used their speed to play hit-and-run baseball. They would beat you by scratching out runs and cutting your batters down with strong pitching.

The A's also knew that the Orioles were the hottest team in baseball at the moment. They had won their last nine games and run away with the division title, finishing 97–65, eight games ahead of the Red Sox. In August, the Orioles had won 14 straight, the longest winning streak in the majors since 1965. They had won three straight AL pennants and one world championship in the past four years. The A's knew the 7 of 12 games they took from Baltimore during the regular season meant nothing now. The Orioles were 11–10 favorites to beat the A's for the AL pennant and the chance to play the Mets in the World Series.

Dick Williams picked Vida Blue, the hottest A's pitcher down the stretch, to go against the Orioles' best, Jim Palmer. Palmer, already in his eighth big league season at twenty-seven, would win the AL Cy Young award that season. With his 22–9 record and 2.40 ERA, Palmer would finish second to Reggie in the MVP voting. Palmer's .685 career winning percentage was the best among active major league pitchers. *The Sporting News* stated simply, "Jim Palmer is programmed to win."[68]

He was properly programmed Saturday afternoon, October 6, at Memorial Stadium. Palmer struck out six batters in the first two innings. Blue struck out two batters himself in the first inning, but he also threw a wild pitch, walked two batters, gave up three hits, and was responsible for four Oriole runs by the time Williams yanked him with one out to go in the first.

Apparently, Blue had brought his billfold, not his heart. "I'm looking forward to the playoff because it's a money series," Blue had told reporters beforehand. "I'm not going to lie to the Little Leaguers by saying anything else than it's the money. It's a business, my job."[69]

Sorry, kids. Like the man said, today's ballplayer isn't on the field simply for your viewing pleasure; he's in it for himself. Welcome to the new age of baseball.

Palmer ended the day with a masterpiece five-hit shutout. He struck out 12—without the assistance of shadows and slanted light Seaver had later in the day when he struck out 13 Reds batters. Reggie Jackson was the only A's batter to connect solidly off Palmer. After striking out in his first two at bats, Reggie slammed a shot directly back at Palmer's face in the sixth. Palmer threw up his glove in defense. The ball struck his glove and caromed into center.[70] Reggie got a single, and Palmer avoided decapitation. In the end, the Orioles pocketed a 6–0 win.

The A's countered with a 6–3 win the next day behind Catfish Hunter, but the game exposed their weakness in center field. In the sixth inning with two men on, Orioles catcher Earl Williams lofted a pop fly into short center. The injured Billy North's replacement, Angel Mangual, advanced tentatively on the ball. He did not see shortstop Bert Campaneris moving into position to make the catch. Nor did Mangual hear Campy call for the ball. Just as the ball hit Campy's glove, Mangual barged into him and knocked it loose. The ball dropped, a run scored, and the Orioles had whittled Oakland's lead to one, 3–2. Williams could only watch in exasperation from the dugout.

Mangual could have learned something from watching the Orioles left fielder, Al Bumbry. The fleet-footed twenty-six-year-old had stolen 23 bases, led the league in triples with 11, and batted .337. He would be voted the AL Rookie of the Year. That day, the Orioles' leadoff hitter had already scored a run in the first. In the third inning, he added a great catch to his day's accomplishments. Sal Bando, the A's third baseman, slugged a drive to deep left field. Bumbry ran back to the wall and waited—"staring up and tensing and poising like a cat about to leap onto a bureau—and ascended perfectly to pluck back Sal Bando's drive just as it was departing the premises," Roger Angell observed.[71] Bumbry saved his team two runs.

Bando vented his frustration with two more blasts, one in the sixth and another in the eighth, that traveled farther and escaped Bumbry's reach. Campaneris and Joe Rudi also homered off losing pitcher Dave McNally. Rollie Fingers, the man with the best mustache in baseball, recorded the save for the A's.

With the series tied at one game apiece, both teams caught late afternoon flights for the next day's game in Oakland. "We had to get them before we left," Reggie said with characteristic swagger, even though he went oh-for-five that day. "We'll finish them at home. It won't be easy. It never is, the way we play. We just win the ones we have to win."[72] That had been true for the A's all season, but Reggie's statement would prove prophetic.

Charlie Finley, still not 100 percent after his heart attack two months earlier, had received clearance from his doctors to attend the playoff games, provided he followed their instructions. He was to take his medication faithfully and not get too excited. Charlie brought with him to the ballpark a cardiologist, who monitored his pulse between innings. He was under doctors' orders to leave the game if his heart raced too fast. He also brought along an off-duty Oakland police officer for security—those days, you never knew what might happen to a guy reviled like Charlie.[73]

Finley still used the wheelchair, but he also found spurts of energy to stand and wave his A's pennant with a group of sexy young cheerleaders. If the cardiologist at his side couldn't remind him to relax, his body did. In Baltimore, Finley became dizzy walking down a flight of stairs, lost his balance, and "fell flat on my face."[74] He left with a bloody nose.

Game three was supposed to be played at the Oakland Coliseum on Monday afternoon, October 8. It rained heavily the night before and throughout the morning. That left the game in doubt and Charlie Finley in a foul mood.

Monday was Columbus Day, and with people off work, Finley had sold 30,000 advance tickets—a windfall in the Oakland market. If Monday's game was postponed, he did not think he would be able to sell that many tickets to a make-up game on a workday.[75]

Finley had trouble selling tickets. When he bought the team, attendance went from poor to lousy in Kansas City. The A's drew about 680,000 fans in 1961, a 50,000 drop from the previous year. When he moved the team to greener pastures, so to speak, in Oakland, and the team started winning regularly, attendance picked up, but nowhere near the level that a world champion should be attracting. In 1973, Finley wanted to draw one million fans for the first time. He announced the final home game attendance at 7,422, which seemed a "fantastic exaggeration" to those who covered the team—they figured there were closer to 1,000 fans in attendance—but it was enough to boost the season total to 1,000,761.[76]

The million mark may have been a matter of pride, but the ticket sales were a major source of revenue. Finley didn't want Monday's game to be called. Twenty-three minutes before its scheduled start, AL president Joe Cronin, who had toured the field twice, decided it was too waterlogged to play and postponed the game.[77]

Finley confronted Cronin in the tunnel outside of the A's clubhouse door. Several reporters, a few A's players, and Dick Williams stood by.

"Why didn't you consult me?" Finley said.[78]

"It was my decision to make," Cronin said.

"I think your decision to call it off a half hour before game time was very premature," Finley said.

"I want the fans to see a full game," Cronin said.

"A lot of these people are off work on Columbus Day and might not be able to come back tomorrow," Finley said. His voice rose.

"How can you expect to play a game under these conditions?" Cronin said. He turned to walk away.

"You sanctimonious little shit!" Finley yelled.

Cronin stopped. "Let's not yell about this," he said angrily. "Let's not discuss it in public."

"I don't give a damn what you think," Finley said. He walked away angrily. This wasn't good for his heart.

The rain continued the rest of the day.[79]

The two teams played game three of the pennant playoff on Tuesday, October 9. The sun shone brightly on an announced crowd of 34,367 and lots of empty seats. The A's Ken Holtzman engaged the Orioles' Mike Cuellar in a pitching duel. In the first inning, Billy Conigliaro, who had replaced Mangual in center field, made a diving catch on a sinking liner to save a run. But Billy C. could do nothing to stop a solo home run by Orioles catcher Earl Williams in the second inning. Cuellar protected the 1–0 lead with a no-hitter going into the eighth inning, which Finley spoiled with his cunning.

Jesus Alou, one of Finley's firesale acquisitions, pinch hit a single. Mike Andrews, the second baseman who supposedly couldn't throw anymore—another late Finley acquisition—pinch hit and laid down a sacrifice bunt to advance the runner. Ted Kubiak would replace Andrews when the A's took the field. Meanwhile, regular Joe Rudi hit a two-out single to left field to score the runner from second and even the score.

The game remained tied until the bottom of the 11th. Holtzman and Cuellar had each only given up three hits and one run. Bert Campaneris led off the A's half of the frame. He was not a home run hitter. The 5-foot, 10-inch shortstop had hit only four home runs all season long in more than 600 at bats. But he was a clutch hitter. He knocked a Cuellar pitch over the left-field fence to win the game, 2–1.

Dick Williams was so delighted to see Campy hit his second homer in two games that he turned to Holtzman next to him in the dugout and kissed the pitcher.[80] The A's were one win away from returning to the World Series.

An announced crowd of 27,497 fans—a healthy but not highly profitable gate for Finley—watched Jim Palmer and Vida Blue duel for the fourth game on Wednesday, October 10. This time, the A's pounced on Palmer early. They scored three runs and chased the Orioles ace from the game in the second inning. They scored another run in the sixth. Meanwhile, Vida Blue seemed to be cruising along the road to redemption, giving up only two hits through six innings to protect the A's 4–0 lead.

Tommy Davis, the Baltimore designated hitter, led off the seventh inning with a fly ball to right field that Reggie Jackson snared for the first out. An A's victory was starting to look routine. But then Blue stumbled.

He walked the next batter, Earl Williams, then gave up a pair of singles that brought Williams home. The tally spoiled Blue's shutout, but that was okay. He got paid the same for the win no matter what the score. The A's still led by three runs. Andy Etchebarren, a backup catcher with a .235 career average, came to bat with one out and two runners on. The scouting report the players read on their flight to Baltimore noted Etchebarren had hit only two home runs all year in his 152 at bats. No problem, Blue must have thought.

Until he watched the backup catcher slug his first pitch over the left-field wall for a three-run homer that suddenly tied the game, 4–4. Dick Williams replaced Blue with reliever Rollie Fingers. Once again, Williams's hottest pitcher had failed to win a big game for the team.

While the Metsomaniacs trashed Shea Stadium in their victory revelry, the Oakland fans had their gratification delayed. Etchebarren's homer postponed what had seemed a certain pennant celebration. When Rollie Fingers served up a solo home run to Baltimore second baseman Bobby Grich in the eighth and the A's failed to make up the difference, the Oakland fans filed out of the Coliseum with disappointment. The Orioles had stolen a 5–4 win and evened the pennant playoff.

Charlie Finley, who would've gladly risked a rapid pulse to celebrate a return to the World Series, exited the stadium with his cardiologist and bodyguard. He left without talking to the team.[81]

Rollie Fingers may have lost the game, but Vida Blue had blown it. Dispirited, the relief pitcher walked into the clubhouse past the unopened crates of champagne. Passing Blue Moon Odom's stall, Fingers muttered to himself, "We had them by the nostrils, and we let them get away from us."[82]

The way Odom heard it, Fingers was blaming Blue, Odom's friend. He jumped at Fingers. "You shouldn't be talking," Odom said. "If you don't give up that homer, we don't lose the game."[83]

Fingers confronted Odom. The two pitchers shouted at one another. Before the shouts escalated to punches, Reggie Jackson broke in. He managed to talk them down.[84]

Jackson also tried to cheer Blue. "You're my man," Reggie told the pitcher. "You're still my man." But the words didn't register.

Blue undressed silently, his anger turned inward.[85]

The press wanted to know if the fight would defeat or ignite the team. "The pressure can't be much higher," Reggie said. "There's only one game left, and that's it. But when the pressure is on, this team is unstoppable."[86]

Big words from a man who had responded to the playoff pressure so far with only two singles in 17 at bats for a measly .118 average. Reggie had driven in no runs, and he had struck out six times. His leg may have been fine, but his bat had gone limp. This was not the way to the big stage.

Thursday afternoon, October 11, fewer than 25,000 fans—actually, 24,265 by Finley's count—passed through the Oakland Coliseum turnstiles. That was the smallest crowd in the five-year history of the major league pennant playoffs. Here it was, the deciding game in the AL pennant playoff, and the A's couldn't draw half of the fans they had in Baltimore. Finley made it into the record books for his ability to keep fans away.

The A's scored one run in the third inning on an error, a sacrifice bunt, and a Joe Rudi single. They scored two more on a three-hit rally in the fourth. Jim Palmer, who had finished his start quickly the day before, came on in relief. He blanked the A's the rest of the way.

Meanwhile, Catfish Hunter had pitched a four-hit shutout going into the ninth. He needed only three outs to convert the A's 3–0 lead into a return trip to the World Series. The smell of victory had resuscitated the Oakland fans. They bunched on top of the outfield walls. A section of the wall collapsed under their weight. The umpires, fearing a repeat of the Shea Stadium pandemonium, chased the fans from the edges of the walls. The grounds crew hurriedly repaired the wall.[87]

Earl Williams led off the Orioles ninth with a ground ball to short. Campaneris scooped it up and threw to Gene Tenace at first. One away.

The excited fans pushed open a gate in the outfield. The umpires called time. Vic Davalillo, the A's center fielder du jour, ran over to shut the gate. Hunter waited patiently on the mound.

All at once, the moment struck Reggie Jackson in right field. "I suddenly realized we were going to be the American League champions," he said later. "My heart started pounding. I got terribly nervous. All I wanted was for someone to hit me the ball."[88]

Paul Blair, the Orioles' All-Star center fielder, grounded out to third, Bando to Tenace. Two away.

Brooks Robinson batted. *Hit it to me*, Reggie thought, *hit it to me*. He wanted to make the final out. His heart raced.

Robinson hit the ball to Reggie, but it wasn't one he could catch. By the time Reggie returned the ball to the infield, Robinson was at second with a double.

The fans in the outfield bleachers danced with urgent anticipation. *C'mon, Catfish. One more out. C'mon!*

Bobby Grich, yesterday's home run hero, batted. *Hit it to me*, Reggie thought. *Something I can catch.*

Grich grounded to Campaneris. He threw to Tenace. Three away.

Reggie was headed to the World Series! This time he would get to play. His dream was unfolding. As the fans danced onto the field—more of a light and happy West Coast two-step than the violent East Coast slam dance—Reggie wanted to be part of them. "I felt so great, all I wanted to do was be a fan, run wild out there with all those other people and scream and yell."[89]

Instead, Jackson ran to the clubhouse to celebrate with his mates. They broke the champagne out of the crates and sprayed it jubilantly. Finley was there, his doctors be damned. He pushed through the reporters crowding Hunter and hugged the winning pitcher. Hunter looked embarrassed, like an eighth-grader kissed by his mom.[90]

A reporter asked one player if the A's could beat the amazing Mets. The player nodded toward Finley. "It's him we have to beat, not them. He's our obstacle. He's our handicap, the burden we have to bear. The Mets are easy. Charlie's something else. You have to wonder what the hell he'll do next."[91]

At that moment, the player didn't know how true his

statement was. Finley would outdo himself at the Series, ignominiously grabbing the spotlight, antagonizing his team, angering his manager beyond the point of no return, and nearly costing his team a game.

But none of that had happened yet. At this point, the A's had just captured the AL flag, punched their ticket to the World Series, and made Reggie Jackson's dream come true. That made Reggie one happy man. He walked around the clubhouse and sprayed champagne. "Fabulous, fabulous," he said. "This is what life's all about—playing under pressure and producing. Winning when you have to win."[92]

He must have been speaking about his teammates, not himself, because the 1973 AL MVP finished the five-game pennant playoff with three singles in 21 at bats, good for a .143 average. He hadn't figured in any of the A's runs—neither scoring nor knocking in a single one. His teammates had won when they had to win, but Reggie, in fact, had not produced under the pressure. The Fall Classic would be an even bigger test of his aspiration for greatness. Nowhere was the pressure greater than in the World Series.

In Game Two of the World Series, **Willie Mays** argues with home plate umpire **Augie Donatelli** that Oakland catcher **Ray Fosse** missed the tag on **Buddy Harrelson**. Mays had a better vantage point than Donatelli of the play. Fosse wisely walks away. Later, he claimed he tagged Harrelson on the jersey.

Chapter Seventeen

A CLASSIC FALL CLASSIC

The seventieth edition of the Fall Classic witnessed a changing of the superstar guard. Willie Mays played his fourth and final World Series; Reggie Jackson played the first of his five. Reggie was five years old, a kindergartner, when Willie played in his first Series as a midseason call-up for the 1951 New York Giants. Willie would be fifty years old when Reggie, by then the legendary Mr. October, played in his last. A full thirty years spanned their World Series glories, but the fulcrum, when Willie bowed out and Reggie jumped in, was the 1973 World Series.

Mays hadn't played in the World Series since 1962, when the San Francisco Giants lost to the New York Yankees in seven games. He was delighted to be back. "I came in with a winner, and I'm going out with a winner," he said.[1] Even though Mays had announced his retirement, he was willing to extend his goodbye.

Reggie was so excited to have finally realized his World Series dream that he got arrested celebrating the night after the A's captured the AL pennant. Accounts varied on how he wound up behind bars. Recurring details included lips loosened by liquor and impolite remarks Reggie had directed at the Bay Area blue. In an act more self-serving than benevolent, Charlie Finley bailed out his superstar.[2] The press hushed up the incident, but it foretold the days when sports pages would read like police blotters. Willie Mays may have liked to party as much as the next ballplayer, but he never required an owner to post bond for him.

Willie and Reggie both started the World Series in the same unlikely spot: center field. For Willie, who once owned that position, it was unusual because he had not started a game in over a month, and he had not played center since the game of his two strained throws in July. But Yogi needed him. Rusty Staub, who had separated his shoulder in the fourth game of the pennant playoff when he ran into the outfield wall, could not play. Berra put Don Hahn in right field and Willie in center. Playing the percentages, Yogi liked the two right-handed batters' chances against the A's left-handed starter, Ken Holtzman.

Reggie hadn't played center field all season, but the haphazard play there of backups to the injured Billy North forced Dick Williams to move Reggie to center and try Jesus Alou in right. Reggie felt the pressure of his new position, where the extra territory to cover would truly test the health of his legs, and of his playoff slump, having batted only .143 against Cincinnati. If ever a player felt the need to prove himself, Reggie did that October in Oakland.

Reggie also felt the pressure Hank Aaron had lived with every day that season: a threat on his life.

In late September, Finley had urgently summoned Jackson to his office. When Reggie arrived, three FBI agents showed him a letter that threatened his life if he played in the American League playoffs or World Series. Reggie had survived the playoffs, but he didn't know what might happen in this, an even bigger series. The letter writer, who signed his missive, "The Weatherman," said he would have a high-powered rifle with a long-range sight trained on Jackson and shoot him from the stands. The FBI assigned agents to protect Jackson.[3]

The year before, when someone had threatened Gene Tenace, Reggie had comforted him, "Well, if you gotta go, Gene, at least it's on national television."[4] Typical Reggie, thinking first of the image.

This time, though, Reggie wasn't joking. He hired his own personal bodyguard, a 6-foot, 5-inch, 290-pound street fighter named Tony Del Rio.[5]

Reggie would know his share of pressure in the Series.

The Mets and A's had never played before, not even in spring training. The Mets might have the emotional edge, coming off their miraculous division and league wins, but the A's outmatched them in talent, runs scored, and games won. The Mets had the lowest winning percentage of any team ever to play in a World Series. They had only the ninth-best record among the twenty-four major league teams in 1973. But the A's weren't a dominant team. They played just well enough to win, often by only one run. The defending champions were 13–10 favorites, but, as the Mets had shown during the last six weeks, anything could happen when they played baseball.

The A's had the home field advantage, where the large green and gold 1972 champion flag flew. The Series opened in Oakland on Saturday, October 13. Hank Aaron became the first active player to throw out the ceremonial first pitch. Jim Nabors, a.k.a. Gomer Pyle, the goofy private with the golden voice, sang the national anthem from the pitcher's mound.

During the player introductions, the 46,021 fans at the sun-drenched Oakland Coliseum cheered louder for the visiting team's center fielder than they did for their own. They knew this was the final stop on his farewell tour, and they wanted to thank him for the memories, many of which he generated just across the Bay. Mays tipped his lucky hat. The crowd cheered steadily for several minutes.[6]

The A's introductions didn't take as long—they were short a player. When Billy North sprained his ankle late in the season, Finley did not replace him with an outfielder. He had already added reserve outfielders Jesus Alou and Vic Davalillo after the All-Star break. Instead, Charlie replaced North with Manny Trillo, a second baseman. He apparently was not as confident in his other late addition, second baseman Mike Andrews. Finley had picked up Trillo in September. A player added to the roster after September 1 could play in the postseason only if opponents gave permission. That was usually granted routinely when reserves were added to replace injured players. The Orioles had approved Trillo on the A's roster. The Mets hadn't.[7]

Since second base had been the A's Achilles' heel all season, Finley had wanted Trillo on the roster as a balm. Trillo had played 16 games at second in September and scored as a pinch runner in the pennant playoff. An hour before the start of Game One, Finley again petitioned Mets general manager Bob Scheffing to let him use Trillo. Scheffing said no.[8] That left the A's a player short and vulnerable at second.

Finley was pissed. He had the public address announcer tell the Coliseum crowd, "Scratch Manny Trillo from the A's lineup because the Mets have refused to approve him as a replacement for the injured Billy North."[9] The Oakland crowd booed. Charlie was a guy who knew how to play a grudge.

Willie Mays, batting third in the Mets order, walked to the plate in the top half of the first inning. Once again, the Oakland crowd stood and applauded. Mays rapped a sharp grounder between third and short for a single, the first hit of the game. Mays didn't score, but he did give the fans a charge. Maybe this was the Willie who had shown up for the World Series, the one who could charm a crowd with his amazing talents.

The A's pitcher, Ken Holtzman, batted in the third inning. It would be another three years before the National League allowed designated hitters to be used in the World Series, much to the chagrin of those won over by the experiment. "The biggest waste of time in the World Series will be to allow American League pitchers to poke about the rack, selecting a bat," wrote *Sporting News* columnist Melvin Durslag, anticipating the worst. "They may as well send them to the plate with bare fists and hope for a walk."[10]

Holtzman had batted only once all season (and walked), but he and the other A's pitchers had started taking batting practice seriously about two weeks before the playoffs began.[11] He guessed fastball on a three-two pitch and guessed right. Holtzman lined a two-out double into left field that sparked a two-run rally. The unlikeliest of heroes—an AL pitcher at bat—had given the A's a 2–0 lead.

With Joe Rudi on first, Sal Bando rapped a single to center field. Mays advanced on the ground ball, but was unable to field it cleanly. The ball struck him in the chest. Rudi advanced to third on Mays's error. This wasn't the Willie the crowd had cheered.

Reggie Jackson came to the plate with Rudi on third and Bando on first, two out. He had the chance to bust open the game. Instead, Jackson hit a popup beyond the left field foul line that shortstop Buddy Harrelson caught to squash the rally.

The Mets came right back with a run in the fourth. With a runner on second, catcher Jerry Grote hit a drive to deep center field. Reggie turned and sprinted toward the wall. He snagged the ball on the fly—a catch the scribes called "stunning"[12] and "dazzling."[13] Reggie explained after the game how he made it, "No short cuts, no science, no guessing. My only chance was to outrun the ball."[14]

The catch saved one run, easy, maybe two. Holtzman pitched out of the jam, and the A's escaped the inning with a 2–1 lead. The Mets threatened again in the next inning, but, with the tying run ninety feet away on third, Willie flew out to right field and ended the inning. In the eighth, Mays faced Rollie Fingers, who had relieved Holtzman in the sixth inning. In what the media speculated might be the last at bat of his career, Willie struck out looking.

Meanwhile, Jon Matlack pitched well for the Mets, yielding only three hits in six innings, before he was lifted for a pinch hitter. Both A's runs had resulted from errors and been unearned. Matlack had finished the season 14–16, and some criticized Yogi for starting him in Game One. It was only the fourth time that a losing pitcher had started a World Series opener.[15] Tug McGraw shut out the A's the last two innings, but the Mets could not score any more runs for him, allowing the A's to squeak out a 2–1 win.

Reggie had made the dazzling catch, but his postseason batting slump continued. He was oh-for-three with a walk. Twice, he made the final out of the inning with runners on base. "I just hope we win this thing so I won't be the scapegoat," Reggie said.[16]

A rumor started that Dick Williams was interested in the Yankees job, which opened up when Ralph Houk resigned as manager on the last day of the regular season. Some suspected that Williams had been talking secretly with the Yankees.[17] Could be something to it. Williams had confided in Reggie and others that he was fed up with Finley's obsessive meddling. Williams brushed off the idea. "I'm happy where I am," he said. "To tell you the truth, I haven't thought about anything lately except the playoffs and World Series."[18]

Happy where I am? The denial didn't ring true. That only fueled the rumor.

Sunday broke beautiful. The October air carried a slight chill, which prompted some players to wear long sleeve T-shirts under their uniforms, but the Indian-summer sun shone warm and bright across the green grass at Oakland Coliseum. The A's looked radiant in their wedding whites—the white top with the green and gold A emblazoned on the left breast and the white pants with the green and gold stripe—that Finley had them wear on Sundays. A whopping—by Oakland standards—49,121 fans drove out to the ballpark to take in Game Two, one of the greatest World Series games ever played.

Many brought signs painted on white bed sheets that carried over the affection from the previous day: "We Love Willie Mays" and "The aMAYSing Mets." But Rusty Staub took three cortisone shots in his shoulder and resolved to play,[19] so Yogi moved Don Hahn back to center field and benched Willie. On the other side, Reggie returned to center field for Oakland.

Vida Blue took the hill for the A's and looked like he had brought his A game, promptly striking out the first two batters. Staub, batting third, grounded out meekly to short. In the A's half, Joe Rudi lofted a fly ball to deep left field. Cleon Jones, the Mets left fielder, backed up to the wall, head upturned, sunlight flickering off his sunglasses, but he could not track the ball in the bright sun. He flinched, the ball dropped, and Rudi stood at second with a double. Sal Bando tripled to the gap in right-center, and Rudi scored. Reggie swung big and struck out. Two down. Gene Tenace walked. Jesus Alou came to the plate. What would Jesus do? He doubled to score Bando and give the A's a 2–0 lead. Jerry Koosman, the Mets starter, walked Ray Fosse intentionally. That brought Dick Green to the plate with the bases loaded.

The A's valued Green more for his glove than his bat. "Green is the Brooks Robinson of second basemen," Reggie Jackson said. "He holds our defense together, and you win with defense as much as you do with offense."[20]

Throughout the season, Dick Williams had started Green at second but usually pinch hit for him later in the game. Sunday, Green had the chance to boost the A's lead. A's broadcaster Monte Moore reminded the millions of NBC-TV viewers that Green had hit four grand slams already in his eleven-year career with the Athletics.[21] But Green struck out to end the inning.

Cleon Jones clubbed a homer to lead off the second inning, the A's countered with a run in their half, and Wayne Garrett touched Blue for another solo homer in the top of the third. A's led 3–2 going into their half of the third. Reggie grounded out to short, extending his seven-game postseason slump to 3-for-26, an anemic .115 average. The A's loaded the bases on a walk, a single, and a throwing error, which brought Dick Green to bat for the second time with the chance to inflate the A's lead.

Dick Williams called for a suicide squeeze. Gene Tenace took off from third with the pitch. The ball broke away from Green. He poked his bat at it but missed. Tenace was picked off in a rundown for the second out. Green watched the next pitch go by for a called third strike. Once again, the A's rally had fizzled with his bat.

In the top of the sixth, Blue's A game vanished, and Williams replaced his starting pitcher after he let two runners reach base. The Mets batted around the order and scored four runs on three singles, a walk, a hit batter, and the pitcher's throwing error. Having survived Dick Green's two bases-loaded at bats, they suddenly led 6–3.

The A's rallied in the bottom of the seventh, and Reggie came to bat with two on and two out. He had singled in the fifth, ending his hitless streak, but still had not contributed a run. Jackson faced Tug McGraw, who had come on in the sixth, the third Mets reliever. Reggie jumped on McGraw's first pitch and cracked a base hit to right field that scored a run, cutting the Mets lead to 6–4. Rusty Staub fielded the hit in right, but with his separated throwing shoulder, he could only flip the ball underhand back to the infield. Reggie dived head first into second with a double, his slump officially ended.

The score remained 6–4, Mets leading, into the top of the ninth. The late afternoon sun dipped in the sky, and the grand-stand shadow edged toward home plate. Rusty Staub led off with a single to right field. Yogi sent in Willie Mays to pinch run for Staub. The sellout Oakland crowd appreciated the opportunity to see Willie one more time. They applauded him as he trotted out of the dugout to first base.

Cleon Jones hit a foul pop that Gene Tenace caught for the first out. John Milner punched a single to right field, and Willie took off for second. Perhaps distracted by the ball going through, Willie neared second base off stride. Jesus Alou juggled the ball in right, giving Mays time to break for third, but Willie tried to correct his footing, stumbled, and fell to the ground rounding the bag. His hat, which used to fly off his head when he rounded the bases, stayed put—lucky no longer. "Here's an unusual thing, one of baseball's all-time greatest runners had an easy shot going first to third," Tony Kubek observed on the NBC-TV broadcast. "And Willie fell down."[22]

The shadows on the field slunk past home plate. The Mets rally died, and the A's batted in the bottom of the ninth, trailing by two runs.

Mays initially jogged out to right field, where a "We Love Willie Mays" banner hung over the railing, but then he switched places with Don Hahn in center field, his natural position once upon a time. Deron Johnson, the A's regular designated hitter, pinch hit for the pitcher to lead off. He lofted a ball out to center field. Willie ran to his right, tried to adjust his angle, but stumbled. He pitched toward the ball and stretched out his hands, glove upturned with hope, but the ball fell several feet out of his reach. Willie landed on his face.

The man—no, the legend—who had made the most famous catch in World Series history had just made the most famous flop. He lifted himself to one knee but could only watch while Cleon Jones scurried to the rescue from left field and threw the ball back to the infield, where Johnson stood on second with a double. "Boy, Curt, this is the thing I think all sports fans in all areas hate to see— a great one playing in his last years having this kind of trouble, standing up and falling down," Tony Kubek remarked to his NBC broadcast partner, Curt Gowdy.[23]

The TV cameras caught Yogi Berra in the dugout, his hand to his chin, his eyes cast down, his expression worried. Here his team had a two-run lead in the bottom of the ninth in a must-win game to tie the Series. They needed only three outs to put away the A's, but his legend-cum-liability center fielder had just muffed one, which brought the tying run to the plate.

McGraw struck out that run in the person of Bert Campaneris and induced the next batter, Joe Rudi, to ground out, third to first. Had Mays made the catch on the leadoff batter, McGraw would have been done, able to come off the mound slapping his glove on his thigh, headed to New York with the series even at a game apiece. Instead, he still needed one more out.

McGraw crept within one strike of that final out, but then, oops, his three-two pitch to Sal Bando missed, and the tying run was on base. McGraw shook his head slightly. *Damn.* But his team still led by two.

Reggie batted. Two out, two on, bottom of the ninth. The world watched. The pressure mounted. This was his hero or goat moment.

Reggie snaked a ground ball between the first and second basemen. One run scored, and the tying run moved to third, almost home. Pressure? Bring it on. That fueled Reggie's October heroics. His single was his third hit in a row. The Oakland fans waved their pennants—a flutter of green and gold and white—and blasted a scattering of air horns.

Gene Tenace followed with a single that drove in the tying run. The A's stayed alive and pushed the game into extra innings.

The shadows on the field slid to the mound, where Rollie Fingers started the tenth. Mets shortstop Buddy Harrelson nicked the A's star reliever for a leadoff single to center field. Tug McGraw bunted the ball back to Fingers, who threw to second, but Harrelson had jumped early, and he beat the throw. Mike Andrews, the A's third second baseman of the day, pivoted cleanly and relayed to first to catch McGraw. One out, runner on second. The next batter, Wayne Garrett, reached when Fingers ran to first to cover on a ground ball hit to Tenace, but the pitcher did not set up properly and, as he caught Tenace's throw, his momentum carried him off the bag. Garrett was safe, and Harrelson moved to third.

This wasn't good for Charlie Finley's heart. He watched with disappointment and frustration from his box seat above the A's dugout, his bright green sport coat blazing among the crowd. His team should have been out of the inning. Instead, the go-ahead run threatened at third with only one out.

Mets second baseman Felix Millan batted, clutching his bat eight inches above the knob in his distinctive choke-up stance. Millan lofted a ball to left field. Not too deep. Harrelson tagged at the base, poised to break for home. Rudi caught the ball. Harrelson took off. Rudi threw to the plate. Ray Fosse waited.

So did ump Augie Donatelli, who lay down on his belly behind the plate, watching Harrelson come toward him, for a clean view. Willie Mays, the on-deck batter, moved in to clear Millan's bat out of the way and took a knee nearly in the batter's box to the left of the plate, his eyes following the runner and the ball.

Rudi's throw bounced once and beat the runner, but it hopped to Fosse's left. The catcher stabbed the ball. Harrelson, coming straight down the line, swerved to Fosse's right. Fosse swung his glove across his body at Harrelson, who crossed the plate standing up.

Out! Augie Donatelli called.

Willie dropped to his knees in front of Donatelli's face. He smacked the ground with his palm and shouted at the ump. *No way! He didn't touch him!* [24]

Donatelli stood up. He had not been in the best position to see whether or not Fosse's glove had tagged Harrelson. Willie had perhaps the best view in the stadium. The television cameras from two angles seemed to confirm what he believed: Harrelson had slipped by the tag. Willie, still on his knees, raised his hands in the air in dramatic protest. *No way!*

Yogi rushed out of the dugout to protest. Other Mets players and coaches rushed over. Several umps rushed to Donatelli's defense.

Fosse, wisely, stepped aside. He thought he had caught Harrelson on the blouse of his uniform.[25] The Mets, of course, saw it differently.

Harrelson insisted that Fosse hadn't tagged him.[26] "I'm not going to pay for your incompetence," Harrelson shouted at Donatelli.[27]

Berra hopped around angrily. "Where did he touch him?" Yogi demanded. "Where did he touch him?"

Donatelli patted Yogi's backside. "Right here," the ump said. "On the ass."[28]

Berra and the Mets were not appeased, but the call stood. Instead of being up a run with a runner at second and Mays at bat, they took the field for the bottom of the tenth with the game still tied.

Mike Andrews batted with one out. The A's second baseman had entered the game in the eighth, pinch hitting for Ted Kubiak. In the revolving door approach Williams took to second base, he had sent Kubiak to second after sending up a pinch hitter for Dick Green, whose bat Williams didn't trust after his two bases-loaded strikeouts. But Green didn't like Kubiak's bat either, so he pinch hit for him and sent Andrews out to the field. In nine games at second for the A's, Andrews had made one error. Williams had said in August, after watching Andrews's troubled throws, that he would not play Andrews again at second, but without Manny Trillo as an option, Williams had no other choice.

"Mike Andrews was on Dick Williams's 1967 Boston Red Sox miracle championship team in the American League," Tony Kubek commented during Andrews's tenth-inning at bat.

"He did a good job that year for the Red Sox, especially with the bat," Curt Gowdy responded. "A manager never forgets a player who does a good job. He really has confidence in him."[29]

Andrews checked his swing on a three-two pitch, but Donatelli called, Strike three!

Rollie Fingers lifted a fly to short center field. Mays ran in, lost the ball briefly in the sharp sun, hitched his stride for an instant, but then caught the ball for the third out.

Mays led off the 11th. Here was a chance for redemption after his stumbles in the field and on the base path. He swung big at a two-oh pitch, trying to jack one out of the park for a legitimate heroic blow. Willie had hit more extra-inning home runs than anyone in history. He wanted one more to boost his record total to 23. But Willie's bat caught only a piece of the ball and fouled it back. On his next cut, he clipped the bottom of the ball and popped it up to the right of the mound. Tenace caught it and deferred Mays's redemption.

The Mets put two runners on but failed to score. In the bottom half, McGraw set down the A's in order. The game remained tied 6–6.

Mays batted again in the top of the twelfth. There were two out, runners at first and third. Redemption was once again within reach.

The shadows reached out to second base. The sun slanted across the field.

"I can't see, man," Mays said to Fosse.

The catcher called for a fastball. That was by the book on Mays: pitch fast to the old man, he can't get around on the ball. Besides, Fingers threw mostly fastballs anyway.[30] If Mays was having trouble seeing, Fingers could blow one by him now.

Willie's cap poked out of his back pocket. He took several quick chomps on his gum, then tucked it into his cheek. He cocked his bat, hands back, and waited for the fastball.

Fingers delivered. Willie swung. His bat connected for a ground ball that skipped over the pitcher's head into center field. Fingers flung his glove into the air in frustration. Mays stumbled out of the batter's box. He broke his fall with his hands and right knee. His helmet bobbled off. He pushed himself up and rushed to first. His clumsy single had scored Harrelson from third—this time without question—and given his team a 7–6 lead. Standing at first, Willie rubbed his sore right knee. He suffered even in his redemption.

Cleon Jones singled to move Tug McGraw to third and Mays to second. Paul Lindblad relieved Fingers with the bases loaded. He needed one out to escape the inning. He seemed to get it when the next batter, John Milner, hit a routine ground ball to second base. Well, routine if hit to any second baseman other than Mike Andrews, whose erratic play made every ball hit to him a gamble.

The ball bounced toward Mike Andrews. He figured the ball was either going to stay low or bounce up.[31] He adjusted his glove to collect the ball on the hop—but it glanced off the tip and rolled between his legs into right field. E-4. McGraw scored. Mays scored. The Mets led 9–6.

Finley fumed. Although he was a rookie, Trillo was an excellent fielder. He would go on to play seventeen seasons and win three Gold Gloves at second base. Finley couldn't help but think, *If Trillo had been out there, that wouldn't have happened. The inning would be over, and the A's would need only one run in their half to tie the game. Damn the Mets!*

The next batter, Jerry Grote, hit another ground ball to second. Still shaken by the one that scooted through his legs, Andrews hurried in to his right, snared the ball, and side-armed a throw on the run to first. Wide. The throw pulled Tenace off the bag. Grote was safe. Another E-4, another Mets run, and the A's trailed 10–6.

By then, the A's had committed five errors, but only the last two would remain stained in people's memory. Andrews stared at the ground, his face hidden by the bill of his cap. He couldn't look at his teammates. His glove pressed to his hip, his shoulders slumped. He looked like he wanted to disappear.

Finley reached for the phone he had stashed in his private box.[32] He summoned Harry Walker, MD, the team physician, from the stands and into the A's clubhouse.[33]

When the next batter grounded out to third to finish the Mets' rally, Andrews walked sadly off the field. He sat alone on the bench, smothered his face with a towel and wept. His teammates did not look at him.[34]

Reggie Jackson led off the A's half of the twelfth. By now, his bat was hot. He smashed a drive to deep center. Willie ran back to the wall and followed it along the warning track. Head uplifted, his eyes groped the bright sky for the ball. They didn't find it. The ball bounced in front of him, out of reach. His spikes caught the dirt and he stutter-stepped. Once again, he could only watch Cleon Jones collect the ball and heave it back to the infield. Reggie pulled into third with a triple. Twice now, the old man in center had been unable to bring in the young buck's drives.

McGraw walked Tenace, and George Stone replaced him, becoming the 11th pitcher of the day, which tied a World Series record. Stone gave up a single to Jesus Alou, which scored Jackson. Vic Davalillo pinch hit for the pitcher, becoming the thirty-eighth player in the game, the most ever to play in a World Series game. The A's managed to load the bases, but they didn't score again. The 12-inning game lasted four hours and thirteen minutes, the longest postseason game in the Series' seventy-year history. The Mets had evened the series with a marathon 10–7 victory.

A dejected Mike Andrews answered reporters' questions in the clubhouse. "I plain kicked things around," he told them. "I'm the goat, and I'm sorry as hell about it."[35]

"Injured?" he responded to another question. "No, my shoulder bothered me last year, but it's been fine this year."[36]

Somebody told Andrews the doctor wanted to see him in the trainer's room. He walked in looking confused and saying, "There's nothing wrong with me." Dr. Walker, whom Finley had summoned out of the stands, examined Andrews's throwing arm and shoulder. Then, Andrews was told to report to the manager's office. Charlie Finley and Dick Williams waited for him there.[37]

Finley told Andrews he wanted to put him on the disabled list, based on the doctor's report that his shoulder injury prevented him from playing. That would allow the A's to subvert the Mets and finally add Manny Trillo to the roster. The rules allowed a substitution for a player injured in the Series without requiring the opposing team's permission. Finley told Andrews he could "help the club," by letting Trillo substitute for him.

"You want me to lie?" Andrews asked.

"No," Finley said.

"How else can you explain it to me?"

"You want to help the ball club?"

"Yes, but not this way," Andrews said.[38]

Williams watched silently. The exchange pained him. He liked Andrews. He couldn't stand watching Finley bully him.[39]

Perhaps, too, Williams felt guilty for setting up Andrews for failure. He could have left Kubiak in the game. Or Green. *Sports Illustrated* writer William Leggett blamed Williams for having Andrews at second for the last four innings of the game. "By tinkering with his second basemen—a well-documented Williams obsession—he ended up with the wrong man in the wrong place at exactly the wrong time," Leggett wrote.[40]

Finley wouldn't let up. After thirty-five minutes of getting nowhere with Andrews, he told him, "I have a statement from the doctor upstairs in my office. At least go up and read it."[41]

Andrews read the statement, already signed by Dr. Harry Walker: "Mike Andrews has a history of chronic shoulder disability. He attempted to play but was unable physically to play his position because of a biceps groove tenosynovitis of the right shoulder. It is my opinion he is disabled for the rest of the year."[42]

Andrews didn't want to sign what he considered a lie. Finley badgered Andrews for another half an hour to sign the doctor's statement. Andrews resisted. Finley threatened to destroy the thirty-year-old's baseball career. Andrews felt sick to his stomach. He couldn't believe this was happening to him.[43] "Okay, fine, don't sign it," Finley finally said. "I'll get it through without you."[44] Finley told his secretary to send out copies of the statement anyway, without Andrews's signature.[45]

What do I do now? Andrews thought. *I'm dead anyhow. Maybe Trillo can help the team.* "Give me the damn thing," he said. "I'll sign it."[46]

He wrote his name next to the line that said, "I agree to the above."[47]

Andrews wasn't on the team bus to the airport, and he wasn't on the flight to New York. While the team headed to Shea for the next three games, the A's ex-second baseman headed home to

Peabody, Massachusetts. The players talked about what had happened to their teammate and pieced together how Finley had forced him out. They were shocked—"I've never heard of firing a player in the middle of the World Series," Reggie said.[48] They were scared—"It could have been any of us," Reggie said.[49] And they were angry. "That's the way Charlie treats people," Reggie said. "There are times I feel he's a good old guy who's just eccentric, and then times when I feel he's a miserable man, or is corrupted by his power."[50] By the time the plane landed, the remaining players had plotted a revolt.

Reggie, the team's player representative, planned to file a grievance with the Players Association, and the team discussed the possibility of striking unless Finley brought back Andrews.[51]

They worked out at Shea Stadium the next day with Andrews's number, 17, taped to their shoulders.[52] Even Manny Trillo, who worked out in uniform in anticipation of Finley's plan being approved, wore Andrews's number taped to his left shoulder. The players' impudence infuriated the owner. "He went absolutely berserk when he saw that," Ray Fosse said.[53]

Reggie, the team rep and Most Valuable Quote, unloaded on Finley. "This thing is a real embarrassment and a disappointment," Reggie told the national and local press gathered at Shea on Monday. "A team is a team. Finley doesn't seem to understand that. The other players won't stand for it. We won't just take it and shut up.

"This team has endured a lot of incidents from Finley, but this may be the last straw. I've never seen the mood of a team so mean. We're near to mutiny. Some of the guys want to follow Mike and walk right out of this World Series. I've got a moral obligation to telephone Marvin Miller, the players' counsel, and report to him on this. Thank God, it's a guy like me. Suppose a fringe player had to make the phone call? He'd be shipped so far you couldn't find him in the back pages of *The Sporting News*."[54]

The commissioner didn't like what was happening. Bowie Kuhn asked Andrews and Dr. Walker for their versions of what happened, then denied Finley's request to substitute Trillo for Andrews. Yes, the rules allowed a team to substitute a player for one injured during the World Series, but, Kuhn pointed out, Andrews had not been injured during the Series. Whatever his arm troubles, they had existed when Finley signed him. The commissioner denounced Finley in a public letter to the Oakland club for "unfairly embarrassing a player who has given many years of able service to professional baseball." Kuhn demanded that Finley reinstate Andrews at once.[55]

Two and a half hours before Game Three on Tuesday night, Mike Andrews phoned the A's clubhouse at Shea and asked to speak to the team rep. "The only reason I signed it," Andrews explained to Reggie Jackson, "was because he (Finley) threatened to destroy me and end my career in baseball if I didn't." Reggie encouraged Andrews to return to New York for the next night's game. He told him he was still a member of the team. "We'd love to have you back," Reggie said.[56] Andrews agreed to rejoin the team if he could tell his side of the story.[57]

The Andrews Affair, as the media called it, had taken its toll on Dick Williams. Finley had dispatched his manager to defend his dirty work. Williams had done so loyally, but it had torn him up inside. He considered Andrews, who had done a good job for him in Boston, a friend. "I hate to see him go this way," he told reporters.[58]

Worse, he hated the way Finley ran the club. Williams couldn't take it any longer.

After Andrews's phone call to the clubhouse, the manager called a closed-door team meeting. Williams told the players Finley's version of Andrews's departure. Then, he told them he disagreed with the way the owner had handled it. Finally, he dropped the bomb. "I'm going to deny this if it leaks out of this room," he told them, his voice tinged by tears, "but I'm resigning after the Series—win, lose, or draw."[59]

His announcement stunned the players. Here was Williams, who had won the last World Series and was only three games away from winning another, telling them he was going to quit. He was where every manager wanted to be—at the helm of a winner—but he was going to walk away. They figured he must be hurting awfully bad to do that.

Amidst all of the hubbub about Andrews, Finley, and now Williams, there was still a World Series to play. They would play three night games at Shea. Finley had advocated for postseason games to be played at night to draw larger crowds at the park and in front of the televisions. The TV networks had loved the idea, but critics pointed to the late start time—8:30 p.m. EST so it would catch prime time across the country's four time zones—as proof that the tail wagged the dog. "That is what the television overlords have decreed and obedient baseball serfs touch their cowlicks in total subservience," Arthur Daley chafed in his *New York Times* column.[60]

Reggie didn't like that. Oh, he didn't mind the television part. No, the added exposure was good for the image. The night part was what he objected to. He hit better in the daytime. "My only weakness is night games," Reggie wrote in his memoir, *Season with a Superstar*. "I wear glasses because I have bad eyesight. I don't see as well at night. If I played all day games I'd rip this sport apart."

He had broken out of his postseason slump with four straight power drives on Sunday—good for two singles, a double, and a triple—but he hit those in the daylight. The nighttime might mess with his hitting. Besides, those hits were for naught. His team had lost. He wanted to bust some purposeful, game-winning shots. Also, pain had stabbed his leg on the way into third on his last hit. He'd hobbled the last few steps to the bag. He told the press it was a cramp, and it had felt better during Monday's workout, but now he had that to worry about.[61] And there was still the death threat that weighed on him.[62] Reggie had a lot on his mind as the Series resumed in New York.

When Bowie Kuhn agreed to the late start for the game, he was not thinking about New York weather on October nights, which often dipped into the fifties. Tuesday night, October 16, nearly 55,000 fans braved the windy cold—wearing parkas and huddling under blankets—and the Mets had 1,000 security guards and police officers on hand to make sure they behaved.[63] The grounds crew had patched up the field from the raucous Metsomaniac pennant celebration six days earlier. Billie Jean King, Battle of the Sexes champ, threw out the first pitch.

Game Three featured the marquee pitching matchup of Tom Seaver versus Catfish Hunter. Catfish, that season's pitcher most likely to win, appeared rattled by Williams's private resignation announcement moments earlier. He watched Wayne Garrett, who had homered off Blue in Game Two, drive Hunter's second pitch into the upper deck in right field. Catfish gave up two singles and heaved a wild pitch that scored another run to put the A's down 2–0 after the first inning.

Seaver, after enjoying a week's rest for his sore shoulder, had brought his fastball. He struck out two A's in the first and three in the second. After five innings, he had rung up nine batters, including Reggie Jackson twice. In the sixth, Sal Bando doubled, Reggie struck out again, and Gene Tenace doubled to score Bando. The A's pulled within one.

Catfish had settled down and blanked the Mets for the next five innings. He left the game for a pinch hitter in the A's half of the seventh with the A's trailing 2–1. In the eighth inning, Bert Campaneris singled, stole second, then scored the tying run on Joe Rudi's single. Reggie flied out to center, and Seaver fanned Tenace for his twelfth strikeout to end the rally.

The game remained tied 2–2 through the ninth inning. When the game went into the tenth, it was the first time in forty years that two teams had played back-to-back extra-inning games in the World Series.[64] Buddy Harrelson singled with two out in the tenth, and Yogi sent Willie Mays to the plate to pinch hit.

Willie had the chance to win the game once again in extra innings. One more chance to club another extra-inning homer or contribute a meaningful base hit. Mr. Clutch had come through in the deciding game of the pennant playoff and again in Sunday's game. Could he do it once more?

Willie ended the inning with a ground ball to short.

In the top of the 11th, Tony Kubiak, who had replaced Dick Green at second base in the seventh inning, walked. Angel Mangual, who had pinch hit in the ninth and stayed in the game at center field (Reggie had started the night in right field), struck out, but Kubiak stole second when Mets catcher Jerry Grote couldn't hold onto the third strike. Kubiak scored on Campaneris's single to center field, and the A's led 3–2.

The Mets failed to score in the home half of the inning. The Metsomaniacs, subdued by the wind chill and defeat, left without incident. The A's took a 2–1 lead in the Series.

But afterward, the talk reverted to the A's circus. The players hadn't been able to keep Williams's pending resignation a secret. Good to his word, Williams denied it. And he denied the rumors he would manage the Yankees. Reggie, who had resumed his slump that night, going oh-for-five with three strikeouts, was in the mood to vent.

"He's going, and I'd like to go with him," Reggie told the press. "I've asked to be traded, but Finley has told me I'll die in the gold and green. No, I haven't talked to Finley about this. What's the point? You never get nowhere talking to that man. And I'm not going to kiss his butt.

"This is not the first thing he's done that's wrong, you know. When I had my big year in 1969, he treated me badly afterward. When Vida Blue had his big year in 1971, he treated him badly. But we were big enough to stay on our feet. Andrews is a little guy, so he got knocked out. He's not important to Finley, so Finley finishes him off.

"Finley's done a thousand wrong things to a hundred guys and we're fed up with it, but there's not much we can do about it. We're playing because we have to play. It wouldn't be fair to baseball, to the fans, or ourselves not to play. Andrews wouldn't want us not to play. But we'd like not to play. Finley takes all the fun out of winning. And we will win because we're big enough to overcome anything he can do to us."[65]

Finley shot back at his superstar: "I don't tell him how to hit home runs, and he shouldn't try to tell me how to run my team. I run it right. I'm not afraid to do what I know is right, no matter what anyone else thinks."[66]

Reggie was unrepentant. The way he saw it, "Finley had fucked us out of the best manager in baseball."[67]

And, he had taken the fun out of the Series. "Something had gone out of the games for us," Jackson reflected. "Our spirit just sagged, and what had been a joy became a job.[68] I wanted to slide and run and hit and get dirty, but the little boy in me was taken out by all the nonsense."[69]

Wednesday, before Game Four, Mike Andrews met with the commissioner then spoke with reporters at a press conference. Finally, he was able to tell his side of the story. Andrews insisted that there was nothing wrong with his shoulder and that the doctor's report was "an outright lie."[70] His voice cracked when he told the assembled reporters how Finley had bullied him while he was down to sign the bogus document to "help the club." "I'm sorry I signed it," he said. "But if I were in the same state, I'd probably do it again."[71]

Then, Mike Andrews went into the clubhouse and put on his A's uniform. No. 17 was back on the team.

Game Four proved a three-way competition for the Comeback Player of the Season award between Jon Matlack, Rusty Staub, and Mike Andrews.

The Mets starting pitcher, Matlack, had suffered a fractured skull in May when a line drive through the box struck his head. He had missed eleven days and returned to pitch wearing a hockey goalie's plastic mask across his forehead. His 14–16 season record belied his contribution—five wins—down the stretch to the Mets division title.

He had won the second game of the pennant playoff, and he had pitched extremely well in the Series opener, losing on an unearned run. Wednesday night, Matlack threw eight innings, allowed only three hits and again endured an unearned run. He had allowed only one legitimate run in his previous 40 innings and none in his last 23.

The Mets right fielder, Rusty Staub, helped Matlack's cause. Still unable to throw with the shoulder he separated in his abrupt meeting with the outfield wall in the pennant playoff, the red-haired Canadian went four-for-four in Game Four, slugging a three-run homer in the first inning and singling in two more runs in the fourth. Staub would finish the Series with six runs batted in and an impressive .423 average on 11 hits.

But Andrews proved the crowd's sentimental choice. Finley had ordered Williams to keep Andrews on the bench.[72] Down 6–1, Williams sent No. 17 in to bat for the pitcher to start the eighth inning. Williams's two-fold message was clear: "Mike, we stand with you," and "Fuck you, Charlie." The players loved it.[73] They cheered their mate from the dugout.

The 54,817 fans at Shea loved it, too, when they heard Mike Andrews announced as a pinch hitter. They rose to their feet and applauded. Even the opposition was rooting for him. "We were hoping he would get a hit," the Mets utility infielder Ted Martinez admitted afterward. "Then he could show up Finley."[74] Everybody seemed to love seeing the little guy stick it to the tyrant.

Andrews grounded out modestly, third to first. When he jogged back to the dugout, the fans stood and roared again. Reggie Jackson, also on his feet and cheering, was the first to greet Andrews with a big smile on his face when he returned to the dugout. The ovation persisted, and Andrews stepped out of the dugout to wave.[75] He'd heard applause like that for Reggie or Catfish, but never for himself. The cheers gave him chills.[76]

The crowd's response overwhelmed his teammates, too. "I couldn't believe they would treat him like that in a visiting city," Gene Tenace said. "Like he was Mickey Mantle."[77]

It warmed even the coldest of hearts on a night when temperatures dropped to forty degrees on the field. "The cheers got bigger and bigger—from everybody except Finley, his lord and master, sitting in a green jacket and hat under a blanket near the Oakland dugout," Joseph Durso reported in *The New York Times*. "But at last, Andrews's moment was complete. Finley yielded to the judgment of history, applauded tentatively, then more boldly and finally gave it a flourish by twirling a green and gold pennant around for the prodigal son."[78]

Durso described the moment as "indisputably the social highlight of the Seventieth World Series."[79] The emotional climax of the Andrews Affair almost obscured the Mets' 6–1 win to even the Series.

Jerry Koosman and Vida Blue started Game Five for a rematch of the previous Sunday's game. Koosman, who lasted less than three innings in Game Two, pitched six-and-a-third shutout innings before Tug McGraw took over in the seventh. The Mets scored one run off Blue in the second and another in the sixth that knocked him out of the game.

When McGraw entered in the seventh, the A's had two runners on base and only one out. He promptly walked Deron Johnson to load the bases. But then McGraw got Angel Mangual to pop up to short for the second out. He struck out Campaneris on a fastball over the outside corner to escape the inning. New York mayor John Lindsay stood up in his box seat and waved a banner that read, "Ya Gotta Believe!"[80]

In the ninth, still protecting the fragile 2–0 lead, McGraw watched the leadoff batter, Ray Fosse, line out to Cleon Jones in left field. Another sellout crowd of nearly 55,000 Metsomaniacs sang, "Goodbye, Charlie, we hate to see you go!"[81] McGraw fanned the last two batters and came off the mound slapping his thigh with his glove. The amazing Mets had come from behind to lead the Series, three games to two. The Metsomaniacs roared in delight but did not destroy anything. One more victory, and the Mets would complete their miraculous rise from last place to top of the world. Can you believe it?

Reggie didn't. "We've had our backs to the wall before, and we win when we have to win," Reggie told the reporters. "I thought I was a stud who wouldn't feel pressure, but I feel it now, and I'll respond to it.

"I waited too long for this to let the team or myself down. We're not gonna let the Mets beat us. We're the best. We've just been toying with them. The way we play, there ain't no way we're gonna go less than seven, but we'll win in seven."[82]

After his big game the previous Sunday in Oakland, Jackson had managed only one hit in 12 at bats during the cold nights in New York. That had not dimmed his bravado, but it had irked his teammates. "He better stop talking and start hitting," one of them said, "Or pretty soon he'll be sitting in our clubhouse all alone, talking to himself."[83]

Amidst the backdrop of signs at Oakland Coliseum that blared, "Keep A's, Trade Finley," Reggie backed up his bravado with his bat in Game Six. He laid the cornerstone to his Mr. October reputation with three big hits. He figured in all of the A's runs, knocking in a run apiece with two doubles and scoring the final one himself. The game ended Reggie 3, Mets 1. He had responded to the pressure when it was greatest and saved the A's from elimination. Just like he said he would. Reggie would not have to sit alone in the clubhouse. His teammates looked to him to deliver the goods once again in Game Seven.

The Mets, on the other hand, were left second-guessing Yogi Berra's decision to start Tom Seaver on three days rest. That had not been enough for his tired arm and sore shoulder. They thought Yogi should have given Seaver another day off. Save him for Game Seven. Game Six had not been a must-win game for the Mets. Now, Game Seven was, and they had to do it without their ace. Yogi looked to Jon Matlack, the hottest Mets pitcher of the past seven weeks, for one last stunning performance to crown the 1973 season.

"We've been doing what we weren't supposed to do all season," Yogi said. "You gotta believe."[84]

Dick Williams named Ken Holtzman his starter for Game Seven. But the talk about Williams centered on his future. The press had glommed onto the idea that he would trade in Finley's gaudy green and gold for Steinbrenner's classic pinstripes. Gabe Paul, George's right hand man in New York, denied that he had spoken with Williams about the Yankees job, but many, including Finley, suspected otherwise.[85]

The Oakland owner told reporters that the new contract he had given his manager after Reggie's midsummer tantrum still had two years left on it. "I told Dick two things: One, I'd like to keep you with me," Finley said before Game Seven. "Two, should you prefer to go to the Yankees if you're offered the Yankee job, I certainly won't stand in your way."[86] That statement would soon echo Steinbrenner's early assertion that he would stick to building ships.

Sunday morning, October 21, the nation awoke to front-page headlines about the "Saturday Night Massacre." President Nixon had fired Watergate prosecutor Archibald Cox. Attorney General Eliot Richardson and Deputy Attorney General William Ruckelshaus had resigned rather than do Nixon's bidding. Cox had refused Nixon's offer to provide a summary of the infamous White House tapes rather than answer questions about them. A week earlier, on the eve of the Series opener, the U.S. Court of Appeals had ordered Nixon to hand over the tapes. The President's retaliation intensified calls for his impeachment. Nixon would outlast Williams at his post, but not Berra.

A sellout crowd of 49,333 filled the Oakland Coliseum on another sunny afternoon. The air smelled fresh after recent rain, and several puffs of clouds scudded across the blue sky. The day was warm, far more comfortable than the frigid night temps in

New York. Before the game began, a group of fans in the bleachers clustered around a portable television to watch Archibald Cox speak to the press.[87]

Gene Tenace was scheduled to start the game at catcher. The man whose arm Charlie O. had declared shot before the start of the season would be behind the plate for the A's most critical game of the year. Tenace had caught Game Six as well as 33 regular season games in 1973. In the wake of the Andrews Affair, Tenace's place behind the plate was an irony not to be overlooked.

Reggie fidgeted impatiently during the New Christy Minstrels' slow rendition of the national anthem.[88] Ten grand was on the line. That was the difference between the winner's individual shares of $25,000 and the loser's share of $15,000—a lot of money in the day when a gallon of gas cost 32 cents. Even bigger was the glory to be won or lost on the field that day. The singing of the national anthem seemed to take forever.

The game finally began and Reggie batted in the first inning. Matlack continued his mastery of Reggie. Fooled by a Matlack pitch, Reggie checked his swing but too late. He was thrown out easily on his weak grounder, third to first. The Mets pitcher extended his streak of innings without giving up an earned run to 25—until the bottom of the third.

That's when the A's broke their homerless streak. They had hit more home runs than any other team in the AL the past two seasons but not managed to hit one out during the Series in 218 tries.[89] Finally, Bert Campaneris parked one over the right-field fence in the bottom of the third to score himself and Holtzman, the pitcher who seemed to be vying for the team's DH role. Holtzman had doubled and scored in the first game. He had doubled and scored again in the seventh. Campy's homer put the A's up 2–0.

Joe Rudi singled. Sal Bando popped out. Reggie batted with two out. With the count at one ball, one strike, Matlack threw a curve that hung by Jackson's eyes. Reggie took a good look and crushed it with his big swing ten rows deep into the right-center bleachers. Reggie knew from the moment he made contact that the ball was gone. He knew it and wanted everybody to know it. This was the longest hit of the Series.

Yogi Berra turned away.[90]

Reggie dropped his 37-ounce bat and stood in the box to watch the trajectory of the ball against the blue sky. Look at that! The pose would become familiar, repeated with increasing frequency throughout the decades, not just in baseball but across all sports: the superstar standing in awe of his own accomplishment, the ego swollen and paused in admiration of his feat. There, in the box stood Narcissus overcome by his own beauty. Reggie watched his ball soar its full 400 feet.

Then, the hot-dogging began. Reggie pranced around the bases exuberantly. When he reached home, where Joe Rudi, who had just scored, and Gene Tenace, the on-deck batter, waited to congratulate him, Reggie jumped high in the air, bringing his knees up, then slammed both feet emphatically onto the plate. A's 4, Mets 0. Reggie's enthusiastic score would be replayed countless times in highlight reels, an enduring image of his heroics.

He ran into the dugout and hugged Williams to the accompaniment of airhorns, fireworks, and fans on their feet waving white pennants. This one was theirs!

Yogi lifted Matlack. The A's added a run in the fifth to build their lead to 5–0. Rusty Staub doubled in a run in the top of the sixth. That chased Holtzman from the game, but the Mets still trailed by four.

The A's took the field in the top of the ninth leading 5–1. Tug McGraw warmed up in the Mets bullpen, just in case his team pulled off another one of its miracles and he needed to pitch the bottom of the ninth. Reggie, who had shifted to right field in the fourth inning, called over to the bullpen across the right field foul line, "Tug, don't bother. We got you now!"[91]

But then, the Mets mounted one last charge. John Milner walked. Jerry Grote flew out to left. Don Hahn singled. Buddy Harrelson grounded out to the pitcher, but the runners advanced to second and third. Ed Kranepool pinch hit a ground ball that Gene Tenace flubbed at first, and a Mets run leaked across the plate, 5–2. McGraw shouted back at Jackson, "Hey, Reggie! We're going to get you now!"[92]

When it had looked like Tenace would scoop up Kranepool's grounder for the third and final out of the game, a dozen fans spilled onto the field to celebrate prematurely. The umpires had to shoo them away.[93] Dick Williams called in Darold Knowles, a left-hander, to pitch to the left-handed-hitting Wayne Garrett. Knowles had missed the 1972 Series with an injury, but when he entered Game Seven, he made history as the only pitcher to appear in seven games of a single World Series.

While Knowles warmed up, the Oakland fans could not contain their anticipation. A man slipped out of the outfield bleachers and ran over to Reggie. He snatched the superstar's hat, but Reggie chased him down and retrieved his cap. A woman snatched his glove, which he had dropped to chase the man.

Finally, Knowles was ready, Reggie was back in position with his hat and glove, and the Mets were down to their last out, perhaps their last at bat. The 49,333 fans at the Oakland Coliseum and the millions watching across the country tensed with the drama.

A Syracuse college student watching the game on TV at a friend's house sensed the possibility in the moment. Pinch hit Willie Mays. Sure, Garrett hits with power and had already slugged two homers in the Series, but he had managed only 7 hits in 29 at bats. And, he batted left. Send in a right-handed batter against the left-handed pitcher. That's how Yogi had generally selected his pinch hitters throughout the postseason. Send up Mays, and you've got the all-time greatest clutch hitter at bat representing the tying run in Game Seven of the World Series in what could be the final at bat of his storied career. "Statistically, it doesn't make sense," Bob Costas, the Syracuse student, said. "But emotionally, it does. The whole run of the team was so improbable, why not let the movie script play out and pinch hit Willie Mays? If he gets a hit, he's the hero. You've got the movie ending. If he doesn't, you still have a dramatic ending."[94]

Willie knew the possibility in the moment. He waited for Yogi's call. He was ready.[95] But the call didn't come. The emotional appeal of the moment was lost on Yogi. For the last time, he looked past Willie on the bench. He stuck with Garrett at bat. Willie accepted that his day was done. He was no longer the man.

The critics were quick to second-guess Yogi's final decision of the 1973 season. Yes, Willie was only a shadow of his former glory, and he had performed embarrassingly poorly a week earlier. But he was still Willie. "I don't care if he was in a body cast, I would've sent him up to the plate—he was Willie Mays," said Lon Simmons, the former Giants' radio broadcaster. "If you had Willie Mays in the stadium, why would you think there would be somebody else who could rise to the occasion like he did?"[96]

Garrett stepped into the box. The runners at first and third took generous leads. Darold Knowles threw a slider. Garrett swung, but he had expected a fastball.[97] He popped the ball up to short. Bert Campaneris caught it for the final out of the 1973 World Series. Ray Fosse and Gene Tenace rushed to the mound to congratulate Knowles. Dick Williams came out of the dugout to shake Knowles's hand. Campy ran off with the ball squeezed in his glove.[98] The fans poured onto the field to celebrate Seventies-style.

Reggie ran in from the outfield. Tony Del Rio, his personal bodyguard, dropped out of the right field stands to carry him.[99] A group of uniformed policemen, the death threat against Jackson foremost on their minds, ringed him and ushered Reggie to the safety of the clubhouse.[100]

He had dodged the threatened bullet and finally revealed to the press the danger he had played under. "If I had got knocked off, I'd rather it be on the field," Reggie said.[101] That was probably true. He would have preferred to die dramatically in the spotlight than unceremoniously in isolation, unseen and unnoticed—that would have been a fate worse than death to him.

Willie Mays, whose baseball career had expired that day, took off his Mets uniform for the final time as a player. He folded it and tucked No. 24 inside his New York Mets equipment bag alongside his locker in the visiting clubhouse. "I don't feel nothin' yet, man," he told the reporters who gathered around him. "I probably won't feel nothin' until next spring training."[102]

Maybe he was numb. Or maybe he just didn't want to reveal the sting of his feelings at the moment. But Mays's fans and Mets fans would never forget that final summer of his career when their team had made such a spectacular and dramatic grab for the world title. "As for the Mets—ah, the Mets!" Roger Angell wrote in an elegy to the New York team. "What can one feel for them but gratitude for such a season of prizes, for a summer that lasted, in the end, just two afternoons too long?"[103]

The same could be said for Willie. Sorry to see you go, old friend, but ah, what a career, even if it had stretched two summers too long. We will remember it by the swift feats of your youth and not the stumbles of your old age. The bounty of those glorious memories fills our minds. For them and to you, we'll be forever grateful.

———————

Over in the A's clubhouse, amidst the spray of champagne and the glare of television lights, the insanity of the A's season continued. "There's no way I can describe the thrill of winning a second World Series," said the manager on national television. "But in my heart it is a sad thing for me." Williams finally confirmed his resignation but took the high road and did not blame Finley.[104]

The owner grabbed the microphone and said to Williams, "Even though you're not going to be with us next year, I want to thank you for the great job you've done for the three years you've been with me."[105]

"Thank you, Charlie, very much, and I'm going to miss being with you, but I've made a decision, and I'm going to stay with it," Williams said.[106]

The superstar hugged the ex-manager—still live on national television. "I'm sorry, sorry, sorry he's leaving us," Reggie said.

Tears clotted Williams's eyes. "I am, too, Reggie," he said. "I really am."[107]

Finley approached Reggie off-camera. "Congratulations for a great job," the owner told his superstar. "Thanks for an outstanding performance. You are the greatest player in the game."

"Thank you," Reggie replied matter-of-factly. Even if it came from Finley, he liked hearing it, *the greatest player in the game.* "Thank you, I appreciate it."

Williams had graciously credited Finley with getting the team to the World Series by dealing for Ray Fosse and Billy North, who had become stalwarts in the A's success. But when somebody asked Reggie if Finley deserved recognition for motivating the club with his shenanigans, the superstar snubbed the owner. "Please don't give that man the credit," Reggie said. "That takes away from what the guys have done. It would have been the easiest thing in the world for this team to lie down because of what that man did. He spoiled what should have been a beautiful thing. We went on and did what we could do because we have character."[108]

Reggie was given the credit he deserved for his World Series contribution. Despite his New York slump, he slugged five extra-base hits, batted .310, scored three runs, and knocked in six. Most importantly, he had come through in the final two games when the A's needed him most. *Sport* magazine named him the Series' Most Valuable Player and gave him the keys to a new car. Reggie had made an impressive debut in his first Fall Classic en route to establishing himself as Mr. October. The All-Star Game may have been invented for Willie Mays, but the World Series was created for Reggie Jackson.

The future Mr. October in New York seated atop the car he won for his MVP performance in his first World Series.

Chapter Eighteen

EXTRA INNINGS

F ive days after Bowie Kuhn presented Finley with the Commissioner's Trophy for winning the Series, he fined the Oakland owner $7,000. Five grand was punishment for the way Finley treated Mike Andrews, one thousand was for his PA announcement blaming the Mets for not approving Manny Trillo on the A's roster, and another grand was for turning on the field lights when he wasn't supposed to.[1] The commissioner was so fed up with baseball's problem child that he threatened to kick him out of the game.[2] Soon another owner on the other side of the country would be giving him fits.

The rowdy and wrasslin' A's, stirred by their owner's antics and stoked by their victory, celebrated at a Bay Area restaurant after Game Seven. Most of the players were still partying with their wives and girlfriends around midnight. Reggie was running his mouth, spraying profanity freely. Blue Moon Odom asked him to clean up his language. "Just respect the wives if you don't respect me," Odom said.

Reggie cussed at Blue Moon. Odom was not intimidated by his larger, more muscular teammate, who outweighed him by 20 pounds. They got into it, shouting at one another. Teammates restrained them before they traded blows.[3] The A's closed out the season true to form: winners, fighters, and unable to restrain Reggie's mouth.

It was goodbye to all that for Dick Williams. The A's ex-manager was indeed headed to the Yankees, or so he thought. Charlie Finley thought otherwise.

When Finley hadn't been able to convince Williams to stay with the A's, he had told him, "Should you prefer to go to the Yankees if you're offered the Yankee job, I certainly won't stand in your way."[4] Later, in the television interview after Game Seven, Charlie seemed to have accepted Williams's resignation. Well, the irascible owner changed his mind. Two days after the A's won the World Series, Finley pulled aside Yankees owner George Steinbrenner at a league meeting in Chicago and told the Boss that Williams wasn't for hire. "If you go ahead and try to sign Williams, I'll charge the Yankees with tampering," Charlie told George.[5]

Showdown. Charlie contended that Williams was still under contract with the A's and that he would not release his manager unless the club that signed him compensated Finley.

Oh, if that's the way it is, then I deserve compensation for Ralph Houk leaving me, Steinbrenner figured. The next moment, he demanded such from Jim Campbell, the Detroit general manager who had hired Houk, the ex-Yankees skipper, to manage the Tigers. Not surprisingly, Campbell didn't view the situation the same way George did. Campbell refused Steinbrenner.

For his part, Williams had made it clear that he would not return to the A's, no matter what. "That's one decision that can't change," Williams said.[6]

Two months later, the Yankees, fixated on Williams, offered Finley two minor league players and $150,000 as compensation for his manager. Nope, Finley said. He didn't think the minor league players would ever break the A's lineup, so they were worthless.[7] "The Yankees had hoped to resolve their problem with Finley on an amicable basis, but Charlie O. was asking for the moon as compensation for Williams," *The Sporting News* reported.[8]

Okay, George said. We'll fight.

Steinbrenner rented out the Terrace in the Park, overlooking the World's Fair grounds, for a "massive" news conference on December 18.[9] There, the Yankees announced that they had signed a new manager, Dick Williams. Steinbrenner gave Williams a three-year, $100,000-a-year contract, which made him the highest paid manager in baseball. Provided Finley let him.

He didn't. As expected, Finley dug in. He filed a federal court complaint to block the hiring. In the complaint, he argued that Williams's departure would cause "irreparable injury and damage to the Oakland club," given his ability to win.[10] Finley submitted the consecutive world champion titles as evidence.

Ultimately, Williams's fate fell to Joe Cronin. In his final days as American League president, Cronin ruled that the Tigers owed the Yankees nothing because the team had accepted Houk's resignation and had not filed a complaint until two weeks after Houk signed with the Tigers. Cronin also ruled that Finley had never accepted Williams's resignation, so the manager was not eligible to sign with the Yankees absent Finley's release.[11] Steinbrenner lost on both fronts.

The Yankees hired Bill Virdon instead. So, when the 1974 baseball season started, Ralph Houk was in Detroit, Bill Virdon was in New York, Alvin Dark was in Oakland, and Dick Williams was in Florida, held hostage by Charlie Finley. "Finley fucked Williams," Reggie Jackson wrote in his diary of the 1974 season. "The best manager in baseball is selling insurance in Florida. It's a shame."[12]

By midseason, Gene Autry, the "Singing Cowboy," ransomed Williams and hired the former Oakland manager to skipper the California Angels. Williams managed another fifteen seasons with the Angels, Expos, Padres, and Mariners before retiring in 1988. He was elected to the National Baseball Hall of Fame by the Veterans Committee as part of the Class of 2008. The A's refuted Finley's argument that Williams's departure would cause irreparable harm by winning the 1974 World Series under new manager Alvin

Dark. In doing so, they joined the New York Yankees as the only team to win three consecutive World Series.

In December, Finley sent out contracts to the players from his '73 championship team. Many of the players were unhappy with the pay he offered. Joe Rudi was one of those. The A's left fielder had been sick and injured much of 1973, playing only 119 games, but he had played strong the final weeks of the season and through the postseason. He had expected a raise. Finley hadn't offered one. Rudi sent back the contract unsigned.[13]

A day or two later, Rudi was at home, setting the table for a family meal, when the phone rang. "How the hell can you send the contract back?" Charlie Finley hollered on the other end. "You're lucky I didn't cut you 20 percent!"

Rudi couldn't break into the torrent of profanity, complaints, and insults. Finally, Rudi yelled back at Charlie.

Finley immediately switched tactics. "How's the family?" he asked.

"As soon as I got mad," Rudi recalled years later, "he became totally charming. Obviously, he'd thought about how he would buffalo me into signing the contract. That's just the way he was. He'd try one approach. If that didn't work, he'd flip the switch."[14]

Rudi wouldn't be buffaloed. He took Finley to arbitration, the option opened to players by the new basic agreement signed at the start of the 1973 season. Rudi did not win his case, but he did earn an additional $5,000. That was the amount Finley upped his offer going into arbitration, not confident in his initial amount.

More A's players than from any other team sought arbitration after the 1973 season, a sign of their dissatisfaction with Finley's tight- and iron-fisted rein on the club. Seven players, including Rudi, took Finley to arbitration. Four of them won, but all of them received raises that would not have been available otherwise.[15]

Reggie Jackson was one of the players to win his arbitration. He figured his $100,000 had been worth $135,000, considering he had been named the Most Valuable Player of both the regular season and the Fall Classic. Finley offered $100,000. Reggie asked for—and won—a contract for $135,000. He was edging toward the big money.[16]

At the start of the 1973 season, Yankees president Gabe Paul had insisted on complete assurance from the new owner that nothing would happen to general manager Lee MacPhail, "one of my closest friends," or to Ralph Houk, "whom I consider the best manager in baseball."[17] Steinbrenner hadn't fired "the best manager in baseball," but he had forced him out with his meddling. Before the year ended, Lee MacPhail also resigned to become the American League president when Joe Cronin left. Gabe Paul's two untouchables lasted only a year under Steinbrenner.

Once George said hello, other Yankees leadership started saying goodbye. Mike Burke was first. Then Houk and MacPhail. *The Sporting News* compared the Yankees management to an Agatha Christie mystery: "like the ten little Indians, they disappeared one by one."[18] But, unlike a Christie novel, the person responsible for the Yankees departures was clear. "Steinbrenner, a highly successful businessman, doesn't like the slow-motion way in which baseball people move," *The Sporting News* observed. "He is a do-it-now guy, while MacPhail and Houk were both methodical, slow-moving and conservative."[19]

The result was a split from the past and the dawn of a new dynasty. By the close of 1973, the change of leadership signaled a shift in Yankees history. Steinbrenner had severed ties to the past. "The Yankees have broken almost completely away from the club tradition since Col. Jacob Ruppert purchased the Yankees in 1915 and began to build that tradition," *The Sporting News* observed. "It really is a whole new ball game for the pinstripers."[20]

Steinbrenner was not on hand to watch his team play the next phase of that new ball game. The day before the Yankees opened the 1974 season, a federal grand jury in Cleveland indicted the Yankee owner on five counts of violating campaign contribution laws, two counts of aiding and abetting false statements to the FBI, four counts of obstruction of justice, two counts of obstructing a criminal investigation, and one count of conspiracy. If convicted on all fourteen counts, Steinbrenner could spend fifty-five years in prison and pay $100,000 in fines—on top of the hundred grand he had illegally given the Nixon campaign and tried to cover up.[21]

Steinbrenner defiantly insisted that he had done nothing wrong. "I am totally innocent, and will prove it in court," he said.[22] "No one wants to go through the agony of a trial, but I feel strongly that I must stand and fight for what I believe is right. I am confident that I will be found innocent of the charges."[23]

He changed his mind when his lawyer, the high-powered Edward Bennett Williams, was unable to have the charges dropped. On August 23, 1974, two weeks after Nixon resigned, Steinbrenner pleaded guilty to one count of conspiracy to violate the campaign contribution laws—a felony—and one count of aiding and abetting obstruction of an investigation—reduced to a misdemeanor. He avoided the agony of a trial, but he faced up to six years in prison. The government's prosecutors were confident that federal judge Leroy Contie would sentence Steinbrenner to a jail term.[24] Instead, Judge Contie fined Steinbrenner $15,000—the most levied against any corporate officer—and fined AmShip an additional $20,000. The Securities and Exchange Commission also recommended that Steinbrenner reimburse the company the $42,325.17 in bogus bonuses, and he did.[25] The Boss wrote a few more checks but avoided hard time.

Two months later, Bowie Kuhn suspended the Yankees owner and convicted felon from baseball for two years. Kuhn allowed Steinbrenner to retain his stock (i.e., his controlling interest), but the suspension was supposed to bar the Boss from the team's operations.

"He is declared ineligible and incompetent to manage or advise in the management of the affairs of the New York Yankees," Kuhn said.[26]

Impossible. Might as well suspend sunlight from the daytime. During his "suspension," the convicted felon recorded pep talks and sent them to his new manager, Bill Virdon, to play for the team in the clubhouse. The felon traded the $100,000 center fielder Bobby Murcer for Bobby Bonds. The felon fired Virdon and hired Billy Martin. The felon choreographed Martin's memorable introduction at the Old-Timers game in August 1975. The felon also met with Sparky Lyle at the end of 1974—with the commissioner's special permission—to convince the pitcher to sign his contract.[27] During this period, the team flashed lots of smoke and mirrors—Gabe Paul said this, Gabe Paul did this—but for all the attribution to the team president, there were no illusions about who actually ran the team during Steinbrenner's suspension. There was only one Boss.

George's greatest coup during his suspension established the new tradition of the contemporary Yankees dynasty. When Charlie Finley let Catfish Hunter slip from his grasp by failing to pay an annuity clause specified in Hunter's contract, Steinbrenner snatched Catfish for the whopping sum—at the time—of $3.75 million and became the first owner to sign a free agent in the new era. Charlie may have won Round One with Williams, but George laughed last with Catfish.

Luring a superstar into pinstripes with a hefty sum would become Steinbrenner's *modus operandi* and his means to rebuilding the Yankees glory. The highest payroll in baseball, established in his first year of ownership, would skyrocket to unfathomable heights with other teams frantically trying to keep pace at the bank and in the standings. That would prove the undoing of Finley, among other owners, and sweet revenge for Steinbrenner. He was on his way to becoming the most hated man in baseball with the best team that money could buy.

In 1975, Finley had led a coup d'etat against Kuhn. Steinbrenner had initially joined the rebel ranks, but when the National League owners balked and doomed the coup, George switched sides. His support solidified Kuhn's standing. Then, in the way these things tend to play out, the commissioner knocked eight months off Steinbrenner's suspension for his good behavior and reinstated the Yankees owner in time for Opening Day 1976.[28]

Of course, George still had that felony rap on his record, something his manager famously reminded him of, when Billy Martin complained about Steinbrenner and the superstar he had acquired for the 1977 season, Reggie Jackson, "The two of them deserve each other. One of them's a born liar, the other's a convicted liar."[29]

George wanted to shake that felony from his reputation. He applied for a presidential pardon from President Jimmy Carter, but the man highly lauded for his morals turned down Steinbrenner's request. George tried again when Ronald Reagan occupied the White House. "I have come to fully accept that my actions or lack of actions in what occurred was in fact criminal conduct," Steinbrenner wrote penitently—or calculatingly—in his application for clemency. President Reagan was sufficiently moved. On January 18, 1989, he granted George's wish as one of his final acts in office.[30] The convicted felon was back to being just George again. In other words, he didn't seem to have changed.

———————

In related news, Steinbrenner achieved a measure of vindication against Gaylord Perry, the man he and the Yankees suspected of throwing spitballs. Perry confessed in his 1974 memoir, *Me and the Spitter*, to throwing spitballs—though insisted he had reformed and no longer threw them. Since umpires had such trouble catching Perry and his like in the act, Major League Baseball's rules committee gave umps the discretion to rule a pitch illegal if it simply acted like a spitball—mysteriously dropping a foot or so on its way to the plate. For the first offense, the pitcher had his pitch called a "ball"; for the second offense, the pitcher was ejected.

On Opening Day 1974, home plate ump Marty Springstead became the first to invoke the rule. He called a ball against Gaylord Perry.[31]

The Indians invited umpires to a demonstration where Perry showed them how his forkball dropped a foot or so. That prompted AL president Lee MacPhail to draft a memo to league umps that informed them how Perry's forkball acted a lot like a spitball.[32] Perry never did manage to shake his reputation for doctoring baseballs, but that did not keep him out of the Hall of Fame. He was inducted in 1991. Former manager Gene Mauch thought a fitting asterisk to Perry's induction would be a "tube of K-Y jelly attached to his plaque."[33]

Before the 1977 season, Steinbrenner lured Reggie Jackson to New York with a $2.9 million contract and a Rolls-Royce. It wasn't a tough sell. Ever since his big series against the Yankees in mid-August 1973, Reggie had made it clear that he would love to play on the nation's grandest stage, to be the straw that stirred the drink of America's team. The bright lights and big city played to Reggie's appetite for attention. There, in the expensive, new Yankee Stadium, on the night of October 18, in Game Six of the 1977 World Series, Reggie solidified his Mr. October reputation with three home runs on three swings against three different pitchers. Only the mighty Babe Ruth had hit three home runs in a single Series game, but not even the Babe had done it in consecutive at bats the way Reggie had. On that night in that place, Mr. October achieved immortality as a World Series legend.

Orlando Cepeda, the "Outstanding Designated Hitter" in the rule's first year, had enjoyed his last good season in Boston. By spring training of 1974, his knees could no longer carry him. "I'd never seen a guy's legs go down that fast," observed Bill Lee, Cepeda's teammate and friend. "He just couldn't run any more on those pins. He could still hit. He just couldn't get to first base."[34]

After Boston released Cepeda, the Kansas City Royals gave him one last chance, but Cepeda managed only 23 hits in 33 games during the 1974 season. Darrell Johnson, the new Red Sox manager, had been right. Cepeda was finished as a big-leaguer.

The transition to retirement did not go smoothly. Cepeda, who had smoked pot to unwind during his playing days, was busted at the San Juan airport in December 1975 and charged with complicity in transporting 170 pounds of marijuana from Colombia. "I told him not to pick up his mail," Lee joked.[35]

But the Court wasn't laughing. When the case finally went to trial in 1978, Cepeda was found guilty, fined $10,000, and sentenced to five years in prison. He appealed and lost. Cha Cha served his time in a minimum-security prison at Eglin Air Force Base in Fort Walton, Florida, the same place where Charles Colson and Howard Hunt, a pair of President Nixon's fall guys in the Watergate scandal, served their time.[36]

Cepeda had retired with Hall of Fame credentials. He'd been the only unanimous selection as both Rookie of the Year (1958) and Most Valuable Player (1967), a seven-time All-Star and the "Most Outstanding Designated Hitter" (1973). He had led the league in doubles (1958), home runs (1961), and RBIs (1961 and 1967). Over seventeen seasons, he had a career batting average of .297 with 379 home runs and 1,365 runs batted in. But there was one record the voting members of the Baseball Writers' Association of America didn't like: his drug conviction. They did not endorse his induction.

As time ran out on his eligibility, celebrities and Hall members campaigned for Cepeda's induction. In 1994, his last year on the ballot, Cepeda fell seven votes short of the 75 percent requirement.[37] He wrote *Baby Bull*, an autobiography published in 1998 to clear his name and petition his cause. Finally, in 1999, the Hall of Fame's Veterans Committee elected him in, and Orlando Cepeda entered the Cooperstown shrine.

———

After spending the winter stalled at 713, Hank Aaron did not take long to pass Babe Ruth once the 1974 season started. Aaron hit No. 714 on Opening Day in Cincinnati. Red Smith, America's most widely read sportswriter, put the home run in perspective. Not only had Aaron caught the mighty Ruth, Smith wrote, "what really counts is that when Henry laid the wood on Jack Billingham's fastball, he struck a blow for the integrity of the game and for public faith in the game."[38]

Aaron completed his humanitarian effort four days later at Atlanta Stadium. In the fourth inning, Hammerin' Hank clubbed Al Downing's second pitch, a fastball, over the left-field fence for No. 715. Finally, Hank Aaron had become the Home Run King, the bigots be damned.

Aaron returned to Milwaukee for his final two seasons. Playing for the Brewers in the American League, he benefited from the designated hitter rule and added 22 home runs to his total. Aaron retired after the 1976 season with 755 career home runs. He held more records than any player in baseball history, including Willie Mays. Over twenty-three seasons, Aaron had not only hit more home runs than anyone else, he had knocked in more runs (2,297), hit more extra-base hits (1,477), and batted for more total bases (6,856) than any other player. He was elected to the Hall of Fame his first year on the ballot with 97.8 percent of the vote, second only to Ty Cobb's 98.2 percent in 1936.

As soon as Aaron passed Ruth on April 8, 1974, the speculation began: Will anybody be able to pass Aaron? Johnny Bench and Bobby Bonds were considered the two most likely candidates to do so, if it could be done. Bench, the Reds catcher, was only twenty-five years old and had already hit 154 home runs. Bonds, the Giants outfielder, was twenty-six and had hit 126. Both had the potential, but neither was moving at a pace fast enough. "Already they were starting to say that this new record which Aaron was writing into the books was unstoppable—just as it was said forty years ago that Ruth's mark of 714 would stand for all time," sportswriter Fred Down observed.[39]

During the winter of his long wait, when the calendar turned from 1973 to 1974, Aaron spoke at a banquet in Modesto, California. Someone asked him, "Would you breaking Ruth's record stand as a shrine for all blacks?"

"It would be a great thing for blacks, giving black children hope that no matter how high the mountain, they can climb it," Aaron said. "I'm hoping someday that some kid, black or white, will hit more home runs than myself. Whoever it is, I'd be pulling for him."[40]

Nobody guessed at the time that kid, who had turned nine years old the day his father, Bobby Bonds, was named Most Valuable Player of the 1973 All-Star Game, would pass Aaron on August 7, 2007, only thirty-three years later. Forty-three-year-old Barry Bonds topped the mountain when he slugged No. 756 at San Francisco's AT&T Park. His godfather, Willie Mays, stood with him at home plate afterward, when Barry thanked the crowd and paid tribute to his father, Bobby, who had died of cancer four years earlier.

Hank Aaron was not there. It was uncertain whether or not the Home Run King was pulling for Bonds to reach the summit. As Barry Bonds neared Aaron's mark and evidence mounted that Bonds had used illegal performance-enhancing substances, Aaron had withdrawn his support. He did, however, in his characteristically gracious fashion, tape a video tribute to the new record-holder that played in the San Francisco stadium after Bonds's historic homer.

"I would like to offer my congratulations to Barry Bonds on becoming baseball's career home run leader," the seventy-three-year-old Aaron said. "I move over now and offer my best wishes to Barry and his family on this historic achievement. My hope today, as it was on that April evening in 1974, is that the achievement of this record will inspire others to chase their own dreams."[41]

The two standing ovations for Aaron's message demonstrated that even in Barryland, Hank Aaron remained the true king. He had conquered racism when he played. And now, he had set down the cheating zeitgeist of the day. His mark—achieved during the summers of the Fifties, Sixties, and Seventies—stood for a time when the game was played on different terms. There will never be another Hank Aaron, and there will never be baseball like it was played in 1973, the season the game changed forever.

BIBLIOGRAPHY

BOOKS

Aaron, Hank with Dick Schaap. *Home Run: My Life in Pictures.* Kingston, NY: Total Sports, 1999.

Aaron, Hank with Lonnie Wheeler. *I Had a Hammer: The Hank Aaron Story.* New York: HarperCollins, 1991.

Adelman, Bob and Susan Hall. *Out of Left Field: Willie Stargell and the Pittsburgh Pirates.* New York: Two Continents, 1976.

Adelman, Tom. *Black and Blue: The Golden Arm, the Robinson Boys and the 1966 World Series that Stunned America.* New York: Little Brown, 2006.

Allen, Maury. *All Roads Lead to October: Boss Steinbrenner's 25-Year Reign over the New York Yankees.* New York: St. Martin's, 2000.

Allen, Maury. *Mr. October: The Reggie Jackson Story.* New York: Times, 1981.

Anderson, Ken. *Nolan Ryan: Texas Fastball to Cooperstown.* Austin: Eakin, 2000.

Angell, Roger. *Five Seasons: A Baseball Companion.* New York: Simon and Schuster, 1977.

Baldwin, Stan and Jerry Jenkins with Hank Aaron. *Bad Henry.* Radnor, PA: Chilton, 1974.

Berra, Yogi with Tom Horton. *Yogi: It Ain't Over . . .* New York: McGraw-Hill, 1989.

Bjarkman, Peter C. *The New York Mets Encyclopedia.* Champaign: Sports Publishing, 2003.

Burke, Michael. *Outrageous Good Fortune.* Boston: Little, Brown, 1984.

Cepeda, Orlando with Bob Markus. *High & Inside: Orlando Cepeda's Story.* South Bend: Icarus, 1983.

Cepeda, Orlando with Herb Fagen. *Baby Bull: From Hardball to Hard Time and Back.* Dallas: Taylor, 1998.

Clark, Tom. *Champagne and Baloney: The Rise and Fall of Finley's A's.* New York: Harper & Row, 1976.

Cooper, Elisha. "Ballpark." New York: Greenwillow, 1998.

Dickey, Glenn. *Champions: The Story of the First Two Oakland A's Dynasties—and the Building of the Third.* Chicago: Triumph, 2002.

Drucker, Malka with Tom Seaver. *Tom Seaver: Portrait of a Pitcher.* New York: Holiday, 1978.

Einstein, Charles. *Willie Mays: My Life In and Out of Baseball.* New York: Dutton, 1966.

Einstein, Charles. *Willie's Time: A Memoir.* New York: Lippincott, 1979.

Fetter, Henry D. *Taking on the Yankees: Winning and Losing in the Business of Baseball.* New York: Norton, 2003.

Garner, Joe. *And the Crowd Goes Wild.* Naperville: Sourcebooks, 1999.

Jackson, Reggie. *Reggie: A Season with a Superstar.* Chicago: Playboy Press, 1975.

Jackson, Reggie with Mike Lupica. *Reggie: The Autobiography.* New York: Villard, 1984.

James, Bill. *The Bill James Historical Baseball Abstract.* New York: Free Press, 1986.

Kahn, Roger. *The Boys of Summer.* New York: Harper & Row, 1971.

Kahn, Roger. *October Men: Reggie Jackson, George Steinbrenner, Billy Martin, and the Yankees' Miraculous Finish in 1978*. New York: Harcourt, 2003.

Kuhn, Bowie. *Hardball: The Education of a Baseball Commissioner*. New York: Times, 1987.

Libby, Bill. *Charlie O. & the Angry A's: The Low and Inside Story of Charlie O. Finley and Baseball's Most Colorful Team*. New York: Doubleday, 1975.

Linn, Ed. *Steinbrenner's Yankees: An Inside Account*. New York: Holt, Rinehart and Winston, 1982.

Mahler, Jonathan. *The Bronx is Burning: 1977, Baseball, Politics and the Battle for the Soul of a City*. New York: Picador, 2006.

Maraniss, David. *Clemente: The Passion and Grace of Baseball's Last Hero*. New York: Simon & Schuster, 2006.

Marcin, Joe et al. *Official Baseball Guide 1974*. St. Louis: Sporting News, 1974.

Markusen, Bruce. *The Orlando Cepeda Story*. Houston: Piñata, 2001.

Mays, Willie with Lou Sahadi. *Say Hey: The Autobiography of Willie Mays*. New York: Simon and Schuster, 1988.

McGraw, Tug and Joseph Durso. *Screwball*. Boston: Houghton Mifflin, 1974.

McKelvey, G. Richard. *All Bat, No Glove: A History of the Designated Hitter*. Jefferson: McFarland, 2004.

Neft, David, et al. *The Sports Encyclopedia: Baseball 2001*. New York: St. Martin's, 2001.

Olney, Buster. *The Last Night of the Yankee Dynasty: The Game, the Team, and the Cost of Greatness*. New York: HarperCollins, 2004.

Pepe, Phil. *Catfish, Yaz and Hammerin' Hank: The Unforgettable Era That Transformed Baseball*. Chicago: Triumph, 2005.

Perry, Gaylord and Bob Surdyk. *Me and the Spitter: An Autobiographical Confession*. New York: Dutton, 1974.

Preston, Joseph G. *Major League Baseball in the 1970s: A Modern Game Emerges*. Jefferson: McFarland, 2004.

Reichler, Joseph. *Baseball's Great Moments*. New York: Crown, 1979.

Reshen, Pat, editor. *Hank Aaron 715*. New York: Arco, 1974.

Ryan, Nolan and Harvey Frommer. *Throwing Heat: The Autobiography of Nolan Ryan*. New York: Avon, 1988.

Ryan, Nolan. *Miracle Man: The Autobiography*. Dallas: Word, 1992.

Schaap, Dick. *Steinbrenner!* New York: Putnam, 1982.

Scheinin, Richard. *Field of Screams: The Dark Underside of America's National Pastime*. New York: Norton, 1994.

Schoor, Gene. *Seaver: A Biography*. New York: Contemporary, 1986.

Schoor, Gene. *Willie Mays: Modest Champion*. New York: Putnam, 1960.

Spatz, Lyle, editor. *The SABR Baseball List & Record Book*. New York: Scribner, 2007.

Stanton, Tom. *Hank Aaron and the Home Run that Changed America*. New York: William Morrow, 2004.

Thornley, Stew. *Land of the Giants: New York's Polo Grounds*. Philadelphia: Temple, 2000.

Ward, Geoffrey C. and Ken Burns. *Baseball: An Illustrated History*. New York: Knopf, 2000.

Williams, Dick and Bill Plaschke. *No More Mr. Nice Guy: A Life of Hardball*. New York: Harcourt Brace Jovanavich, 1990.

Zagaris, Michael. *Oakland A's*. San Francisco: Chronicle, 1991.

1974 World Book Year Book: A Review of the Events of 1973. Chicago: Field Enterprises, 1974.

Baseball: Four decades of Sports Illustrated's finest writing on America's favorite pastime. Birmingham: Oxmoor, 1993.

AUDIO CASSETTES, COMPACT DISCS, AND DVDS

"A History of Baseball with Greg Proops." New Street Productions, 2002.

"Baseball Comes of Age." Koster Films, 2006.

Burns, Ken. "Baseball." Florentine Films, 1994.

ESPN Classics, Game Two, 1973 World Series, Mets vs. A's, October 14, 1973. The Miley Collection.

ESPN Classics, Game Seven, 1973 World Series, Mets vs. A's, October 21, 1973. The Miley Collection.

MLB copyrighted radio broadcast, Braves vs. Phillies, July 21, 1973, The Miley Collection.

MLB copyrighted radio broadcast, Mets vs. Pirates, September 18, 1973, The Miley Collection.

MLB copyrighted radio broadcast, Mets vs. Pirates, September 20, 1973, The Miley Collection.

MLB copyrighted radio broadcast, Mets vs. Pirates, September 21, 1973, The Miley Collection.

MLB copyrighted radio broadcast, Mets vs. Reds, October 8, 1973, The Miley Collection.

MLB copyrighted radio broadcast, Mets vs. Reds, October 9, 1973, The Miley Collection.

MLB copyrighted radio broadcast, Mets vs. Reds, October 10, 1973, The Miley Collection.

PERIODICALS AND MAGAZINES

Atlanta Constitution
Atlanta Journal
Baseball Digest
Ebony
History Channel Magazine
Inside Sports
Journal News
Los Angeles Times
Minneapolis Star
Minneapolis Star Tribune
Minneapolis Tribune
New York Daily News
New York Times
New Yorker
Newsweek
Record-Searchlight
Sport
Sporting News
Sports Illustrated

Time
USA Today
Washington Post

WEBSITES

www.baseball-almanac.com
www.baseballlibrary.com
www.baseball-reference.com
www.ESPN.com
mlb.mlb.com
www.oswego.edu/~dighe
kansascity.royals.mlb.com
www.sabr.org
www.thebaseballpage.com
www.thesmokinggun.com
www.tvhistory.com
www.watergate.info/judiciary
en.wikipedia.org

INTERVIEWS

Dick Bresciani, Boston Red Sox historian
Fred Claire, former Los Angeles Dodgers executive
Bob Costas, television broadcaster
Ray Fosse, former MLB player
Ed Kranepool, former MLB player
Bill Lee, former MLB player
Paul Levy, former *Trentonian* staff writer
Matt Merola, agent for Reggie Jackson and Hank Aaron
John Odom, former MLB player
Tony Oliva, former MLB player
Joe Rudi, former MLB player
Robert Sahr, economist, University of Oregon
Lon Simmons, San Francisco Giants radio announcer
Art Stewart, Kansas City Royals scout
Gene Tenace, former MLB player

ENDNOTES

CHAPTER ONE

[1] Allen, Maury. *Mr. October: The Reggie Jackson Story*

[2] Jackson, Reggie, with Mike Lupica. *Reggie: The Autobiography*

[3] Blount, Roy. *Sport*

[4] Jackson, Reggie. *Reggie: A Season with a Superstar*

[5] baseballlibrary.com

[6] baseball-almanac.com

[7] Jackson, *Season with a Superstar*

CHAPTER TWO

[1] Kahn, Roger. *October Men: Reggie Jackson, George Steinbrenner, Billy Martin, and the Yankees' Miraculous Finish in 1978*

[2] *Daily News*, April 22, 2006

[3] *New York Times*, January 4, 1973

[4] *Ibid.*

[5] Kahn, *October Men*

[6] Mahler, Jonathan. *The Bronx is Burning: 1977, Baseball, Politics, and the Battle for the Soul of a City*

[7] *Daily News*, April 22, 2006

[8] Allen, Maury. *All Roads Lead to October: Boss Steinbrenner's 25-Year Reign over the New York Yankees*

[9] Olney, Buster. *The Last Night of the Yankee Dynasty: The Game, the Team, and the Cost of Greatness*

[10] Schaap, Dick. *Steinbrenner!*

[11] Olney, *The Last Night of the Yankee Dynasty*

[12] *Ibid.*

[13] Kahn, *October Men*

[14] *Ibid.*

[15] *New York Times*, January 4, 1973

[16] *Ibid.*

[17] *USA Today*, May 8, 2002

[18] Schaap, *Steinbrenner!*

[19] Pepe, Phil. *Catfish, Yaz, and Hammerin' Hank: The Unforgettable Era that Transformed Baseball*

[20] Schaap, *Steinbrenner!*

[21] *New York Times*, January 4, 1973

[22] Kahn, *October Men*

[23] *Ibid.*

[24] *Daily News*, April 22, 2006

[25] *Ibid.*

[26] Olney, *Last Night*

[27] *Sporting News*, Date of issue unknown.

[28] *New York Times*, January 4, 1973

[29] Olney, *Last Night*

[30] Dighe, Ranjit S. "The Economics of Baseball"

[31] Ward, Geoffrey C., and Ken Burns. *Baseball: An Illustrated History*

[32] *Sporting News*, March 10, 1973

[33] *New York Times*, April 14, 1972

[34] *Ibid.*

[35] *Sporting News*, March 3, 1973

[36] baseballlibrary.com

[37] *New York Times*, February 9, 1973

[38] *Sporting News*, March 3, 1973

[39] *New York Times*, February 8, 1973

[40] Author interview with Robert Sahr, economist, University of Oregon

[41] *New York Times*, March 2, 1973

[42] Burke, Michael. *Outrageous Good Fortune*

[43] *Ibid.*

[44] *New York Daily News*, December 30, 2002

[45] Allen, *All Roads*

[46] *New York Times*, March 5, 1973

[47] Pepe, *Catfish, Yaz*

[48] Allen, *All Roads*

[49] Pepe, *Catfish, Yaz*

[50] *Ibid.*

[51] Allen, *All Roads*

[52] *New York Times*, March 5 and 6, 1973
[53] Pepe, *Catfish, Yaz*
[54] *New York Times*, March 11, 1973
[55] *New York Times*, March 20, 1973
[56] Angell, Roger. *Five Seasons: A Baseball Companion*
[57] *New York Times*, March 5 and 6, 1973
[58] *Sporting News*, April 21, 1973
[59] Proops, Greg. *A History of Baseball with Greg Proops*
[60] 1974 World Book
[61] *Ibid.*

CHAPTER THREE

[1] Jackson, *Season with a Superstar*
[2] *Ibid.*
[3] *Ibid.*
[4] Kahn, *October Men*
[5] Olderman, Murray. "Reggie Jackson: The Blood and Guts of the Fighting A's," *Sport Magazine*, October 1974
[6] *Sporting News*, April 21, 1973
[7] Olderman, "Blood and Guts"
[8] tvhistory.com
[9] Angell, Roger. *Five Seasons: A Baseball Companion*
[10] *Baseball Digest*, date of issue unknown
[11] Markusen, Bruce. "Thirty Years Ago: The Birth of the Mustache Gang," baseballlibrary.com
[12] *Ibid.*
[13] Kates, Maxwell. "A Brief History of the Changing Attitudes Towards Facial Hair in Baseball," baseballlibrary.com
[14] Markusen, "Thirty Years Ago"
[15] Williams, Dick, and Bill Plaschke. *No More Mr. Nice Guy: A Life of Hardball*
[16] Markusen, "Thirty Years Ago"
[17] Ward, Geoffrey, and Ken Burns. *Baseball: An Illustrated History*
[18] *Sporting News*, January 27, 1973
[19] Markusen, "Thirty Years Ago"
[20] Kates, "A Brief History"
[21] Allen, *Mr. October*

[22] *Ibid.*
[23] *Sporting News*, January 27, 1973
[24] Markusen, "Thirty Years Ago"
[25] Williams, *No More Mr. Nice Guy*
[26] Kates, "A Brief History"
[27] *Sporting News*, April 14, 1973
[28] *Ibid.*
[29] *Ibid.*
[30] Dickey, Glenn. "Reggie Jackson Superstar (Not Yet)," *Sport Magazine*, Date of issue unknown.
[31] *Time*, August 18, 1975
[32] Scheinin, Richard. *Field of Screams: The Dark Underside of America's National Pastime*
[33] *Sporting News*, April 21, 1973
[34] Williams, *No More Mr. Nice Guy*
[35] *Sporting News*, March 17, 1973
[36] Jackson, Reggie, with Mike Lupica. *Reggie: The Autobiography*
[37] Dickey, Glenn. *Champions: The Story of the First Two Oakland A's Dynasties—and the Building of the Third*
[38] *Time*, August 18, 1975
[39] *Ibid.*
[40] *Sporting News*, January 27, 1973
[41] *Sporting News*, March 3, 1973
[42] *Sporting News*, January 27, 1973
[43] *Sporting News*, September 26, 1970
[44] *Time*, August 18, 1975
[45] Dickey, "Reggie Jackson Superstar"
[46] *Ibid.*
[47] Scheinin, *Field of Screams*
[48] *Time*, August 18, 1975
[49] Dickey, *Champions*
[50] Clark, Tom. *Champagne and Baloney: The Rise and Fall of Finley's A's*
[51] *Ibid.*
[52] Ward, *Baseball*
[53] Dickey, "Reggie Jackson Superstar"
[54] *Sporting News*, January 27, 1973
[55] Williams, *No More Mr. Nice Guy*
[56] Dickey, "Reggie Jackson Superstar"
[57] Clark, *Champagne and Baloney*

[58] Jackson, *The Autobiography*
[59] *Sporting News*, March 17, 1973
[60] *Sporting News*, April 21, 1973
[61] *Sports Illustrated*, April 9, 1973
[62] Dickey, *Champions*
[63] *Sporting News*, April 14, 1973
[64] Clark, *Champagne and Baloney*
[65] Author interview with Gene Tenace
[66] *Sporting News*, March 24, 1973
[67] *Minneapolis Star*, April 6, 1973
[68] Dickey, *Champions*
[69] *Sporting News*, April 21, 1973

CHAPTER FOUR

[1] *Sporting News*, June 30, 1973
[2] *New York Times*, April 6, 1973
[3] mlb.com
[4] *Sporting News*, April 14, 1973
[5] *Sports Illustrated*, April 9, 1973
[6] *Sporting News*, April 7, 1973
[7] *Sporting News*, March 10, 1973
[8] *Sporting News*, March 3, 1973
[9] baseball-reference.com
[10] Preston, Joseph G. *Major League Baseball in the 1970s: A Modern Game Emerges*
[11] ESPN.com
[12] *Sports Illustrated*, April 9, 1973
[13] Holtzman, Jerome. "Review of 1973," in Official Baseball Guide
[14] Kuhn, Bowie. *Hardball: The Education of a Baseball Commissioner*
[15] Preston, *Major League Baseball*
[16] *Sporting News*, February 10, 1973
[17] Preston, *Major League Baseball*
[18] *Sporting News*, February 10, 1973
[19] baseball-almanac.com
[20] *Sporting News*, February 3, 1973
[21] *Baseball Digest*, April 1973
[22] Holtzman, "Review of 1973," in Official Baseball Guide
[23] *Sports Illustrated*, April 9, 1973
[24] *Sporting News*, March 3, 1973
[25] Markusen, Bruce. *The Orlando Cepeda Story*

[26] Cepeda, Orlando, with Herb Fagen. *Baby Bull: From Hardball to Hard Time and Back*
[27] Markusen, Bruce. "1972: McLain for Cepeda," baseballlibrary.com
[28] *Ibid.*
[29] Dickey, *Champions*
[30] *Sporting News*, February 10, 1973
[31] *Sporting News*, January 20, 1973
[32] *Sporting News*, February 10, 1973
[33] Dickey, *Champions*
[34] Cepeda, *Baby Bull*
[35] *Ibid.*
[36] *Sporting News*, September 1, 1973
[37] *Ibid.*
[38] Cepeda, Orlando with Bob Markus. *High & Inside: Orlando Cepeda's Story*
[39] *Sporting News*, February 3, 1973
[40] Markusen. *The Orlando Cepeda Story*
[41] Holtzman, "Review of 1973," in Official Baseball Guide
[42] *Sporting News*, February 2, 1973
[43] Markusen, *The Orlando Cepeda Story*
[44] *Sporting News*, September 1, 1973
[45] *Sporting News*, May 19, 1973
[46] *Sporting News*, February 3, 1973
[47] Cepeda, *High & Inside*
[48] *Ibid.*
[49] *New York Times*, April 9, 1973

CHAPTER FIVE

[1] Stanton, Tom. *Hank Aaron and the Home Run that Changed America*
[2] *Sports Illustrated*, August 6, 1973
[3] Aaron, Hank, with Lonnie Wheeler. *I Had a Hammer: The Hank Aaron Story*
[4] Baldwin, Stan and Jerry Jenkins, with Hank Aaron. *Bad Henry*
[5] Aaron, Hank with Dick Schaap. *Home Run: My Life in Pictures*
[6] Aaron, *I Had a Hammer*
[7] *Newsweek*, August 13, 1973
[8] Aaron, *I Had a Hammer*
[9] *Ibid.*

[10] Aaron, *Home Run*
[11] Aaron, *I Had a Hammer*
[12] Stanton, *Hank Aaron*
[13] Aaron, *I Had a Hammer*
[14] *Ibid.*
[15] *Sports Illustrated*, May 28, 1973
[16] Aaron, *Home Run*
[17] Stanton, *Hank Aaron*
[18] Aaron, *I Had a Hammer*
[19] Stanton, *Hank Aaron*; Aaron, *Hammer*
[20] Stanton, *Hank Aaron*
[21] *Ibid.*
[22] *Sports Illustrated*, May 28, 1973
[23] *Atlanta Journal*, August 7, 1973
[24] Aaron, *I Had a Hammer*
[25] *Sporting News*, May 26, 1973
[26] Aaron, *Home Run*
[27] *Sports Illustrated*, May 28, 1973
[28] Aaron, *I Had a Hammer*
[29] *New York Times*, April 30, 1973

CHAPTER SIX

[1] *New York Times*, May 1, 1973
[2] Burke, Michael. *Outrageous Good Fortune*
[3] Holtzman, "Review of 1973," in Official Baseball Guide
[4] *New York Times*, May 1, 1973
[5] Linn, Ed. *Steinbrenner's Yankees: An Inside Account*
[6] Holtzman, "Review of 1973," in Official Baseball Guide
[7] baseballlibrary.com
[8] ESPN.com
[9] *New York Times*, May 1, 1973
[10] Linn, *Steinbrenner's Yankees*
[11] Schaap, *Steinbrenner!*
[12] Linn, *Steinbrenner's Yankees*
[13] Holtzman, "Review of 1973," in Official Baseball Guide
[14] *Sporting News*
[15] Preston, Joseph G. *Major League Baseball in the 1970s: A Modern Game Emerges*
[16] Linn, *Steinbrenner's Yankees*
[17] *Sporting News*, January 27, 1973

[18] *New York Times*, May 1, 1973
[19] Linn, *Steinbrenner's Yankees*
[20] *New York Times*, May 1, 1973
[21] *New York Times*, April 30, 1973
[22] *Ibid.*
[23] Linn, *Steinbrenner's Yankees*
[24] *New York Times*, May 14, 1973
[25] *Ibid.*
[26] *Ibid.*
[27] *Ibid.*
[28] Schaap, *Steinbrenner!*
[29] Kahn, *October Men*
[30] Burke, *Outrageous Good Fortune*
[31] *Sporting News*, May 19, 1973
[32] *New York Times*, May 14, 1973
[33] *Ibid.*
[34] *1974 World Book*
[35] Schaap, *Steinbrenner!*
[36] Linn, *Steinbrenner's Yankees*
[37] Schaap, *Steinbrenner!*
[38] Kahn, *October Men*
[39] Schaap, *Steinbrenner!*
[40] *Ibid.*
[41] *Ibid.*
[42] Linn, *Steinbrenner's Yankees*
[43] Schaap, *Steinbrenner!*
[44] Linn, *Steinbrenner's Yankees*
[45] *Ibid.*
[46] *Ibid.*
[47] *Ibid.*

CHAPTER SEVEN

[1] Cepeda, *High & Inside*
[2] *Ibid.*
[3] *Ibid.*
[4] *Ibid.*
[5] *Ibid.*
[6] *Sporting News*, April 28, 1973
[7] Cepeda, *High & Inside*
[8] Cepeda, Orlando, *Baby Bull*
[9] Cepeda, *High & Inside*
[10] *Sporting News*, June 9, 1973
[11] *Sporting News*, May 12, 1973
[12] Einstein, Charles. *Willie's Time: A Memoir*

[13] Mays, *Say Hey*
[14] Einstein, *Willie's Time*
[15] *New York Times*, May 12, 1972
[16] Author interview with Lon Simmons
[17] Mays, *Say Hey*
[18] *Sporting News*, March 17, 1973
[19] Mays, *Say Hey*
[20] *Sports Illustrated*, April 9, 1973
[21] *New York Times*, April 8, 1973
[22] Einstein, *Willie's Time*
[23] *Ibid.*
[24] *Sporting News*, May 26, 1973
[25] *Ibid.*
[26] Einstein, *Willie's Time*
[27] *Sporting News*, May 26, 1973
[28] *Sporting News*, June 23, 1973
[29] *Sporting News*, March 17, 1973
[30] *Sporting News*, June 23, 1973
[31] *New York Times*, June 10, 1973
[32] *Ibid.*
[33] *New York Times*, June 12, 1973
[34] *Ibid.*
[35] *New Yorker*, July 1973
[36] *Record-Searchlight*, May 21, 1973
[37] *1974 World Book*

CHAPTER EIGHT

[1] *Sporting News*, April 28, 1973
[2] *Ibid.*
[3] Libby, *Charlie O.*
[4] *New York Times*, October 22, 1973
[5] Libby, *Charlie O.*
[6] *Ibid.*
[7] Author interview with Joe Rudi
[8] Author interview with John "Blue Moon" Odom
[9] *Ibid.*
[10] Allen. *Mr. October*
[11] Jackson, *Season with a Superstar*
[12] Allen, *Mr. October*
[13] Author interview with Joe Rudi
[14] *Ibid.*
[15] Allen, *Mr. October*
[16] Dickey, *Champions*

[17] Allen, *Mr. October*
[18] *Minneapolis Tribune*, April 15, 1973
[19] Clark, *Champagne and Baloney*
[20] *Sporting News*, May 26, 1973
[21] *Sporting News*, June 2, 1973
[22] *Ibid.*
[23] Allen, *Mr. October*
[24] Dickey, *Champions*
[25] *Sporting News*, May 26, 1973
[26] Clark, *Champagne and Baloney*
[27] *Sporting News*, June 9, 1973
[28] *Sporting News*, June 30, 1973
[29] *Ibid.*
[30] *Sporting News*, June 2, 1973
[31] Libby, *Charlie O.*
[32] *Sporting News*, June 16, 1973
[33] *Sporting News*, June 30, 1973
[34] Kahn, *October Men*
[35] Clark, *Champagne and Baloney*
[36] *Ibid.*
[37] *Ibid.*
[38] *Ibid.*
[39] *Sporting News*, August 11, 1973

CHAPTER NINE

[1] *Sports Illustrated*, May 28, 1973
[2] Aaron, *Home Run*
[3] Stanton, *Hank Aaron*
[4] Aaron, *I Had a Hammer*
[5] *Sporting News*, July 14, 1973
[6] Stanton, *Hank Aaron*
[7] *Newsweek*, August 13, 1973
[8] Stanton, *Hank Aaron*
[9] *Sporting News*, May 26, 1973
[10] *Atlanta Constitution*, May 8, 1973
[11] *Ibid.*
[12] Stanton, *Hank Aaron*
[13] Aaron, *I Had a Hammer*
[14] *Ibid.*
[15] Stanton, *Hank Aaron*
[16] *Ibid.*
[17] *Atlanta Journal*, May 9, 1973
[18] Aaron, *Home Run*
[19] Stanton, *Hank Aaron*

[20] Aaron, *I Had a Hammer*

[21] *Sporting News*, June 30, 1973

[22] Aaron, *I Had a Hammer*

[23] *Washington Post*, November 24, 1973

[24] Stanton, *Hank Aaron*

[25] *Ibid.*

[26] *History Channel Magazine*, May/June 2007

[27] Ward, Geoffrey C., and Ken Burns. *Baseball: An Illustrated History*

[28] Stanton, *Hank Aaron*

[29] *Ibid.*

[30] *Ebony*, September 1973

[31] Aaron, *Home Run*

[32] Aaron, *I Had a Hammer*

[33] *Ibid.*

[34] *Ibid.*

[35] Stanton, *Hank Aaron*

[36] Aaron, *I Had a Hammer*

[37] *Ibid.*

[38] Libby, *Charlie O.*

[39] Aaron, *I Had a Hammer*

[40] *Ibid.*

[41] Stanton, *Hank Aaron*

[42] Aaron, *I Had a Hammer*

[43] *Ebony*, September 1973

[44] *Time*, July 9, 1973

[45] *Newsweek*, June 4, 1973

[46] *Sporting News*, June 30, 1973

[47] *Ebony*, September 1973

[48] *New York Times*, July 8, 1973

[49] Stanton, Hank Aaron

[50] *New York Times*, July 8, 1973

[51] Aaron, *I Had a Hammer*

[52] *Ibid.*

[53] *Ibid.*

[54] *Newsweek*, June 4, 1973

[55] *Newsweek*, August 13, 1973

[56] *Sports Illustrated*, May 28, 1973

[57] Reshen, Pat, editor. *Hank Aaron 715*

[58] *Sporting News*, January 5, 1974

[59] Aaron, *Home Run*

[60] *Los Angeles Times*, June 18, 1973

[61] Aaron, *Home Run*

[62] MLB copyright radio broadcast, The Miley Collection

[63] *Sporting News*, July 14, 1973

[64] Stanton, *Hank Aaron*

[65] MLB copyright radio broadcast, The Miley Collection

[66] Aaron, *I Had a Hammer*

[67] *New York Times*, July 22, 1973

[68] *Sporting News*, August 4, 1973

[69] Stanton, *Hank Aaron*

[70] *New York Times*, July 22, 1973

[71] Holtzman, Jerome. "Review of 1973," in Official Baseball Guide

[72] *New York Times*, July 22, 1973

[73] Aaron, *I Had a Hammer*

[74] Reshen, *Hank Aaron 715*

[75] Aaron, *I Had a Hammer*

[76] *Newsweek*, August 13, 1973

CHAPTER TEN

[1] Libby, *Charlie O.*

[2] *Sporting News*, June 30, 1973

[3] *Sporting News*, July 28, 1973

[4] *Sporting News*, July 28, 1973

[5] *Sporting News*, August 18, 1973

[6] Ryan, Nolan, and Harvey Frommer. *Throwing Heat: The Autobiography of Nolan Ryan*

[7] *Ibid.*

[8] *Sporting News*, August 11, 1973

[9] Ryan, *Throwing Heat*

[10] *Ibid.*

[11] *Sporting News*, August 11, 1973

[12] *Atlanta Journal*, July 24, 1973

[13] *Sporting News*, August 11, 1973

[14] baseball-almanac.com

[15] Stanton, Tom. *Hank Aaron and the Home Run that Changed America*

[16] *Sports Illustrated*, April 9, 1973

[17] *Sporting News*, August 11, 1973

[18] Stanton, *Hank Aaron*

[19] *Sporting News*, August 11, 1973

[20] *New York Times*, July 24, 1973

[21] *Ibid.*

22 *Sporting News*, August 11, 1973
23 *Atlanta Constitution*, July 25, 1973
24 *New York Times*, July 24, 1973
25 *Ibid.*
26 *Sporting News*, August 11, 1973
27 *1974 World Book*
28 *Minneapolis Star*, July 25, 1973
29 *1974 World Book*
30 *Minneapolis Star*, July 25, 1973
31 *New York Times*, September 9, 1973
32 Schaap, *Steinbrenner!*
33 *Minneapolis Star*, July 25, 1973
34 *Sporting News*, August 11, 1973
35 *Atlanta Journal*, July 25, 1973
36 *Sports Illustrated*, August 6, 1973
37 *Ibid.*
38 royals.mlb.com
39 *Sporting News*, July 28, 1973
40 *Ibid.*
41 *Ibid.*
42 *1974 World Book*
43 *Sporting News*, July 28, 1973
44 *Ibid.*
45 *Sporting News*, August 11, 1973
46 Author interview with Art Stewart
47 *Sporting News*, August 11, 1973
48 *Sporting News*, July 28, 1973
49 *Sporting News*, August 11, 1973
50 *Ibid.*
51 *Ibid.*
52 Author interview with Stewart
53 *Atlanta Journal*, July 25, 1973
54 *Sporting News*, August 11, 1973
55 *New York Times*, July 25, 1973
56 *Atlanta Constitution*, July 24, 1973
57 Dickey, *Champions*
58 Author interview with Stewart
59 *Sports Illustrated*, August 6, 1973
60 *Sporting News*, June 30, 1973
61 *Minneapolis Star*, July 25, 1973
62 Author interview with Stewart
63 *Atlanta Journal*, July 25, 1973
64 *New York Times*, July 25, 1973 and *Sporting News*, August 11, 1973
65 *Atlanta Constitution*, July 26, 1973
66 *New York Times*, July 25, 1973
67 *New York Times*, July 26, 1973 and *Sporting News*, July 28, 1973
68 *Atlanta Journal*, July 24, 1973
69 *Sporting News*, August 11, 1973
70 *Minneapolis Star*, July 25, 1973
71 *Atlanta Journal*, July 26, 1973
72 *Sporting News*, August 11, 1973
73 *Atlanta Constitution*, July 26, 1973
74 *New York Times*, July 26, 1973
75 *Ibid.*
76 *Atlanta Journal*, July 25, 1973
77 *Minneapolis Tribune*, July 25, 1973
78 Stanton, *Hank Aaron*

CHAPTER ELEVEN

1 *New York Times*, June 10, 1973
2 *New York Times*, June 7, 1973
3 *New York Times*, June 10, 1973
4 *Ibid.*
5 *Ibid.*
6 *Ibid.*
7 Schaap, *Steinbrenner!*
8 *Sporting News*, July 28, 1973
9 Schaap, *Steinbrenner!*
10 *Sporting News*, June 30, 1973
11 *Sporting News*, August 4, 1973
12 baseball-almanac.com
13 Armour, Mark. "Gaylord Perry," SABR Baseball Biography Project
14 *New York Times*, June 26, 1973
15 *Sporting News*, July 21, 1973
16 Armour, "Gaylord Perry"
17 *New York Times*, July 15, 1973
18 *New York Times*, June 27, 1973
19 *Sporting News*, July 21, 1973
20 *New York Times*, June 29, 1973
21 *New York Times*, July 21, 1973
22 *New York Times*, June 30, 1973
23 *Ibid.*
24 *Ibid.*
25 *New York Times*, July 1, 1973
26 *Ibid.*

27 *Ibid.*
28 *Sporting News*, July 21, 1973
29 *New York Times*, July 1, 1973
30 *Sporting News*, July 21, 1973
31 Schaap, *Steinbrenner!*
32 *Ibid.*
33 *Ibid.*
34 Linn, *Steinbrenner's Yankees*
35 Schaap, *Steinbrenner!*
36 Linn, *Steinbrenner's Yankees*
37 *Ibid.*
38 Schaap, *Steinbrenner!*
39 *Ibid.*
40 Linn, *Steinbrenner's Yankees*
41 Schaap, *Steinbrenner!*
42 *Ibid.*
43 Armour, "Gaylord Perry"
44 thebaseballpage.com
45 *Sporting News*, October 13, 1973
46 *Ibid.*
47 *Ibid.*

CHAPTER TWELVE

1 *Sporting News*, September 1, 1973
2 *Ibid.*
3 *Sporting News*, August 25, 1973
4 *Sporting News*, September 1, 1973
5 *Ibid.*
6 *Ibid.*
7 *Ibid.*
8 *Sporting News*, August 4, 1973
9 *Sporting News*, September 29, 1973
10 *Sporting News*, September 1, 1973
11 *Sporting News*, September 8, 1973
12 McKelvey, G. Richard. *All Bat, No Glove: A History of the Designated Hitter*
13 *New Yorker*, November 19, 1973
14 *Sporting News*, October 20, 1973
15 McKelvey, *All Bat*
16 *Sporting News*, August 11, 1973
17 *Sporting News*, September 29, 1973
18 *Sporting News*, October 20, 1973
19 *Sporting News*, August 4, 1973
20 *Sporting News*, October 20, 1973

21 Preston, Joseph G. *Major League Baseball in the 1970s: A Modern Game Emerges.*
22 McKelvey, *All Bat*
23 *Ibid.*
24 *Sporting News*, October 27, 1973
25 McKelvey, *All Bat*
26 *Journal News*, May 2003
27 *Sporting News*, October 27, 1973
28 baseball-almanac.com
29 McKelvey, *All Bat*
30 *Time*, December 12, 2004
31 *Sporting News*, October 27, 1973
32 *Ibid.*
33 McKelvey, *All Bat*
34 *Sporting News*, October 20, 1973
35 *Sporting News*, September 22, 1973
36 Author interview with Bill Lee
37 *Sporting News*, December 22, 1973
38 *Sporting News*, October 20, 1973
39 Author interview with Dick Bresciani

CHAPTER THIRTEEN

1 Stanton, *Hank Aaron*
2 *Ibid.*
3 *Time*, September 24, 1973
4 *Sporting News*, October 13, 1973
5 Stanton, *Hank Aaron*
6 *Sporting News*, July 14, 1973
7 *Time*, September 24, 1973
8 Aaron, *I Had a Hammer*
9 Aaron, *I Had a Hammer*
10 *Los Angeles Times*, September 25, 1973
11 Stanton, *Hank Aaron*
12 *Ibid.*
13 *Ibid.*
14 *Ibid.*
15 *Ibid.*
16 Aaron, *I Had a Hammer*
17 Stanton, *Hank Aaron*
18 *Ibid.*
19 *Ibid.*
20 *Time*, September 24, 1973
21 Stanton, *Hank Aaron*
22 Aaron, *Home Run*

[23] *Ibid.*
[24] Stanton, *Hank Aaron*
[25] *Ibid.*
[26] *Ibid.*
[27] Aaron, *I Had a Hammer*
[28] Stanton, *Hank Aaron*
[29] *Los Angeles Times*, September 25, 1973
[30] *Ibid.*
[31] *New Yorker*, November 19, 1973
[32] *Los Angeles Times*, September 25, 1973
[33] Aaron, *I Had a Hammer*
[34] Stanton, *Hank Aaron*
[35] Aaron, *I Had a Hammer*
[36] *Sporting News*, Ocotber 20, 1973
[37] *Los Angeles Times*, September 25, 1973
[38] Aaron, *I Had a Hammer*
[39] Stanton, Hank Aaron
[40] *Ibid.*
[41] *Sporting News*, January 5, 1973
[42] *Sporting News*, October 13, 1973
[43] Stanton, *Hank Aaron*
[44] *Ibid.*
[45] *New Yorker*, November 19, 1973
[46] Aaron, *I Had a Hammer*
[47] *Ibid.*
[48] Stanton, *Hank Aaron*
[49] Aaron, *I Had a Hammer*
[50] Stanton, *Hank Aaron*
[51] Aaron, *I Had a Hammer*
[52] Stanton, *Hank Aaron*
[53] Aaron, *I Had a Hammer*
[54] *Sporting News*, October 13, 1973
[55] Aaron, *I Had a Hammer*
[56] Baldwin, *Bad Henry*
[57] Aaron, *I Had a Hammer*
[58] Stanton, *Hank Aaron*
[59] Aaron, *I Had a Hammer*
[60] *Ibid.*

CHAPTER FOURTEEN

[1] *Sports Illustrated*, August 6, 1973
[2] Libby, *Charlie O.*
[3] *Ibid.*
[4] baseball-almanac.com

[5] Clark, *Champagne and Baloney*
[6] Libby, *Charlie O.*
[7] *Sporting News*, September 1, 1973
[8] Clark, *Champagne and Baloney*
[9] Libby, *Charlie O.*
[10] *Ibid.*
[11] Author interview with Ray Fossse
[12] *Ibid.*
[13] Clark, *Champagne and Baloney*
[14] Mahler, *The Bronx is Burning*
[15] Libby, *Charlie O.*
[16] Clark, *Champagne and Baloney*
[17] *Ibid.*
[18] *Sporting News*, October 13, 1973
[19] Clark, *Champagne and Baloney*
[20] Libby, *Charlie O.*
[21] Clark, *Champagne and Baloney*
[22] Libby, *Charlie O.*
[23] *Ibid.*
[24] *Ibid.*
[25] *Ibid.*
[26] *Ibid.*
[27] *Ibid.*
[28] Garner, Joe. *And the Crowd Goes Wild*
[29] *Sporting News*, October 13, 1973
[30] Clark, *Champagne and Baloney*
[31] *Sporting News*, October 13, 1973
[32] *Ibid.*
[33] Clark, *Champagne and Baloney*
[34] Libby, *Charlie O.*
[35] Clark, *Champagne and Baloney*
[36] *Ibid.*

CHAPTER FIFTEEN

[1] *New York Times*, August 1, 1973
[2] *Ibid.*
[3] *New Yorker,* July 1973
[4] *New York Times*, September 23, 1973
[5] *Ibid.*
[6] *Ibid.*
[7] *Sporting News*, August 18, 1973
[8] Mays, *Say Hey*
[9] *Sporting News*, August 18, 1973
[10] *Ibid.*

[11] *Sports Illustrated*, October 1, 1973
[12] Schoor, Gene. *Seaver: A Biography*
[13] *Sport*, July 1974
[14] *Sporting News*, October 20, 1973
[15] *Sporting News*, August 4, 1973
[16] McGraw, Tug, and Joseph Durso. *Screwball*
[17] *Sporting News*, August 4, 1973
[18] *Sporting News*, July 28, 1973
[19] Schoor, *Seaver*
[20] *Sporting News*, August 4, 1973
[21] Schoor, *Seaver*
[22] *Sports Illustrated*, October 1, 1973
[23] McGraw, *Screwball*
[24] Author interview with Paul Levy
[25] McGraw, *Screwball*
[26] *Sports Illustrated*, October 1, 1973
[27] *Ibid.*
[28] McGraw, *Screwball*
[29] *New Yorker*, November 19, 1973
[30] Holtzman, Jerome. "Review of 1973," in Official Baseball Guide
[31] *Sport*, July 1974
[32] Pepe, *Catfish, Yaz*
[33] Schoor, *Seaver*
[34] Einstein, *Willie's Time*
[35] *Sport*, June 1973
[36] wikipedia.org
[37] Drucker, Malka, with Tom Seaver. *Tom Seaver: Portrait of a Pitcher*
[38] ESPN.com
[39] Drucker, *Tom Seaver*
[40] Pepe, *Catfish, Yaz*
[41] *Ibid.*
[42] McGraw, *Screwball*
[43] Pepe, *Catfish, Yaz*
[44] Author interview with Ed Kranepool
[45] McGraw, *Screwball*
[46] Author interview with Kranepool
[47] McGraw, *Screwball*
[48] *Ibid.*
[49] *New York Times*, September 12, 1973
[50] *Ibid.*
[51] *New York Times*, September 21, 1973

[52] *New York Times*, September 13, 1973
[53] *Ibid.*
[54] *Sporting News*, February 10, 1973
[55] *New York Times*, September 14, 1973
[56] *New York Times*, September 18, 1973
[57] *New York Times*, September 19, 1973
[58] MLB copyright radio broadcast, The Miley Collection
[59] *New York Times*, September 19, 1973
[60] *New Yorker*, November 19, 1973
[61] *Sporting News*, October 6, 1973
[62] *New York Times*, September 20, 1973
[63] *Sports Illustrated*, October 1, 1973 and *New Yorker*, November 19, 1973
[64] MLB copyright radio broadcast, The Miley Collection
[65] Pepe, *Catfish, Yaz*
[66] *New Yorker*, November 19, 1973
[67] *Sports Illustrated*, October 1, 1973 and *New York Times*, September 22, 1973
[68] *New Yorker*, November 19, 1973 and Drucker, *Seaver*
[69] *New York Times*, September 22, 1973
[70] *New York Times*, September 21, 1973
[71] *Ibid.*
[72] *Ibid.*
[73] Einstein, *Willie's Time*
[74] Saccoman, John. "Willie Mays," SABR Baseball Biography Project
[75] *Sports Illustrated*, October 1, 1973
[76] *New York Times*, September 26, 1973
[77] *Ibid.*
[78] *Ibid.*
[79] *Sporting News*, October 13, 1973
[80] Mays, *Say Hey*
[81] *New York Times*, September 26, 1973
[82] *Ibid.*
[83] *Ibid.*
[84] Mays, *Say Hey*
[85] Einstein, *Willie's Time*
[86] *New York Times*, September 26, 1973
[87] *Sports Illustrated*, October 8, 1973
[88] Drucker, *Tom Seaver*
[89] McGraw, *Screwball*

[90] *Ibid.*
[91] *Ibid.*
[92] Mays, *Say Hey*
[93] Einstein, *Willie's Time*

CHAPTER SIXTEEN

[1] *Sports Illustrated*, October 8, 1973
[2] Schoor, *Seaver*
[3] *New Yorker*, November 19, 1973
[4] *Sports Illustrated*, October 8, 1973
[5] *Ibid.*
[6] *New Yorker*, November 19, 1973
[7] *New York Times*, October 9, 1973
[8] *Baseball Digest*, August 2005
[9] Schoor, *Seaver*
[10] McGraw, *Screwball*
[11] MLB copyright radio broadcast, The Miley Collection
[12] McGraw, *Screwball*
[13] Schoor, *Seaver*
[14] MLB copyright radio broadcast, The Miley Collection
[15] *New York Times*, October 9, 1973
[16] *Ibid.*
[17] *Sporting News*, October 27, 1973
[18] MLB copyright radio broadcast, The Miley Collection
[19] *New York Times*, October 9, 1973
[20] *Ibid.*
[21] *Ibid.*
[22] Schoor, *Seaver*
[23] *New York Times*, October 9, 1973
[24] *Ibid.*
[25] *Ibid.*
[26] *New Yorker*, November 19, 1973 and *New York Times*, October 10, 1973
[27] *New Yorker*, November 19, 1973
[28] *New York Times*, October 10, 1973
[29] *Sports Illustrated*, October 22, 1973
[30] *New York Times*, October 10, 1973
[31] *Ibid.*
[32] *Ibid.*
[33] *Ibid.*
[34] *New York Times*, October 11, 1973

[35] Schoor, *Seaver*
[36] *New York Times*, October 11, 1973
[37] *Ibid.*
[38] *Ibid.*
[39] *Ibid.*
[40] *New Yorker*, November 19, 1973
[41] Bjarkman, Peter C. *The New York Mets Encyclopedia*
[42] *New Yorker*, November 19, 1973
[43] *New York Times*, October 11, 1973
[44] Schoor, *Seaver*
[45] *New Yorker*, November 19, 1973
[46] *New York Times*, October 11, 1973
[47] *Ibid.*
[48] *New Yorker*, November 19, 1973
[49] *New York Times*, October 11, 1973
[50] Schoor, *Seaver*
[51] *New York Times*, October 11, 1973
[52] *New Yorker*, November 19, 1973
[53] *New York Times*, October 11, 1973
[54] *Sporting News*, October 27, 1973
[55] *Time*, October 15, 1973
[56] Schoor, *Seaver*
[57] *New York Times*, October 11, 1973
[58] Allen, *Mr. October*
[59] *Ibid.*
[60] *Ibid.*
[61] *Ibid.*
[62] *Sports Illustrated*, October 29, 1973
[63] Libby, *Charlie O.*
[64] *Ibid.*
[65] *Sporting News*, November 24, 1973
[66] Clark, *Champagne and Baloney*
[67] *Ibid.*
[68] *Sporting News*, October 13, 1973
[69] *Ibid.*
[70] *New Yorker*, November 19, 1973
[71] *Ibid.*
[72] Libby, *Charlie O.*
[73] *Ibid.*
[74] *Ibid.*
[75] Clark, *Champagne and Baloney*
[76] *Ibid.*
[77] *Ibid.*

[78] Dickey, *Champions*
[79] Libby, *Charlie O.*
[80] Clark, *Champagne and Baloney*
[81] *Ibid.*
[82] Libby, *Charlie O.*
[83] *Ibid.*
[84] Clark, *Champagne and Baloney*
[85] *Ibid.*
[86] Libby, *Charlie O.*
[87] Clark, *Champagne and Baloney*
[88] *Sporting News*, October 27, 1973
[89] *Ibid.*
[90] Libby, *Charlie O.*
[91] *Ibid.*
[92] *Sporting News*, October 27, 1973

CHAPTER SEVENTEEN

[1] *New York Times*, October 14, 1973
[2] Libby, *Charlie O.*
[3] *Sporting News*, November 3, 1973
[4] Libby, *Charlie O.*
[5] *Ibid.*
[6] Clark, *Champagne and Baloney*
[7] *New York Times*, October 17, 1973
[8] Libby, *Charlie O.*
[9] Clark, *Champagne and Baloney*
[10] *Sporting News*, February 10, 1973
[11] Dickey, *Champions*
[12] *New York Times*, October 14, 1973
[13] *New Yorker*, November 19, 1973
[14] Clark, *Champagne and Baloney*
[15] baseball-almanac.com
[16] *Sporting News*, October 27, 1973
[17] Dickey, *Champions*
[18] Clark, *Champagne and Baloney*
[19] Television broadcast, ESPN Classics
[20] Jackson, *Season with a Superstar*
[21] Television broadcast, ESPN Classics
[22] *Ibid.*
[23] *Ibid.*
[24] Author interview with Ray Fosse
[25] *Ibid.*
[26] *New York Times*, October 15, 1973
[27] Television broadcast, ESPN Classics
[28] *Ibid.*
[29] *Ibid.*
[30] interview with Fosse
[31] Libby, *Charlie O.*
[32] Clark, *Champagne and Baloney*
[33] Libby, *Charlie O.*
[34] Clark, *Champagne and Baloney*
[35] *Ibid.*
[36] Libby, *Charlie O.*
[37] Clark, *Champagne and Baloney*
[38] *New York Times*, October 18, 1973
[39] Libby, *Charlie O.*
[40] *Sports Illustrated*, October 29, 1973
[41] *New York Times*, October 18, 1973
[42] Kuhn, *Hardball*
[43] Clark, *Champagne and Baloney*
[44] *New York Times*, October 18, 1973
[45] Clark, *Champagne and Baloney*
[46] *New York Times*, October 18, 1973
[47] Clark, *Champagne and Baloney*
[48] *Sporting News*, November 3, 1973
[49] Jackson, *Season with a Superstar*
[50] *Ibid.*
[51] Clark, *Champagne and Baloney*
[52] *New York Times*, October 16, 1973
[53] Author interview with Fosse
[54] Libby, *Charlie O.*
[55] *New York Times*, October 17, 1973
[56] Clark, *Champagne and Baloney*
[57] *New York Times*, October 17, 1973
[58] Libby, *Charlie O.*
[59] Clark, *Champagne and Baloney*
[60] *New York Times*, October 16, 1973
[61] *Ibid.*
[62] *Sporting News*, November 3, 1973
[63] *New York Times*, October 17, 1973
[64] *Ibid.*
[65] Libby, *Charlie O.*
[66] *Ibid.*
[67] Jackson, *Season with a Superstar*
[68] *Ibid.*
[69] *Sports Illustrated*, October 29, 1973
[70] Clark, *Champagne and Baloney*
[71] *New York Times*, October 18, 1973

[72] Libby, *Charlie O.*
[73] Author interview with Fosse
[74] Libby, *Charlie O.*
[75] Author interview with Gene Tenace
[76] *New York Times*, October 18, 1973
[77] Author interview with Tenace
[78] *New York Times*, October 18, 1973
[79] *Ibid.*
[80] *New York Times*, October 19, 1973
[81] Clark, *Champagne and Baloney*
[82] Libby, *Charlie O.*
[83] *Ibid.*
[84] *Ibid.*
[85] Clark, *Champagne and Baloney*
[86] Libby, *Charlie O.*
[87] Clark, *Champagne and Baloney*
[88] *Ibid.*
[89] *Sports Illustrated*, October 29, 1973
[90] Clark, *Champagne and Baloney*
[91] McGraw, Tug, and Joseph Durso. *Screwball*
[92] *Ibid.*
[93] *New York Times*, October 22, 1973
[94] Author interview with Bob Costas
[95] *Ibid.*
[96] Author interview with Lon Simmons
[97] Clark, *Champagne and Baloney*
[98] *Ibid.*
[99] *Ibid.*
[100] *New York Times*, October 22, 1973
[101] *Ibid.*
[102] *Ibid.*
[103] New Yorker, November 19, 1973
[104] Libby, *Charlie O.*
[105] Holtzman, "Review of 1973," in Official Baseball Guide
[106] *Ibid.*
[107] Libby, *Charlie O.*
[108] *Ibid.*

CHAPTER EIGHTEEN

[1] Kuhn, *Hardball*
[2] *Sporting News*, November 24, 1973
[3] Author interview with John "Blue Moon" Odom
[4] Libby, *Charlie O.*
[5] Holtzman, "Review of 1973," in Official Baseball Guide
[6] *Ibid.*
[7] *Ibid.*
[8] *Sporting News*, December 29, 1973
[9] Schaap, *Steinbrenner!*
[10] Holtzman, "Review of 1973," in Official Baseball Guide
[11] *Ibid.*
[12] Jackson, *Season with a Superstar*
[13] Author interview with Joe Rudi
[14] *Ibid.*
[15] *1975 Sporting News Official Baseball Guide*
[16] *Ibid.*
[17] *New York Times*, April 30, 1973
[18] *Sporting News*, November 10, 1973
[19] *Ibid.*
[20] *Ibid.*
[21] Schaap, *Steinbrenner!*
[22] Linn, *Steinbrenner's Yankees*
[23] Schaap, *Steinbrenner!*
[24] Kahn, *October Men*
[25] Schaap, *Steinbrenner!*
[26] *Ibid.*
[27] Linn, *Steinbrenner's Yankees*
[28] *Ibid.*
[29] ESPN.com
[30] thesmokinggun.com
[31] Armour, Mark. "Gaylord Perry," SABR Baseball Biography Project
[32] *Ibid.*
[33] wikipedia.org
[34] Author interview with Bill Lee
[35] *Ibid.*
[36] Cepeda, *Baby Bull*
[37] wikipedia.org
[38] Aaron, *Home Run*
[39] Reshen, Pat, editor. *Hank Aaron 715*
[40] *Sporting News*, January 5, 1974
[41] *Minneapolis Star Tribune*, August 8, 2007

INDEX

Photo by Scott Streble

John Rosengren is an award-winning journalist and author. He has written five other books, including *Blades of Glory: The True Story of a Young Team Bred to Win*. His articles have appeared in more than one hundred publications, ranging from *Sports Illustrated* to *Reader's Digest*. He is a member of the Society for American Baseball Research and the American Society of Journalists and Authors. A lifelong Twins fan, John lives in Minneapolis with his wife and their two children.

Visit him at www.johnrosengren.net.